BOOMBAY

From Precincts to Sprawl

KAMU IYER

BOOMBAY

From Precincts to Sprawl

KAMU IYER

Popular Prakashan

www.popularprakashan.com

Published by
Harsha Bhatkal for
POPULAR PRAKASHAN PVT. LTD.
301, Mahalaxmi Chambers
22, Bhulabhai Desai Road
Mumbai - 400 026
www.popularprakashan.com

First Published 2014
First Reprint June 2019

(4403)
ISBN: 978-81-7991-844-9

Editors: Vaishnavi Chandrashekar
Radha Rajadhyaksha
Design: Sudhakar Nadkarni

PRINTED IN INDIA
by Thomson Press (I) Ltd.
New Delhi

Sponsored by:
arbour research initiatives architecture
Priyanath Banerjee Memorial Trust

For Lalitha
Without whose patient support throughout
I could not have written this book.

Acknowledgements

A number of people have shown interest in my writing this book and have contributed to it in many ways. It is difficult to thank all but I must, in gratitude, acknowledge particularly:

Charles Correa, for insisting that I put down my experiences in a book. He advised me to make it a written version of conversations that we have had over many years.

Shekhar Krishnan helped me with research and information and frequently discussed various topics pertaining to the city, especially the work done by the Improvement Trust.

My daughter Aditi, despite her busy work schedule, edited all the drafts and made valuable suggestions to improve the script.

My sister, Hema Nadkarni, made a version of the book on 'I books' which gave an idea of what the print version would look like.

Dr. Anuradha Murthy put an embarrassing amount of faith in my ability to write a book. She dug into her collection of old photographs and let me choose from them.

Carmen Kagal, after reading the initial draft, convinced me to rewrite the book in the form of a memoir even though that meant giving up two years of work. She was right and I am thankful to her for the suggestion.

Ameya Athvankar, Shibani Kulkarni and Tejashree Kulkarni who painstakingly and ungrudgingly worked on the many avatars of the dummy. I cannot forget their help.

My colleague, Prateek Bannerjee, took most of the photographs without complaining either about the time he spent on doing it or the time I spent in the office working on the book.

Arun Ranade and Uday Athvankar gave me a lot of information that confirmed what I knew but was unsure of.

Anil Nagrath took me to Chembur Gaothan and showed me another layer of Bombay. He gave me photos and information that clarified some of my doubts.

Prof. Mary Woods of Cornell University read the manuscript of the earlier version and discussed it with me during all her trips to India. Her suggestions on the structure of the book were invaluable.

Sytse de Maat, who has spent a lot of time in India and especially Dharavi, read the current manuscript carefully and made important suggestions that I have incorporated in the final version of the book. I am also grateful to him for letting me use his photographs which have helped illustrate the book so well.

The Kamla Raheja Vidyanidhi Institute of Achitecture gave me free access to its studies of Dadar-Matunga Estate, Ballard Estate and Nariman Point. I am thankful to the institute.

Ipsita Mahajan helped me understand the dynamics of high-rise development from her experience of project management.

Navin Ramani, whose book 'Bombay Art Deco Architecture' formed a source for photographs that I have included in the book. This was possible only with his kind permission.

I have to specially thank Vaishnavi Chandrashekhar who brought her experience and editing skills to make the text crisp and Radha Rajadhyaksha for her contribution and final editing that gave the book a finesse and significantly enhanced it.

And Sudhakar Nadkarni, who so admirably designed the book - to him a special thanks.

Contents

Foreword	10
Introduction	12
Growing Up In A Planned Neighbourhood	13
Studying In South Bombay	33
Learning About The Improvement Trust	65
Marine Drive : Everyone's Icon	81
Art Deco Phase	95
Two Office Districts	109
Living In A Community	117
The Apartment	129
You Can Judge A City By How Its Poor Live	145
Policies Affect The Urban Fabric	165
Opportunities For Growth	177
Epilogue	188
Glossary	189
Credits	191

Foreword
by Charles Correa

The physical aspects of any city, ie its buildings, streets, public spaces etc, don't just spring into being. They are the products of a complex interplay of building materials and technology, municipal regulations, street setbacks and so forth. Most books on Bombay, intended primarily for coffee tables, fill us with nostalgic imagery but provide little or no explanation of the mechanics of that crucial interplay – ie, just **why** in those days, our city looked the way it did.

This book is different. Kamu Iyer is an architect who has lived in Bombay all his life. He is observant, analytical, visual. He understands how people use spaces – especially public spaces. And he has a sense of History.

In Iyer's genealogy of this city, there are of course the usual suspects: Bombay Gothic, Indo-Saracenic, Art Deco and so forth. But there is much more: for instance, the Bombay Improvement Trust – which from 1898 to 1926 was directly responsible for pioneering the new developments that made Bombay the most progressive city in India. Developments that were prime examples for the rest of urban India to follow – from a number of elegantly scaled new streets like Laburnum Road and Alexandra Road in Gamdevi to the creation of whole neighborhoods, like the office area (behind the Bombay Gym) between Waudby and D N Roads, and the Parsi and Hindu housing colonies in Dadar. The Development Department, that followed the B.I.T. was also responsible for Marine Drive – that brilliant urban gesture that has become the iconic image of our city.

This is what made Bombay the magnificent city it was – and this process continued after Independence with the augmentation of these capabilities at state and central government levels. The future of India's cities seemed to be in capable hands. Tragically, in the last few decades, almost all this capacity has been systematically dismantled. And why? Because it comes in the way of corrupt political agendas. So now decisive shifts in the city's development (savage increases in FSI, drastic changes in land use etc) are NOT vetted by any planning agency nor exposed to any public scrutiny but are sent directly from the cabinet to the Urban Secretary to the Municipal Commissioner for implementation.

All this has led to criminally wretched and dehumanising conditions for the have-nots in our cities. And this is why Iyer has a chapter with the laconic title: 'YOU CAN JUDGE A CITY BY HOW ITS POOR LIVE'. That is indeed a profound thought. In his own gentle critique of our city's development, Iyer delivers a lethal punch that takes your breath away.

For we all know we have created a city that only the top 25 per cent of its inhabitants can afford. A city of high-rise towers and high-speed elevators, of flyovers and multi-level car parks – a city that has no connection whatsoever with the actual prevailing income profile of its citizens. This was not the case some decades ago – when Bombay's growth rate was just as high but where the existing rules generated typologies that were affordable to almost all. The problem then was of overcrowding in the rooms – not of whole families being forced to live out on the pavements. This is a problem that we ourselves have created, starting in the 1960s – and we should get full credit for having done so.

Iyer's book is like a leisurely stroll through the city – sometimes in a tram or bus but most often on foot – the schoolboy followed by the college student and finally the curious professional, always looking, questioning, seeking to understand. And as we witness the development of the city, we learn about the gradual metamorphosis of the new typologies that were developed here (for chawls, for apartments, for houses) and about the architects (Claude Batley, G B Mhatre and others) who helped create them.

And throughout, Iyer is like a modern-day Proust – sifting through his memories and insights, presenting them for our consideration. And just like that small Parisian tea-cake more than a century ago, today the sight of a metal railing of a boundary wall recalls to his mind the memory of a schoolboy sitting on that railing, waiting for his turn to bat. It brings back another Bombay. And perhaps reading through this book will help us understand what is going wrong with our city – and provide us with clues on how to reverse the grave (perhaps terminal) blunders we are currently making.

Introduction

" The voyage of discovery is not in seeking new landscapes but having new eyes"
- Marcel Proust

In this book I write about the built form of the city as I have seen it grow and change since the 1940s. It is written largely from my experience through my years as a student, professional architect and teacher in schools of architecture, though I have also drawn from the observations of many others, young and old. I also look at the way in which the Improvement Trust, the Bombay Development Department and the Bombay Municipal Corporation, through their interventions, altered the homes and lives of people over the decades. This book is about a changing order and the city's fabric.

Growing Up In A Planned Neighbourhood

Growing Up In A Planned Neighbourhood

I have lived all my life in Dadar-Matunga in the northern part of the island city of Bombay. I spent my first nine years in Hindu Colony, after which we moved to Parsi Colony, a neighbourhood that stood just across the main road from it. As a child, I would imagine this road, Vincent Road (now called Dr Ambedkar Road), to be a thick black line on which red trams ran. Both Hindu Colony and Parsi Colony, though noticeably different from each other, were part of the Dadar-Matunga Estate Scheme V developed in the 1920s by the Bombay Improvement Trust, the main city development authority of that time. It was set up by the government to replan crowded areas of the city and develop new neighbourhoods.

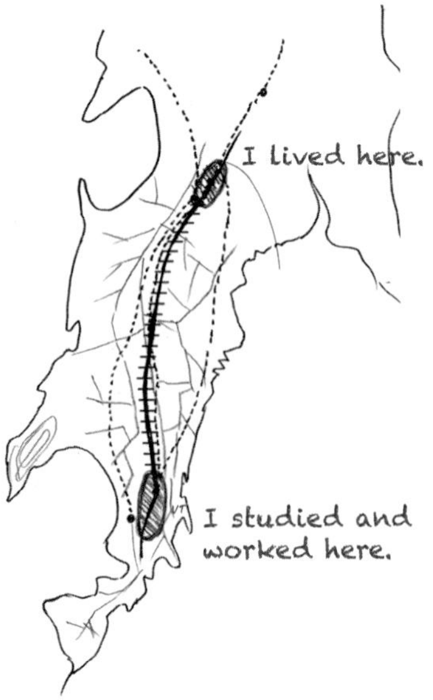

I lived in a planned neighbourhood at the northern end of the island city. The train took me to school.

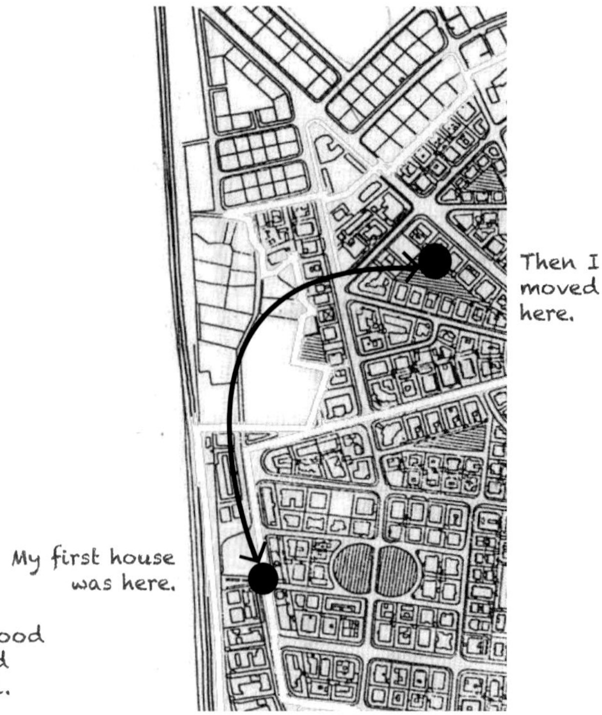

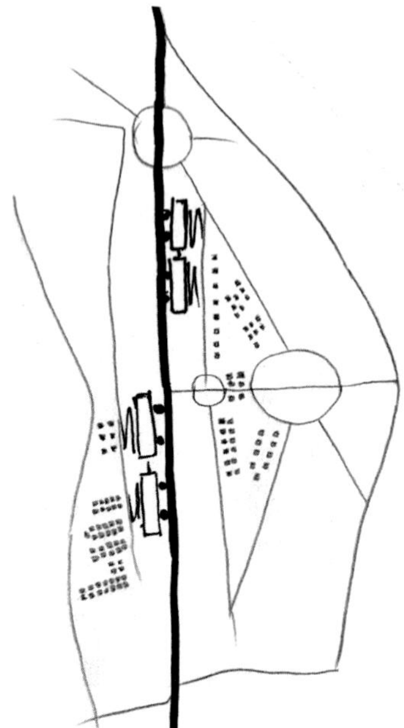

For a child the road was a thick black line on which red trams ran.

Hindu Colony

The precinct was made up of shaded roads, plenty of open space and three-storey buildings. Contrary to its name, Hindu Colony was not meant exclusively for Hindus although the majority of its residents were middle-class Maharashtrians. Perhaps it was so called only to distinguish it from Parsi Colony, which was reserved mostly for members of that community. Several Christians owned houses in Hindu Colony. My early friendships were with the boys of a Goan Christian family that lived down the road. We went to the same school in Dhobi Talao, travelling together by train every day. The family was headed by a stern widow. I used to wonder why a Christian lady would want to bring up her family in a Hindu locality rather than one where her own community resided. To that question my uncle surmised that she probably felt safer among strangers than her own people, especially since she was attractive and without any means. In a Hindu area, she could keep prying neighbours at bay.

Hindu Colony had two main roads that ran north-south. One was Sir Bhalchandra Road and the other was Lakhamsi Napoo Road, which was named after a prosperous trader by the authorities as compensation for acquiring some of his land. The British generally named roads after their officials or those whom the Raj favoured. Between these two roads were six crossroads, each with nine houses on either side. Fourth Road, on which I lived, was wider than the others. This deviation from the layout seemed to have no logical explanation. The only reason I could think of was that all plots in the area were of one size, and making all roads of a uniform width would have resulted in odd dimensions and areas. It was far easier and more practical to make one road wider. The roads were narrow by today's norms but adequate for a time when ownership of cars was rare and everyone travelled by train or tram.

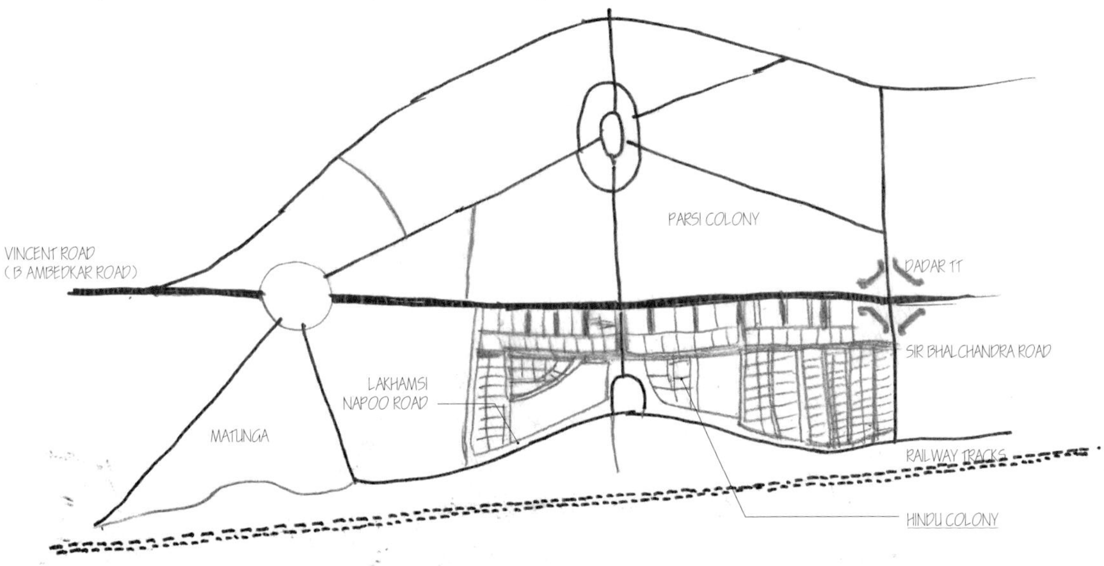

The buildings in Hindu Colony were set back from the road, and the distance between buildings added to the general sense of openness. The roads had footpaths on either side but they were narrow and occupied mostly by trees. The result is that scarcely anyone walked on them. The roads and houses were scaled in such a way that the call of passing hawkers could be heard by housewives inside their homes and they could bargain with them right from their verandahs. Every house had a verandah or a balcony from which you could see the street and activity on it. The balcony in a flat is an idea carried over from the *otla* or verandah in a village house, which was like an outdoor living-room used by male family members. In the city, the *otla* became the balcony.

Hindu Colony did not have a large garden or play area. For more play space, we had to cross Vincent Road, named after a British police commissioner, to Parsi Colony, which had wider roads, more spacious houses and bigger compounds. Years later, I learnt that the plots in Hindu Colony were smaller because the locality itself was smaller than Parsi Colony, with narrower roads and fewer gardens. The reason for this was that middle-class Maharashtrians, who formed the bulk of lessees in Hindu Colony, had a lower paying capacity than their Parsi neighbours.

In Hindu Colony, most of those who leased plots from the Improvement Trust in the 1930s were men who had retired from government service or mercantile companies and had invested their life savings in properties that could be rented out. Property was safer than other forms of investment, especially since bids for leases were low, and the leases themselves were for a humongous 999 years. Buildings then could be

My house in Hindu Colony.

Every house had a balcony from where you could see life on the street.

erected at a relatively low cost, usually between Rs 15,000 and Rs 25,000. Rents were affordable and most renters in the area were middle-class, which brought a certain homogeneity to the neighbourhood.

My father, who was among the early migrants from the South, was from a middle-class family and moved from Bandra to Hindu Colony in order to be closer to Matunga with its sizeable South Indian population. He rented a flat in a three-storeyed (ground-plus-two) building that belonged to P V Kane, a well-known Sanskrit scholar who would ensure that his tenants were middle-class Brahmins. Built in 1931, the building had two apartments on each floor and was crowned with a sloping tiled roof, also called as a 'pitched roof'. Flats on the second floor had high ceilings while those on the ground and first floors were lower. The floor was made of wood joists with boarding over which stone slabs were laid. All buildings before 1940 were constructed in a similar way.

My flat, like all apartments in these buildings, was designed for a traditional way of living. All the rooms were interconnected and used in multiple ways like in village houses, where interior spaces are not designated for any specific use. The kitchen alone was a dedicated space because its location in the house was related to rituals associated with cooking and eating. It was as large as the other rooms because in addition to its primary functions, it was the space where female visitors were received and also doubled up as a makeshift bedroom at night. The kitchen platform was low and suitable for sit-down cooking, and the family sat on the floor for a meal.

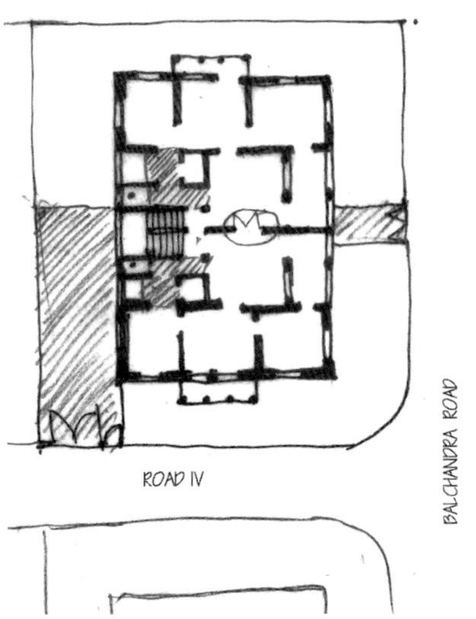

Within the house all rooms were connected by doors ensuring cross-ventilation. You had to close more than one door for privacy.

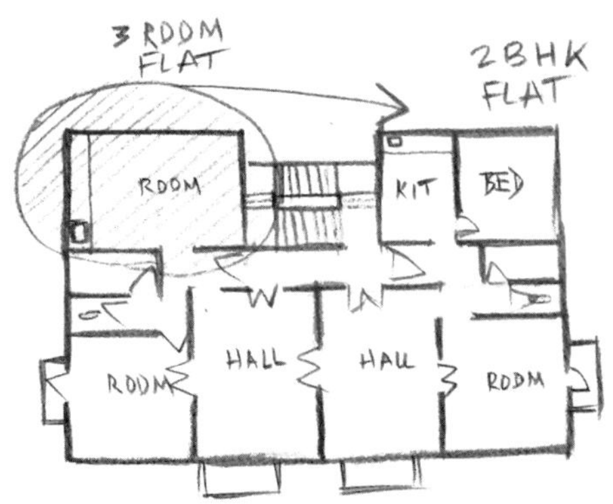

Flats were three- or four-roomed and advertised as such. The kitchen was a room, not just a space for cooking. Later developers halved the kitchen and sold the same flat as a 2BHK.

In the early decades of the century, the size of an apartment was defined by the number of rooms it had. 'To Let' boards in Hindu Colony as well as classified ads in the newspapers mentioned three- and four-room flats that typically consisted of a living room, a bedroom and a kitchen. This nomenclature changed after 1947, when the influx of refugees from neighbouring Pakistan led to an acute housing shortage. Rental flats became scarce and the idea of owning an apartment began to gain currency. The first developers, who were mostly Sindhi businessmen, offered buyers flats along with a share of the land on which the building stood. They built apartments in which the large kitchen of the erstwhile three-room flat was halved in size to accommodate a bedroom. These apartments were then sold as 2BHK (two bedrooms, hall and kitchen), a canny marketing strategy because the area of the apartment remained the same.

The shrinking of the kitchen had a huge impact on lifestyle. Kitchens became narrow, forcing the women of the house to stand and cook on a raised platform. This was not entirely a bad change since sitting on the floor had always carried a greater risk of a sari *pallu* catching fire. Smaller kitchens also meant that dining had to move to another area, usually the living room, a move that was initially resisted since families were used to cooking and eating together. For many years small kitchens were referred to as "Sindhi kitchens" since the common perception was that Sindhi developers had brought in the BHK terminology to make small flats appear big and increase sales. From then on it became a standard practice among all developers, not just the Sindhi ones.

Some houses had bay windows that added area to the living-room. They replaced balconies, and the connection with the street was lost.

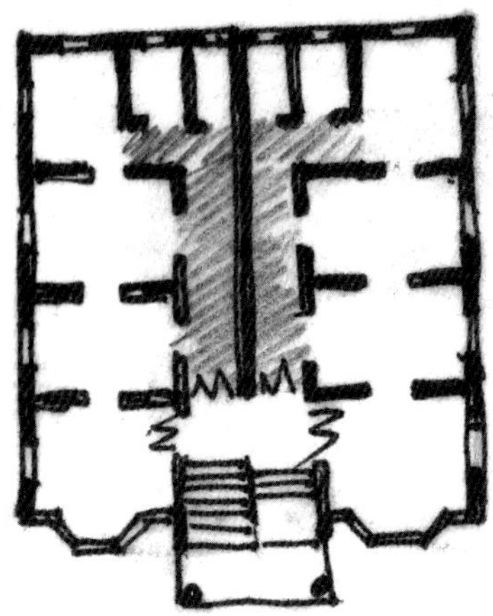

Every flat had two entrance doors. One lead to the main room and the other to the kitchen and toilets at the rear.

Flat Design

A flat in Hindu Colony had two doors opening into the stair lobby: one led to the front room, the other to a corridor connecting the WC, bathroom, washing place (also called a *nahani*) and kitchen. This was the service entrance for sweepers, domestic workers and tradesmen – a hangover from the days of manual scavenging and caste segregation. Locating toilets at one end of the apartment continued for a very long time. None of the houses in Hindu Colony had a toilet attached to a habitable room.

An interesting feature in the design was that flats adjoining one another had an interconnecting door between the living rooms. In my house, as perhaps in several others, the door was always left open during the day, and we walked in and out of one another's houses. It was a wonderful feeling of security both for us and our parents, who could even leave us at home without worrying about our safety. Some of my friends who lived in a chawl in Parel also had a door connecting their rooms to the adjoining ones. This feature, which originated in chawl housing for structural reasons, carried over even in the apartments built till the 1950s.

For a long time I believed that the connecting door was a design innovation meant to enable security and neighbourliness. However, years later when my fellow students and I studied chawl structures, we found that this was mainly to enable tenements to be combined laterally without breaking the intervening wall, which consisted of timber posts and thin infills. Breaking the wall could endanger structural stability. Neighbours living together peaceably was just a byproduct of a structural necessity and not a design innovation.

The balcony was the town equivalent of the 'otla' in the village house. You sat in your balcony and bargained with the hawker on the street or called out to your neighbours passing by. Everyone knew everyone else.

Most houses in Hindu Colony were built with thick load-bearing walls and projecting balconies in wood. Windows were narrow because the lintels above them were made of brick, which could only produce a certain width of arch unlike the more versatile reinforced cement concrete (RCC) which came into popular use in the 1940s. Balconies were made of wood with carved supporting brackets, railings and glass panels called lead lights. Houses were cool because inter-connected rooms provided cross-ventilation. However, the rooms suffered from a paucity of light on account of the narrow windows and the trees outside that reduced the light coming in. The verandahs or balconies made all the difference – we sat there for hours, even slept in them.

Most buildings were constructed by small-time contractors who hired engineers to design them. The engineers, on their part, relied on draftsmen or assistants in architects' offices for the design of the facade (also known as elevation) of a building and its architectural details. The building's facade was generally the combined effort of the draftsman, engineer and the skilled craftsman employed on the job, who was usually a carpenter. While credit is due to the engineers for paying attention to the design of the facade, it was the craftsman whose contribution was often the most important. When RCC-framed buildings appeared in the 1940s, architects used the same designs but constructed balconies, chhajjas and brackets in concrete rather than wood. The mainstay of the construction team shifted from the carpenter to the mason.

All balconies did not look the same. You recognised a house by its balcony.

Balconies were made of wood shaped by the carpenter who played the lead role in construction.

Concrete replaced wood but balconies still looked the same. Now the mason replaced the carpenter in the lead role.

Parsi Colony And The Differences

On the other side of Vincent Road, the thick black line of my childhood imagination, lived some of my good friends from school. Their neighbourhood, Parsi Colony, had more gardens and it was to play in these that I crossed over from the relatively cramped Hindu Colony where I was perforce confined to my compound. My classmate, Darius Engineer, lived in a house that overlooked a vast open playground belonging to the Dadar Parsi Gymkhana. Most Parsis living in the colony were members of this club and would meet there every evening to play cards or share gossip about the community. Hindu Colony had no such den except for Bhagini Samaj, which was exclusively for women. Unlike Parsi Colony, the residents of Hindu Colony were not bound by a single religion, region or subculture – the only commonalities they shared were language, mostly Marathi, and being part of the middle class.

There were physical differences between the two neighbourhoods too. A study by Kamla Raheja Institute of Architecture shows that plots and flats in Hindu Colony were smaller than those in Parsi Colony, which affected the living standards of its residents. While a Hindu Colony resident had a covered space of 11 square metres, his neighbour to the east enjoyed 15 square metres while his relative living in Parel to the south had only five square metres. What did this tell me? Planners see density as the number of persons sharing land for living, utilities and all facilities needed in a city. That is at the scale of a city. Little or no consideration is given to space within a dwelling and space outside in the neighbourhood. The ratio between the two is crucial for the planner to decide on the number and size of residential sites, footprints and heights of buildings and width of streets. This was evident in both the areas I lived in.

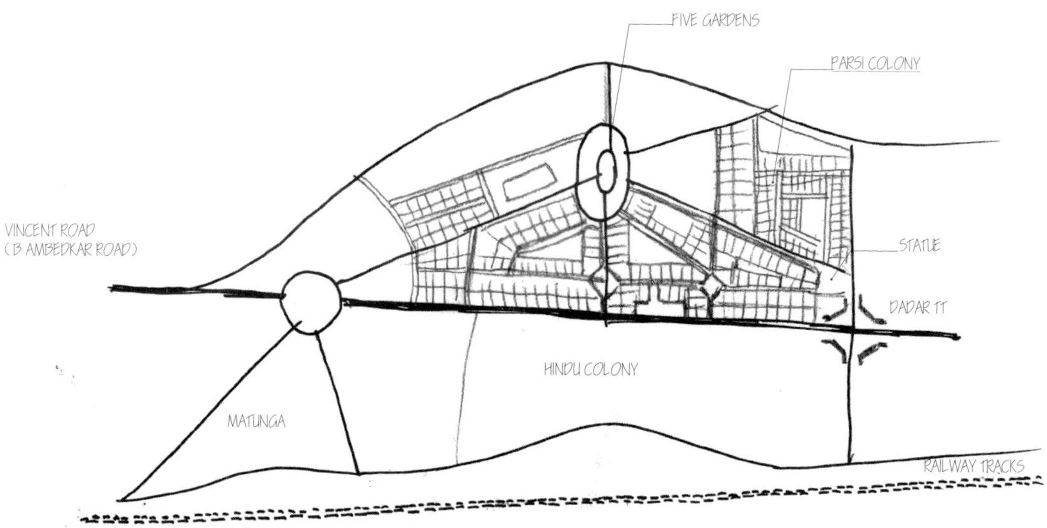

The density ratio became even clearer to me when I shifted from Hindu Colony to a building called Gold Finch at the northern end of Parsi Colony. The road I moved to – and where I have lived ever since – is only nine metres wide, a dimension that allows homes in the three-storey buildings to get adequate light and air while retaining a connection to activity on the street. Living within shouting distance of the street made us feel safe. When an additional floor was subsequently built over the houses, its residents found a disconnect between their flat and the street. People looked smaller and hawkers were out of reach. The additional height of ten feet made all the difference.

The difference between my new and old residence was immediately obvious: the presence of an architect in the former and the absence of one in the latter. Gold Finch, with its large, well-lit and airy flats, was designed by G B Mhatre, a well-known city architect of that time. Built in 1937, the building, which appears modern in design even today, used RCC technology which permitted a boldly cantilevered verandah, skewed on plan, and wide windows – elements that differentiated it from Prabha Sadan, my earlier residence though, like Prabha Sadan, its plan too had interconnected rooms. Although the architectural details of the building are in the Art Deco style, Gold Finch, like many others in the city, is among the early modern buildings that transited from Art Deco to modern.

R P Masani Road, on which Gold Finch stands, was also called Hollywood Lane because several film stars from New Theatres in Calcutta migrated in the 1940s. The most famous of them were Prithviraj Kapoor and the singer K L Saigal. They, along with others, gave the area a cosmopolitan character unlike Parsi and Hindu Colonies, which were, by and large, parochial.

A house by G B Mhatre built in 1937 had verandahs skewed on plan and cantilevered, made possible by using RCC technology which in the '30s was new.

The other buildings in the neighbourhood had exteriors designed in the Art Deco style. This was most visible in the verandah railing

Between the northern and southern parts of the precinct is the seven-acre park named after Mancherji Joshi but popularly called Five Gardens. Joshi was a civil engineer in the Bombay Improvement Trust who used his position to influence the planning of the area south of Five Gardens and get the maximum advantage for his Parsi community. He persuaded the Improvement Trust to approve a covenant for the Parsi Central Association Cooperative Housing Society by which 102 plots in the colony were reserved for the exclusive use of Parsis. His argument was that plots were going abegging, and a concession such as this would help him convince his community to buy them all. He also managed to get the colony a larger share of the open space planned for the Dadar-Matunga Scheme V precinct.

According to Joshi's granddaughter, Zarine Engineer, Joshi had to work hard to persuade the charitable trusts of his community to build houses for their middle-class members. He had to hard-sell them the idea that the Parsi community needed to move out of its small tenements in overcrowded localities in South Bombay to bigger flats in the new Parsi Colony. He also had to plant trees and develop gardens before he could get the plots sold. Joshi was later elected three times to the municipality as a corporator.

As a young student of architecture, I realised that most buildings in the Parsi part of the colony were built by architects who used RCC consultants to design the structure. I later worked on a project with a structural engineer called Jehangir Darukhanawala, who had designed the structures of most buildings in Parsi Colony, including Gold Finch. He told me that RCC buildings came up in Parsi Colony from the mid-1930s, ahead of other areas. Apartments were planned for a western style of living. Flats were larger than in the neighbouring areas, and toilets were located between rooms instead of being at one end of the flat.

Mancherji Joshi was largely responsible for planning and developing Parsi Colony. He got for his community a covenant that reserved several plots for exclusive use by Parsis.

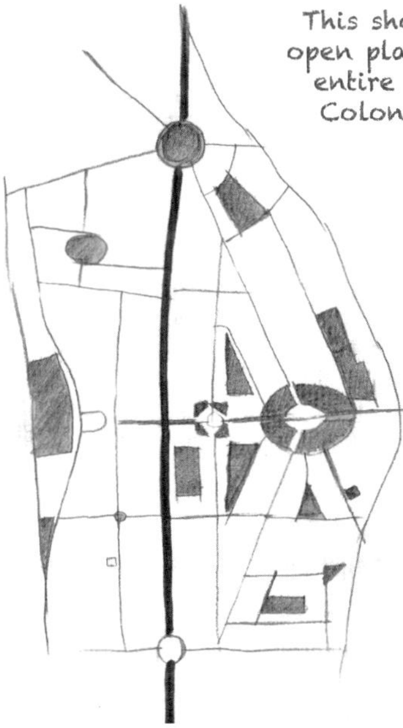

This shows parks and open play areas in the entire precinct. Parsi Colony has a larger share of this.

Flats in Parsi Colony were bigger than those in Hindu Colony. An individual here had a covered area of 15 square metres while a Hindu Colony resident had only 11square metres.

Pitched or sloping roofs, characteristic of buildings of the late 1920s and early 1930s, gave way to flat roofs. The design of balconies, chhajjas and canopies changed. Buildings were designed in a language that used features of the 1930s Art Deco style in their structures, facades and plan arrangements, unlike the 'Indo Deco' buildings in Hindu Colony which retained the plans of earlier buildings and grafted improvised Art Deco facades.

The Improvement Trust had rules that ensured order in the entire precinct as also in all the other schemes developed by it. For instance, buildings could not occupy more than a third of the site and could not be more than three storeys high. The setbacks were fixed on all sides, and it was compulsory to maintain the one on the front even if the rear setback was larger. Buildings had to be kept in a line on the front. In Sion to the north, an enterprising engineer attempted a deviation. He set alternate buildings back a few feet further than the others. But the Improvement Trust allowed this deviation only on one street.

Regularity and order were more visible in Hindu Colony and Parsi Colony than in Matunga, where some roads were narrow and the front setbacks of buildings smaller. Buildings were closer, giving the impression of disorder. What unified the houses on the street in all schemes of the Trust were the compound walls, which had to strictly follow design rules – masonry walls with the upper third done in grillework. It was on this grillework that my friends and I would sit as we waited for our turn to bat in gully cricket matches.

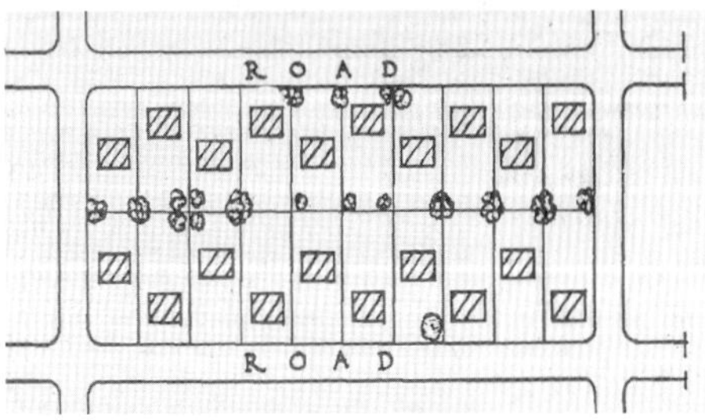

Design rules of the Improvement Trust insisted that buildings be in a line on the front. In Sion, for a change, the building line on the front was broken. Front setbacks were staggered. This was done only once.

Compound walls, like the arcade, unified buildings on a street. They were designed to have grilles on the upper third of their height – nice to sit on while waiting for your turn to bat in gully cricket.

'Pitched' or sloping roofs, characteristic of buildings of the 1920s and early 1930s, later gave way to flat roofs when RCC replaced timber.

Most buildings in Parsi Colony were designed by architects unlike Hindu Colony where they were commissioned to contractors.

Charitable trusts invested in housing for the lower income groups of the community. These were also designed by architects.

Dadar Parsi Colony was, in a sense, a gated community. Most buildings could be owned or rented only by Parsis. Yet, its exclusivity is almost imperceptible as the house and space outside it merge inseparably into the city's fabric unlike other gated communities that stand like lone objects in the city's landscape.

Matunga

Matunga is the northernmost part of the precinct planned by the Improvement Trust. It is also the most interesting. I walked through the area every day to catch a train to school, to run errands or accompany my parents to functions organised by the South Indian community. Till the 1960s, South Indians were the dominant community in Matunga, which was popularly known as 'Mini Madras' on account of its temples, music sabhas, shops and restaurants that were replicas of those in South India. People in dhotis and women in Kanjivaram saris were a common sight. Most South Indian restaurants were located around King's Circle and were patronised by everyone but South Indians, who preferred to have their afternoon tiffin and coffee at home.

Early migrants to the area, including my father, came from the South in the first two decades of the twentieth century. Most were employed as clerks or stenographers in the railways or civil service or in commercial companies. They brought with them nothing but their skills, mostly typing, shorthand and book-keeping. They also brought with them a Brahmanical and ritualistic culture, to sustain which they built institutions for religion, music and education. Initially, cultural activities were carried out in rented premises but over time the community built properties to house the institutions they started.

The South Indian community was not visible in the social order because the positions its members occupied at the workplace were insignificant. They were all called Madrasis, just as those from the North were called bhaiyyas, and were known for their industriousness. In fact, a senior railway officer is known to have asked his junior, "Why are you working hard when there are Madrasis in the department?"

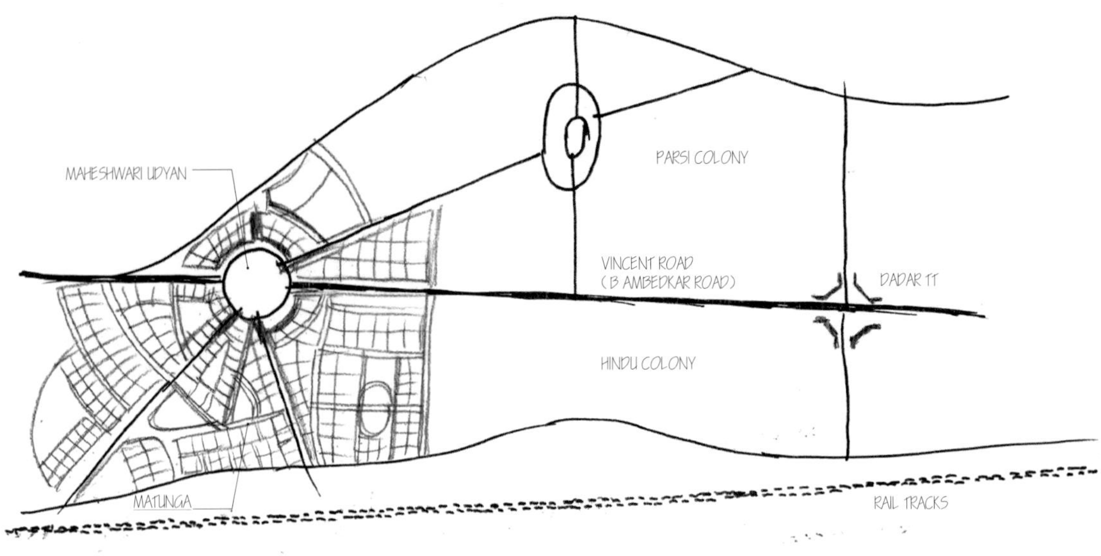

The one thing that gave the community a measure of visibility was the very popular South Indian restaurants in the area. Mani's Lunch Home, for instance, has been in business for over 70 years, serving up delicious fare to several generations of students while the popular Cafe Madras has had the consistent patronage of non-South Indian foodies. Matunga has other interesting places that are part of the collective memory of old-time residents. For me, the wide footpaths around King's Circle Garden (now called Maheshwari Udyan), the plaza outside the railway station and Ruia College, the Indian Gymkhana and Napoo Garden were special. Around King's Circle, the front setbacks of buildings are merged with the footpath, making it a wide urban space where people stroll, vendors sell newspapers, magazines and used books, and stray hawkers try and make quick sales. This is also the place where people meet while waiting for a table in restaurants. It struck me as a simple and effortless way of making an urban space.

Until the 1960s, getting to Matunga Station meant weaving your way through a messy market – as was the case with most railway stations. Then the market was shifted into a new building, leaving an open plaza – one of the few near a railway station on the suburban line, which made arrival and departure a pleasant experience for train commuters. The annual Ganesh festival was also held in this plaza – ten days of festivities, concerts and hawkers selling eatables.

For many years, the festival was sponsored by Varadaraja Mudaliar, an underworld don with political clout. He had total control over major criminal activity in Matunga, Sion and Dharavi and guaranteed votes for whichever party he chose to favour. In the 1970s, his writ prevailed over the market area and all shop owners were forced to fund, among other things, the annual Ganesh festival, although the impression

At King's Circle, the front setbacks of buildings and the footpath merge to make a larger public space. When that happens, it is not just for pedestrian movement. It turns into a place that over time becomes a landmark in the city.

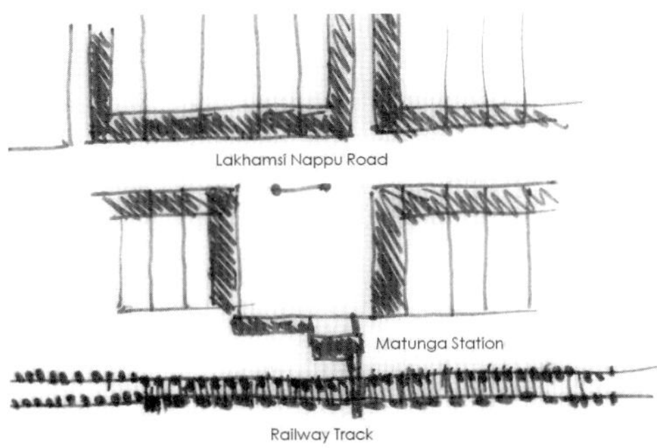

The plaza outside Matunga Station was used to celebrate the Ganpati festival patronised by an underworld don and paid for by shopkeepers in the area. The city lost this public space when it became a parking lot.

created was that he was the main sponsor. To cut him down to size, the police commissioner shifted the police chowky from the north-west corner of the plaza to its centre so that the Ganesh festival could not be held there anymore. We lost an urban space because an administrative act to deal with a don was not revoked even after the don's power faded.

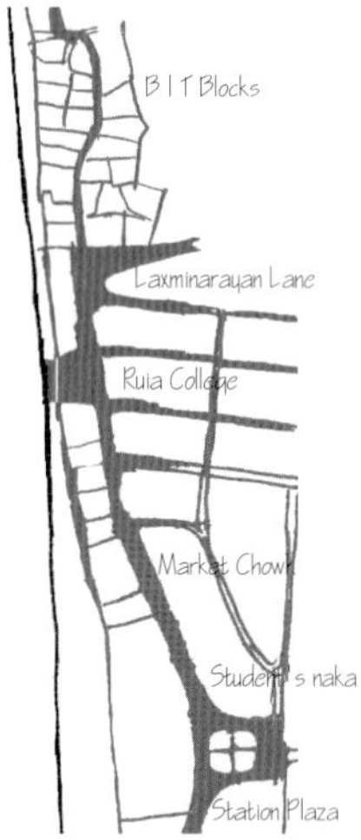

The walk from B I T Blocks in the north through the original Matunga village, to Ruia College is the most interesting walk in Matunga.

There were other public spaces along the western edge of the precinct as well, as a walk from the Bombay Improvement Trust (BIT) Blocks in the north to Hindu Colony in the south reveals. The walk, through the winding Laxminarayan Lane in the original village of Matunga, leads to a public square from where Lakhamsi Napoo Road begins. Down that road, past the station plaza, are colleges abuzz with students who bring life and energy to the place. The space outside Ruia College, especially the wide footpaths outside the Irani restaurant (now an Udupi restaurant) and Mani's Lunch Home, are used by students for chats over tea and snacks. The larger area, planned as a place for students to meet, is on the south-east of Ruia College. This space is not used since its location and the entrance to the college do not face each other and neither is there a restaurant to attract students.

Bombay (now Mumbai), like other cities, has informal public spaces called nakas, where friendships are struck up, news exchanged and issues debated. Nakas are seldom included in development plans because it is difficult to predict how people will use a space, especially if the users are from diverse groups. Planned nakas, or plazas, tend to be successful where there is less diversity in users and where social interaction is a daily routine – Jaipur is a good example of nakas built into the city's plan. With daily use, nakas, whether spontaneous or planned, get woven into the fabric of a city.

The space outside Ruia College is a 'katta' for students. Such spaces are seldom planned because their use cannot be predicted but some become popular and over time become a part of the city's collective memory.

Mani's Lunch Home is more than a good eatery. It is also a place for students to chat over tea and snacks.

At the northern end of Matunga lies Indian Gymkhana, which was one of the earliest sports clubs to host floodlit basketball tournaments – an exciting new event for us young boys at that time. Before the gymkhana lies Napoo Garden, a venue used in the 1940s for political debates between students, young khadi-clad nationalists and fiery leftists. Napoo Garden, tucked away amid houses, was not as large and visible as Five Gardens or King's Circle but it was suitable for small gatherings and did not attract police attention. Meetings were held here to persuade students to take part in the freedom movement and to discuss ideas about post-independence development. I remember political debates centred around the Gandhian ideals of grass-roots development, socialism and even on Karl Marx's theory of dialectical materialism. A story goes that during one of these debates, a South Indian was asked on which side of the political divide his community stood. He replied, "We are neither leftists nor rightists. We are typists." The post-script to that story is that he said this not meekly, as most would assume, but assertively – because no government, left or right, could run without typists.

The garden stood on land owned by Lakhamsi Napoo, the prosperous Kutchi trader after whom a road was named in Hindu Colony. His project for constructing apartment buildings was turned down, and he had to give up his land for public use. Kutchis owned land in and around Matunga village, and acquiring it for the Dadar-Matunga Estate Scheme V was difficult for the Improvement Trust. The Kutchis litigated against acquisition and contested compensation. To reduce delays, the Improvement Trust negotiated prices directly with individual landowners on a case-to-case basis instead of applying standard valuation methods. In many instances, architects mediated between their clients and the Improvement Trust in valuation of properties.

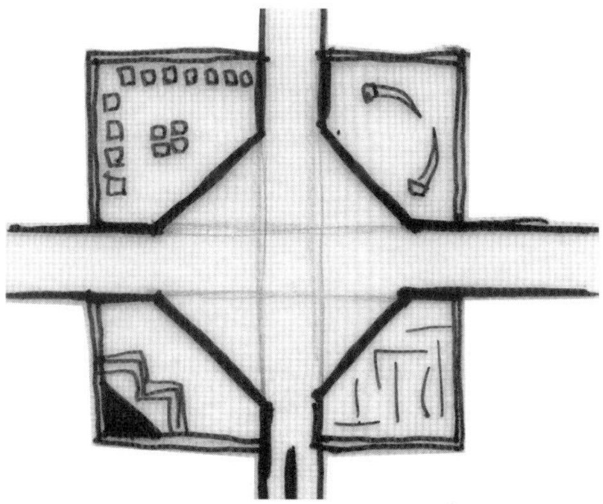

Planned 'naka's seldom work if user groups are diverse. They work better when users are a more homogeneous bunch as in Jaipur.

Napoo was not as educated or professionally qualified as Mancherji Joshi nor did he have connections with officials in the government. Yet, he extracted from the Improvement Trust a concession similar to the covenants in Parsi Colony: twenty plots reserved for the exclusive use of the Kutchi Oswal Jain community to which he belonged. The plots were leased to the Kutchi Visa Oswal Cooperative Society in 1920, on which 22 buildings were subsequently built.

Summation

I had friends in all parts of the Dadar-Matunga area. The three places – Hindu Colony, Parsi Colony and Matunga – were different because the people who lived there brought to them their distinct character and cultures. Parsi Colony was quiet and orderly, Hindu Colony was staid but noisy on festive occasions, while Matunga was vibrant and colourful. Such variety within a planned precinct made me realise early on that an urban space whose design is derived from formulae and abstract ideas becomes meaningful only when a group of people occupy it and give it character.

Today, that variety of people and places is slowly disappearing. This is at least partly due to the government policy, introduced in the 1980s, of allowing old rental housing to be demolished and reconstructed. The resulting new form is inevitably the tower, which is associated with affluence and isolation. Towers are like ghettos, secluded and often occupied by a single community or religious group. Diversity, if any, is accepted only if those who aspire to live there belong to the affluent section of society. The unwritten rule is: you are welcome to stay here if you can afford it.

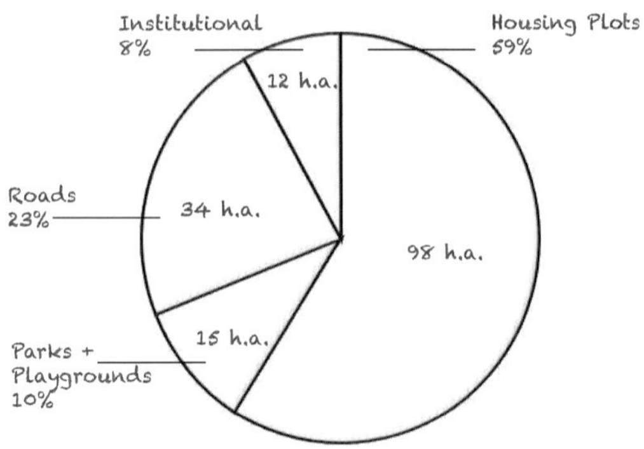

This is how land is shared in the precinct.

An urban space designed from formulae and abstract ideas is cold and heartless. It needs people to occupy it and give it character. It is only then that it becomes human.

Citizens' groups have long debated the redevelopment policy that allows buildings built before the 1950s to be razed and rebuilt – indeed, even buildings built in the '80s are allowed to be redeveloped now. Most of these groups have raised concerns about overcrowding, strain on the infrastructure and the loss of open space. These objections come from those concerned with the larger picture of the ward as a whole. But the majority of residents do not look beyond their own building. Protected tenants are only too happy to convert a tenancy right to ownership in the new building, while landlords are glad to get flats in the new building along with some cash. And the developer can rake in big profits because his selling price is based on the cost of land – for which he does not pay. Everyone gains, or so the government says without stopping to think of the effect of such redevelopment on the entire ward and the city.

The reconstruction policy was brought in because of the collapse of old buildings in some parts of the island city. But the Dadar-Matunga area is not derelict, nor have there been any house collapses here. The application of the redevelopment policy to the Dadar-Matunga area is clearly to benefit developers. Residents of the locality do not have a say in approving a scheme though they are the ones to bear the brunt of the additional load on the infrastructure.

We have come a long way from living in diverse groups within a planned precinct, where everyone had as much space outside his doorstep as he had inside. That is what the Improvement Trust meant when it promoted the Dadar-Matunga Scheme V as a garden suburb. Through its layout and design rules, the precinct showed that development becomes humane when every square metre of built residential space is matched by an equal or larger area of land for all the things that support city life – roads, parks and playgrounds, education and health and infrastructure, which depend on land distribution. The changes that have taken place since the 1980s have shown that increasing built-up residential area reduces the individual's share of common areas. The new rules envisage only one way of living: the stand-alone high-rise apartment building that has little or no connection to its neighbours or locality. It is the exact opposite of what the Improvement Trust's plan intended.

Living in a community has given way to living in isolation. Towers, the opposite of the Garden Suburb concept of the Improvement Trust, are saying: "Forget greenery. Enjoy air space – if you have the money."

Studying In South Bombay

Studying In South Bombay

My school and college were both in South Bombay, some 10 km from where I lived. I travelled by local train every day with friends from my neighbourhood in a 25-minute ride that was long enough for us to catch up on homework, pull one another's legs or play word games. Other commuters would be drowsily nodding off or staring blankly out of the window; the more active ones would play cards or sing devotional songs. I learnt that the players and singers came from the distant suburbs and were a group only because they commuted by the same train every day. Our ride may have been shorter than theirs but it was long enough to make me conscious of a world outside Matunga. The train was a wonderful link between the two worlds of my existence.

Getting out of the train at Victoria Terminus (today's Chhatrapati Shivaji Terminus), I would cross the road, past horse-drawn carriages and trams, then walk along Cruikshank Road (now Mahapalika Marg) named after a Municipal Commissioner. The footpath was wide and buildings abutting it were important and impressive. They were set back from the road, had porticos in front of them and were built in black trap

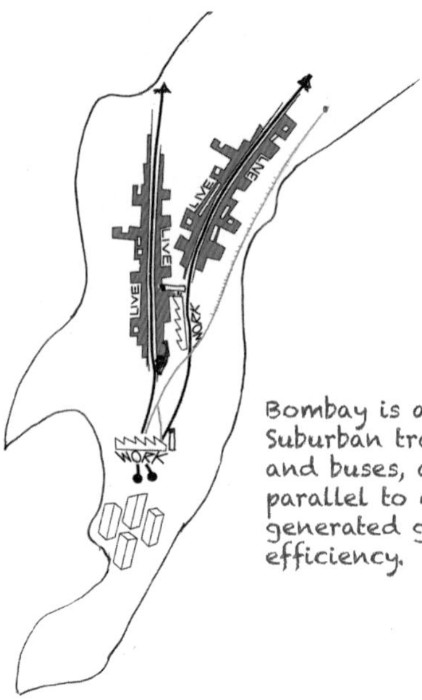

Bombay is a linear city. Suburban trains, trams and buses, all running parallel to one another, generated growth and efficiency.

Going to school in South Bombay meant travelling by local train. The train connected the two worlds of my existence.

stone, which was intimidating because of its colour, scale and size. These buildings defined the edge of the Esplanade, a term that was then used to refer to Azad Maidan and Cross Maidan. I later learnt that the term was often used for the ground around a fort kept open as protection against sudden attacks from "rebellious natives".

My school, St Xavier's High School, was at the junction of Cruikshank Road and Carnac Road (today's Lokmanya Tilak Marg) and abutted two entirely different worlds. To the north of Carnac Road lay a colourful world of winding roads, densely packed buildings and streets bustling with people and hawkers – confused and chaotic compared to the orderly world on the south side of the road. The contrast prompted me to explore both areas.

I discovered that the two best ways to see a city, in two different scales as it were, was to either walk around and get a feel of the various neighbourhoods, nooks and crannies or take a round trip on the upper deck of a tram or bus for a great overhead view. In the 1940s and '50s, you could travel by tram from the city's southern tip (Sassoon Dock) to the northern end (King's Circle) and see most of the island city because the tram ran on three arterial roads. That was how I saw Girgaum, Kalbadevi, Bhendi Bazar, Parel and Dadar – lively places with people of different communities living in varying degrees of overcrowding. Later, I made friends with classmates who lived in Girgaum and Prarthana Samaj and walked with them through their locality's bylanes, eating authentic Marathi lunches at Virkar or batata wadas at Kulkarni's.

After my schooling, I spent a year studying to be an accountant before deciding to switch to architecture, a subject which was then taught only at the Sir J J School of Art. When I visited JJ for the first time to write

Looking out of a tram window on the upper deck showed you another dimension of a street. You could see most of the island city on tram journeys.

Trams, though slow, were inexpensive to travel in. Instead of improving rolling stock and making them faster and efficient, they were discontinued in 1965. Till then, Flora Fountain was a major tram halt.

the entrance exam, I was surprised to see this beautiful wooded campus in Fort, an area which I only knew as crowded and noisy. The entrance examination itself was quite funny. It started with dictation, a subject that I had left behind in my second standard at school. The person dictating was neither loud nor clear in his pronunciation: 'Akbar ' sounded like 'October' and 'monuments' like 'momentous'. I wondered why the test for admitting students to a school of architecture should include dictation but soon realised that it was meant for the many students who came from vernacular-medium schools and were not fluent in English. The other test was freehand drawing, which was a level playing field for all.

The first two years at JJ were spent learning drawing skills since the curriculum emphasised drawing before designing. This system of education was a carryover from the time the architecture department of the school first began in the form of classes for draftsmen. When the curriculum was upgraded in 1908 to become a formal four-year certificate course in architecture, subjects like history of architecture, structural mechanics and building construction were added but the emphasis on drawing continued. Importance was also given to building visits for students to understand the elements that made a building – its style, proportions and history.

Fort

Fort was a good place to start exploring the city because it held stories of enterprise, opportunities and prosperity. It was a planned area with public buildings of a size and scale that overawed the onlooker. Initially I thought this effect was intended to communicate the authority of the ruling British, but after

Public buildings were built in stone masonry. Floor heights were greater to make rooms cool. This made the buildings look impressive. Some historians mistook this for symbols of the rulers' authority.

looking at the buildings closely and finding that most of them were built with thick, load-bearing masonry walls, I discovered that the design had nothing to do with imperialistic haughtiness. The warm climate demanded greater floor heights, and black trap or yellow basalt stone was therefore a stronger and more durable material for external walls. The combination of stone and greater floor heights gave buildings an overbearing appearance that was misread as an expression of the ruler's authority.

But there was more to Fort than what the British had built. My friends and I, driven by the energy and curiosity of youth, would walk through the entire Fort area in order to discover its different facets. We found that orderliness was limited to a few areas and mostly along the main roads – behind it was a more haphazard town with narrow streets chock-a-block with people, handcarts and hawkers. In one such area, Bora Bazaar, people lived above shops, many of them for generations. They followed their daily routine like in other parts of the city: visiting temples and buying wares from hawkers whom they knew by name. There was an order here too, though of another kind.

On the main roads of the city, order was created by the repetition of identical or similar units. Rules ensured that buildings related to neighbouring buildings and streets. People did not matter. But in the organically grown town behind, the order was one of complex relationships between people, places and the daily routine of life. If these were in harmony, buildings and rules did not matter. Neighbourliness was not between buildings but people. Organic growth, apparently disorderly, has within it a dynamic pluralism that comes from a multitude of ideas, each with its own logic. This is unique to Indian towns, most of which do not have any formal planning.

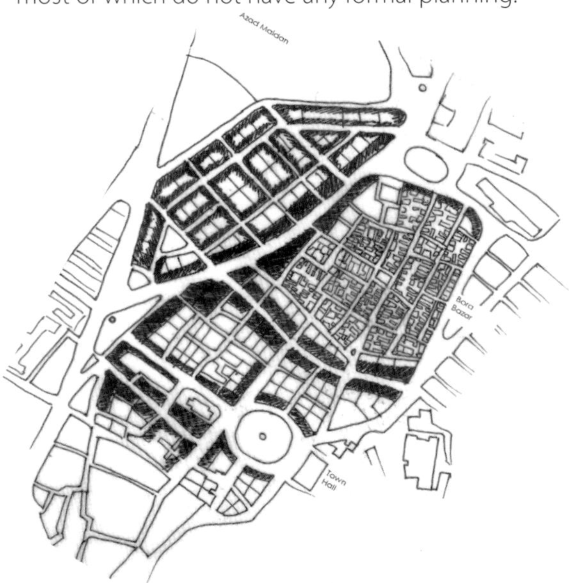

Fort is a planned area with order on the edges of main roads.

There is more to Fort than what the British built. Behind the visible planned order lies a more disorderly town

Many years later, this became clearer to me when I read architect Christopher Alexander's classic essay on the nature of cities titled 'The city is not a tree'. "Cities which are planned by designers and planners are artificial while cities that have arisen more or less spontaneously over many, many years, are natural," he writes. "A natural city has the organisation of a semi-lattice, but when we organise a city artificially, we organise it as a tree. The structural simplicity of trees is like the compulsive desire for neatness and order that insists that the candlesticks on a mantelpiece be perfectly straight and perfectly symmetrical about the centre. The semi-lattice, by comparison, is the structure of a complex fabric. It is the structure of great paintings and symphonies."

The co-existence of planning and informality in Bombay reminded me of Jaipur, where behind the main roads and between the crossroads lies a growth that is indigenous and influenced more by exigencies than by rigid planning rules. I observed this also during my student years through exploring the entire Fort and other areas with Dileep, my classmate. He had seen many towns, especially those that were off the beaten track, and he had a knack of spotting interesting places. During our Fort jaunts, which were frequent, we would invariably end up at Pancham Puriwala, a century-old eatery, for a quick meal and a discussion about what we saw. We asked ourselves: Why and how did informally grown areas come up? Why do people continue to live there? What qualities did informal growth have that planned areas did not? We also wondered if we would opt to live there if we had a choice. These questions did not have easy answers.

The reasons for informal growth are often incidental, not intentional. The 'native' part of Fort area is a case in point.The British allowed some 'native' Indians to live inside the Fort, either because they provided

In the informal town, people, handcarts and hawkers take up the most space on the roads

Life is lived on the street as well.

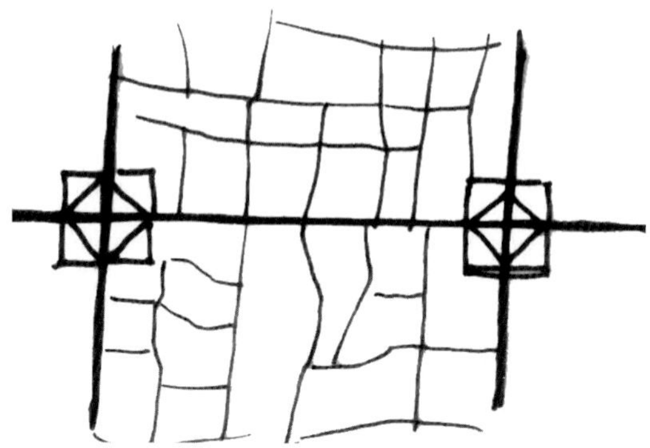

In Jaipur, like Bombay, informality and planning co-exist. In the grid bounded by planned streets is a growth that is not pre-determined but influenced by exigencies.

essential services or because they were traders with whom they did business. The natives had little land to live on but the British did not concern themselves with how they lived or the kind of buildings they built. The latter, therefore, came up in any manner that suited the landlord without any regard for light and air in the tenements or overcrowding and lack of sanitation. It took several fires and minor outbreaks of plague to bring in some semblance of a town. The British introduced bye-laws for orderly development but the town had already taken shape before the laws were sanctioned by the government.

People have lived in Bora Bazaar, Parsi Bazaar and neighbouring areas for generations. Many have businesses there or work nearby. For those whose workplaces are far away, trains and other modes of transport are easily available. With all the conveniences needed for daily life at hand, people opt to stay in these crowded Fort neighbourhoods although buildings there are too close to one another and people are in and out of one another's houses all the time. In such informal towns, individuals have to share their private world with others, make do with less living space and accommodate everyone in their daily routine. In return, they are not lonely and enjoy a greater sense of emotional security in this close-knit, if somewhat insular, group. Today, few would opt to move into an informal town of this sort. They might have felt differently if the area was less dense, buildings were only two storeys high, better maintained and the environment cleaner like in old European towns.

As we walked around Fort, we noticed that the contrast between the planned and unplanned areas was stark. Plots and buildings in the planned areas were bigger and the spaces between them noticeable, unlike Bora Bazaar where it was difficult to make out where one property ended and the other began, and where spaces between buildings were narrow.

Old towns in Europe have the same informality as Indian towns though they are less crowded and cluttered. People also live in close-knit groups.

Like Dadar and Matunga where I lived, Fort was vertically divided by a wide road on which trams and buses ran. Called Hornby Road (later D N Road), this important connector was bordered by office buildings that were built up to the front edge of their plots without any setback. Every building on both sides of the road had an arcade for the full width of the plot on which it stood. This was a wonderful response to the climate and provided a shaded walkway for pedestrians. The arcade was an important urban design idea and we assumed that, like all ideas, it must have been improvised and improved on before it was codified as a rule.

On the main road, buildings had shops on the ground floor and offices on the upper floors. Some buildings, especially those in the area between Hornby Road and the maidans, had residences for the European managers of the companies that occupied the floors below or residences called 'chummeries' for expatriate bachelor employees.

We noticed that the buildings in Fort did not conform to any particular style of architecture even though arcades and the stone masonry walls on the exterior visually unified the buildings on Hornby Road. The styles of some buildings were referred to as Indo-Gothic, Indo-Saracenic or Neo-Classic, 'Indo-This' or ' Indo-That'. For us students, this was confusing because we were studying history from Sir Bannister Fletcher's 'A History of Architecture on the Comparative Method', which looked at history through fixed frames. These frames were either of a period or empire or style and distinctly labelled. It was a rigid way of seeing, and like Fletcher we could not see how styles could blend.

On D N Road, buildings were unified at the eye level by arcades, a compulsory design feature

Buildings were built up to the front edge of the plot and arcades provide a shaded walkway.

However, Claude Batley, a prominent British architect who headed our school till 1944, thought differently about adaptation of a style for new needs. He brought in a subject called specialised history, which looked at how traditional Indian architecture could be adapted for contemporary projects – in this class, we could take liberties with the established orders and innovate within their basic principles. Batley's intention was to remind students that architecture in India needed to transit from its rich past to the modern day through studying the architecture of different parts of the country and by building on its time-tested understanding of materials in new ways, not by blindly copying architecture from the western world.

Batley supported his theory with his book titled 'Design Development of Indian Architecture' – a compilation of measured drawings by his students of lesser known monuments and residential buildings. Most of these monuments were considered relatively unimportant by historians and archaeologists. But we referred to the book often because it contained examples of architecture from different parts of the country, and we gained a better sense of history from it than we did from Fletcher's book although the latter was more comprehensive.

Batley also reminded us to study the theories surrounding architecture during different periods of history. The Hindu temple was of particular interest since it was more than a place of worship – it had a central position in the town and all life revolved around it. In his book, Batley analysed the temple through a series of diagrams to explain the constructs of its various physical elements, especially the shikhara. However, his analysis did not go beyond the geometry of the form.

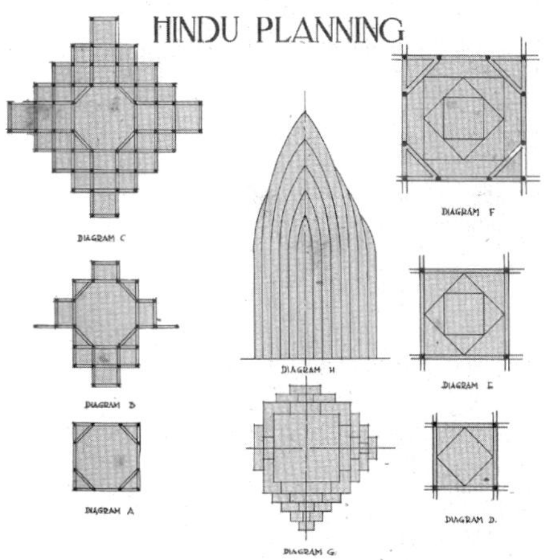

Batley, in his book, analysed the constructs of the temple 'shikhara'. He did not go beyond the geometry of the form.

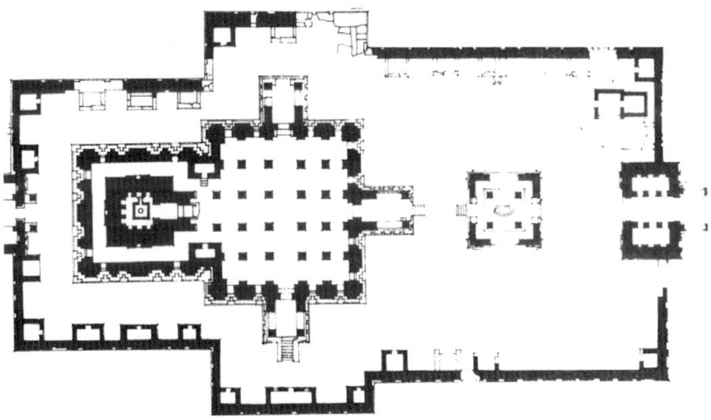

The plan of the Hindu temple is based on a mystical grid of squares called a mandala which diagramatically represent the cosmos. Each square in the grid has a religious significance.

The Hindu temple is the physical expression of a philosophy in which everything in the universe is connected. It is full of symbolism, its plan being derived from a diagram of the cosmos with its planetary positions, each of which is endowed with mystical significance. Its pyramidal tower, the shikhara, is a symbol of Mount Meru, and the finial, the apex of the temple structure, is on the axis connecting the earth to the cosmos. It also symbolises the ascent to enlightenment. However, this spiritual subtext was lost on our professors, who taught us only about the physical aspects of the temple – its form, construction materials and methods – not the significance of the parts that made the whole. The iconography integral to the design of the temple was referred to by them as only decorative elements meant to act as relief to surfaces, while in fact icons were used for depicting events and life during those times as also different manifestations of Divinity. The underlying philosophy of temple design and the role of the architect, who was also sculptor, builder and interpreter of the deeper meaning of symbols, was of interest only to scholars, not our professors.

The studio for specialised history in our third year at school was well intentioned. Batley probably made it interesting and students then perhaps did not question its validity. But we were sceptical about mixing historical baggage with modernity and the effect it could have on our designs and architecture in general. So we embarked on a trek around the city to see if there were buildings that fulfilled the ideal that Batley expounded, particularly the General Post Office, Prince of Wales Museum and Gateway of India which, we had been told, were good examples of the application of historical styles to modern buildings.

The recce, however, did not convince us. All these buildings, constructed in stone with a technology that was outdated, were built before we were born and it was difficult to relate to them. For us, they were like

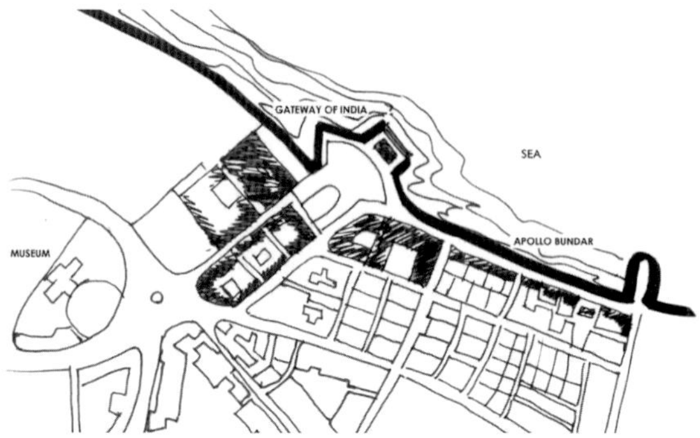

The transition from the vast expanse of the sea to land is through the Gateway of India, a man-made object that belongs only to that site. If it was in the midst of Flora Fountain, it would have been a gateway to nowhere.

any monument from the past. The Gateway of India, though, was an exception because the monument and its location are inseparable – it was singularly appropriate for its site, unlike the others which could have been built anywhere. As its name suggests, the Gateway is a transition from the vast space of the sea to the land through a man-made object – a wonderful symbol of an entrance to a country.

Our professor, G B Mhatre, who conducted the studio in specialised history, dismissed our apprehensions about adapting history to the present. He told us in no uncertain terms that history would become 'baggage from the past' if we only read and talked about buildings instead of seeing, drawing and experiencing them. He was concerned more with the form of a building, its proportions and the way it was built than any classification of its style or discussion on its relevance to the present. He dismissed all our debates with the words, "Roll up your sleeves and start drawing. That is the only way to understand the past, without which you cannot design for the present".

We continued to explore what others, especially practising architects, felt about using a historical style for the facade of a building that was modern in its plan and use. Once, while at the library of the Indian Institute of Architects, I read an article by H J Billimoria in a 1942 issue of the Institute's journal. In his piece, Billimoria cited Kanhaiyalal Vakil, art critic of *Bombay Chronicle*, who made a fervent appeal for an Indian Renaissance through the revival of Indian architecture. Such articles in *Bombay Chronicle* did have an effect, inasmuch as they led to the Improvement Trust conducting competitions that invited Indian-style designs for facades of public buildings. The idea of such a Renaissance, however, was short-lived because traditional forms were not compatible with the complex requirements and technology of modern times.

The dilemma faced by architects was: Are traditional forms compatible with the complexities of present-day buildings? Most architects rejected the idea of facades with features from historical styles grafted on them.

Most architects, barring a few, rejected the idea of grafting a facade from the past on a building of the present.

Through my years at the school of architecture in the 1950s, I visited many buildings which had just been built or were under construction. My friends accompanied me on these visits and we would have intense discussions about them. We saw areas in the city that one would not normally visit.

Roundabouts

Fort was one area that we thoroughly enjoyed spending time in. It had interesting bylanes, street food vendors and some clearly defined urban spaces that became important landmarks because they were used all the time. The character and use of these spaces differed. For instance, Nagar Chowk, the plaza in front of Victoria Terminus (now Chhatrapati Shivaji Terminus) on its west front and Bhatia Baug built in 1894 on its southern front, is perhaps the biggest urban space in the city. It should ideally have been a place for public meetings, citizens' shared activity and a spot for people to interact with one another. Instead, the heavy bus and car traffic that passes through the space leaves very little room for pedestrian movement, let alone public interaction. A civic space has been reduced to a traffic interchange. Despite this, Nagar Chowk is a place that belongs to everyone because, like the Gateway of India which is a symbol of the entrance to the country, the train terminus is the entrance to the city for people who come from other parts of the country.

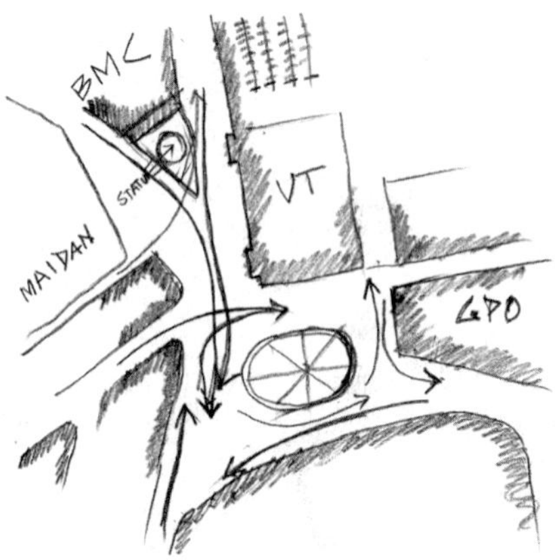

VT, the train terminus, is an entrance to Bombay. Nagar Chowk, the major urban space outside it, could have been available to the people of the city. Instead, it has been lost to motor traffic.

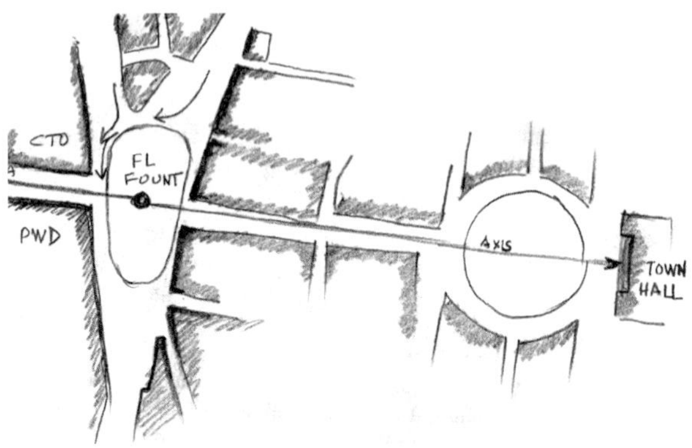

Flora Fountain is a people's place. It has seen many gatherings and political protest rallies which are deeply etched in the memory of the city.

Compared to Nagar Chowk, Flora Fountain (today's Hutatma Chowk), another public space, lent itself more naturally to public use. Political meetings and demonstrations have taken place there at different times. Till 1965, it was also a major halt for trams going further south and the alighting point for most office-goers.

Though all these were public areas, there were few, if any, restrictions on the buildings that abutted them. Any semblance of design order is incidental. For instance, in Nagar Chowk, the train terminal and the office of the Brihanmumbai Municipal Corporation impose themselves on the city square, making all other buildings inconsequential. In contrast, Flora Fountain has its edges better defined. On its eastern edge, buildings follow the rules of the Improvement Trust while on the other sides, buildings with differing facades contain the central space. However, unlike Nagar Chowk and Flora Fountain, the plaza in front of the Gateway of India needs no definition. The monument and the sea are attractive enough to make it a public place worth being in.

While the plazas were defined by the buildings on their edges, they were not compelled to follow facade controls in their design. It was only in the roundabouts, that too major ones like Horniman Circle and Dadar TT, that the Improvement Trust emphasised and insisted on these facade controls (a way to give a uniform appearance to a circle). The first building to come up decided how the circle would look. The architect of this building had to work closely with the Government Architect, who had the last word on the style to be adopted. The one element constant in all buildings on a circle was the arcade. The elevation or facade of the first building had to be repeated for all subsequent buildings.

The plaza in front of the Gateway of India is one of the most used public spaces in Bombay. The structure also serves as an impressive backdrop for the festive events that are sometimes held there.

Facade control on roundabouts was a way of unifying buildings.

Wherever the Improvement Trust developed areas, it designed circles at the junction of four roads and again imposed facade controls. Yet, not all the circles were successful. Buildings at King's Circle were nondescript while those on Sion Circle were not worth a second look. Getting a well-designed circle seemed to be a matter of luck. It depended on the architect who did the first building and the involvement of the approving architect.

Unlike Dadar TT, the style or design for facades at King's Circle and Sion Circle were not specified though all buildings on the circle had to be identical. We compared all the circles and attempted to find out why they came up and how they differed. Barring Horniman Circle, which was built in 1869 to transform the green in front of the Town Hall and give it a structured foreground, the others were merely junctions of roads. Of them, Dadar TT was better designed because the Improvement Trust set out design guidelines. The buildings on the circle were designed to have some Indian features like balconies with arched openings, sloping chhajjas and verandah columns. Their entrances were marked by porticos instead of arcades.

The Improvement Trust certainly paid more attention to Dadar Circle than the others. The spaces between the edges of buildings and the road were wide and put to many uses. Hawkers sold their wares, groups of people, especially the young, gathered there every evening, and some restaurants and shops became convenient spots from where office-goers and others could be picked up or dropped off. Dadar Circle is a successful urban space. It is bustling with people and activity at all times unlike Horniman Circle, which is formal and goes dead after working hours.

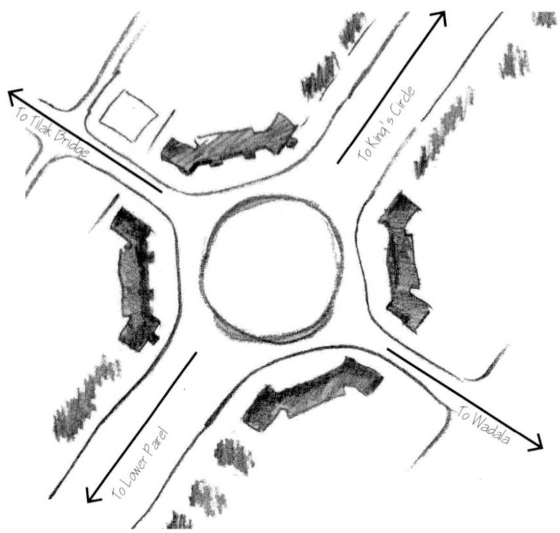

Dadar TT- A circle with facade controls

The Improvement Trust had to choose between the classical and Gothic styles for buildings on Horniman Circle. After a lot of debate in England, the government decided that in Bombay all official and public buildings and those fronting public spaces would have to be designed in the Gothic style. The decision to opt for the classical style for Horniman Circle, which ran counter to official policy, was probably influenced by the style of the Town Hall.

Stevens' Gothic Style And The School Of Architecture

In Bombay, the Gothic style outlived its welcome by the end of the nineteenth century. Some public buildings built during the time that it was the official style are now remembered more for their historical association than for their design merit.

Major buildings began to be designed by architects after F W Stevens built Victoria Terminus in 1888. Before that, most public buildings were designed by Royal Engineers, a corps of military engineers posted in India, who acquired the skill to design from experience and wide exposure to Indian construction methods even though their basic training in engineering was mostly military. They could not deal with the Gothic-style elevations of the buildings, and for these they consulted architects in England when they went on home leave. The architects who were consulted had to make detailed architectural working drawings for local masons who were not familiar with the mouldings, details and proportions of the Gothic style.

Facades had to be designed in Indian style - so the design rules said.

The space between buildings and the street is used in many ways which keeps it lively all the time.

Stevens had a difficult time making drawings for building contractors in the absence of trained architectural draftsmen to help draw the elaborate details he dreamt of. That was the reason the J J School's architecture department was launched, initially as classes for training draftsmen in 1900, which became a regular school of architecture in 1913 with courses leading to a diploma. The certificate course that started in 1908 ceased with the emergence of the diploma course.

Stevens used students from the J J School of Art to make full-scale models of gargoyles, brackets and other sculptural items that he used in the facades of Victoria Terminus. He gave students an opportunity to work on a live project and opened up the possibility of enlarging the scope of the school. But it took many years and the efforts of architects like John Begg, George Wittet, Robert Cable, Foster King and Claude Batley (all except Begg headed the school at some point) to transform those early drafting classes into a full-fledged school of architecture.

Gothic as the official style was discarded in 1900 when Begg became chief architect to the government. He was an adherent of the Indo-Saracenic style of architecture while his protege Wittet was ambivalent in the choice of style. The buildings they designed were quite different. Begg built GPO in 1911 in the style of the Gol Gumbaz in Bijapur and Wittet constructed many buildings between 1904 and 1926, in some of which Indian styles were successfully adapted for the facades. Wittet was eclectic and more concerned with appropriateness than adhering to a style. His buildings, though outstanding in their time for skilful design and exquisite detailing, did not display any noticeable innovation.

F W Stevens detailed VT Station and its offices elaborately. He used students of the Sir J J School of Art to sculpt mock-ups of architectural features. Column capitals, drawn by Stevens himself, were carved in stone.

Gargoyles (rainwater spouts shaped like animals and projected from the building) are a part of the VT design.

By the time we became students, all these architects except Batley were part of history. Batley was more recent, and his work appealed to us because we could see his sincere attempt to find an architectural language using the experience he had gathered in India without imitating past styles as his predecessors did. Begg and Wittet built official buildings and their contact with Bombay was official. But Batley took a broader view because he lived in a cosmopolitan Bombay from 1924 to 1956 and was a practitioner as well as an academic. This enabled him to appreciate the larger issues that affected the city.

Modernism

Foster King, a practitioner, headed the school of architecture between 1914 and 1918, the time that the previous head, Robert Cable, was away on war duty in Mesopotamia. He was the first head to get senior architects from professional firms and the government as well as architects who were practising in the city to teach in the school. That tradition continued while we were students. We had most of the prominent architects of the city giving lectures or conducting design studios.

Younger professors exposed us to some of the ideas of the Modern Movement and the experiments at the Bauhaus, a school in Germany that combined crafts and the fine arts and was one of the most influential currents in modern architecture and design.

One of these professors, Jehangir Bilimoria, a devotee of Sri Aurobindo and a regular member of his ashram, introduced us to Antonin Raymond's work in Pondicherry – the iconic Golconde dormitory in

The J J School of Architecture, like many important buildings in Bombay, was designed by George Wittet. His architectural choices were eclectic unlike his predecessor John Begg who was an adherent of the 'Indo-Saracenic' style.

which Raymond and his associate, George Nakashima, created beauty by using few materials and relying more on proportion and refinement of detail. Bilimoria showed us plans and photographs and analysed the building, from which we concluded that it was a good example on two counts. One, it fulfilled an austere programme with its sparsely furnished rooms and by being strictly functional and minimalist in details and finishes; and two, it responded well to the climate by its orientation and use of moveable louvres for adjusting light and flow of air.

The building was built by the devotees of the ashram since Sri Aurobindo believed that work was sadhana, a form of spiritual practice. For a building to have a spiritual quality, it needs to be minimalist in concept and detail, like Haiku poetry which conveys a lot with few words. The Golconde dormitory lived up to this ideal. Bilimoria's mention of 'spiritual quality' in a building prompted us to ask him about the Greek preoccupation with perfection in the architecture of their temples, especially since we grew up studying Normand's 'Parallel of the Orders', a book on Greek classical orders. The book contained plates with drawings of the elements of the Greek temple. It set out the proportions and relationship between different parts of the building. The Greeks, over the years, had perfected the design and proportions of the column and entablature and codified them into a set of dimensioned relationships.

We asked Bilimoria if he, like us, also saw this as striving for perfection – a journey to a mythical end – and if temple architects in India were on similar missions. He replied that the ancient Greeks had a fixed notion of perfection, which was replicating their gods and the state of heaven. But traditional Indian thought concerned itself with completeness – the inter-relatedness of everything in the universe and continuous

The Golconde dormitory in Pondicherry's Sri Aurobindo Ashram is an early example of modern architecture in India. Designed to suit the climate, it has moveable louvres that modulate light and provide cross-ventilation.

Louvres in Golconde soften the harsh tropical light.

evolution. The ideal, itself only a notion, could therefore change with evolution. The thought was reflected in the Hindu temple, which based its design on a model of the cosmos and assigned positions to the different deities on a mystical grid of squares called a mandala. The position of the deities was hierarchically related to the presiding deity in the temple. In Hindu thought, cosmic evolution is on a time scale that is longer than others and hence positions of deities and planets appear constant.

For most of the years that we spent in the school of architecture, our exposure to modern architecture was mainly the Bauhaus and European modernists like Walter Gropius, Adolf Loos and Ludwig Mies van der Rohe. There were also architects whose work was included in FRS Yorke's book 'The Modern House'. Their rational approach to architecture and advocacy of modern materials and technology appealed to many students. Others were more influenced by Frank Lloyd Wright and his philosophy of 'organic architecture'.

The dichotomy in architectural thought was a central point of debate in the school. The 'rationalists' took the example of Frank Lloyd Wright's 'prairie house' that was preceded by the Oak Park houses in Chicago. They argued that this house, built out of local stone or brick and suiting only its immediate site, was just a rehash of the traditional cottage with its sloping roof and chimney. It was local, not modern or universal, and an example of romanticism, which lacked the intellectual vigour of the 'International Style'. By contrast, they said, the International Style (sometimes derisively called the European 'box' building) was a product of the machine age and built with products of industry and was therefore universal: It could be located anywhere because it was derived from an understanding of people's needs, which are the same everywhere. This International Style looked at architecture as a bridge between the impersonal world of industry and the people who benefit from it.

Modern architecture in Europe was called the "dumb box". To most architects, the box symbolised everything modern. To others it was cold and soulless.

For followers of Frank Lloyd Wright, 'organic architecture' was based on universal values which could give one a glimpse of the truth.

Wright supporters, on the other hand, argued that his "organic architecture" relied on understanding universal values. Wright's philosophy was about developing a sense for the nature of materials and structure; it had more to do with feeling than reason. The modern buildings in Europe, they argued, were impersonal, cold and soulless. They appealed only to the intellect, leaving little room for the indefinable quality that one can experience in art or music.

These perceptions of architecture among both groups of students – votaries of 'rationalist' and 'organic' architecture alike – as well as some of the younger architects changed when Le Corbusier started work at Chandigarh in 1951. Brochures containing the plan of the new city and sketches of housing and other buildings did not tell us much about his work; neither did we pay much heed initially. It was an exhibition, held in 1953 at the Indian Institute of Architects, of Le Corbusier's drawings for the High Court at Chandigarh, which opened a door for us. The rigid orthogonal plan and strictly functional elevation and roof line associated with the International Style were not sacred anymore. The Chandigarh High Court, with its combination of rigid boxes and free-flowing spaces and ramps, its monumental, yet human, entrance and its great roof, both arched and sloped down to the centre of the building, showed us an architecture that dislodged our earlier notions of form and function. It forced us to rethink the 'box', the machine and universality. It was new for all and reactions differed from architect to architect, person to person.

Some architects wondered why there wasn't a proper entrance to the building, why the elevation appeared crude, why Indian art forms or craftsmanship were not employed and so on. One observer said that the design of the entrance and ramps was a way of democratising public space, and cynically added

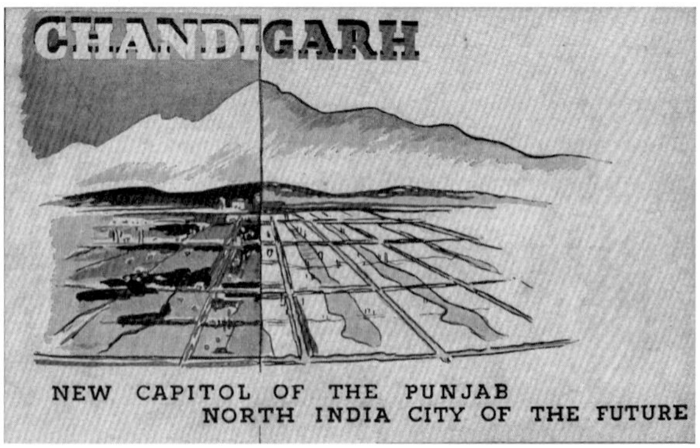

Brochures announced the Chandigarh project and invited people to settle in the city designed by Le Corbusier.

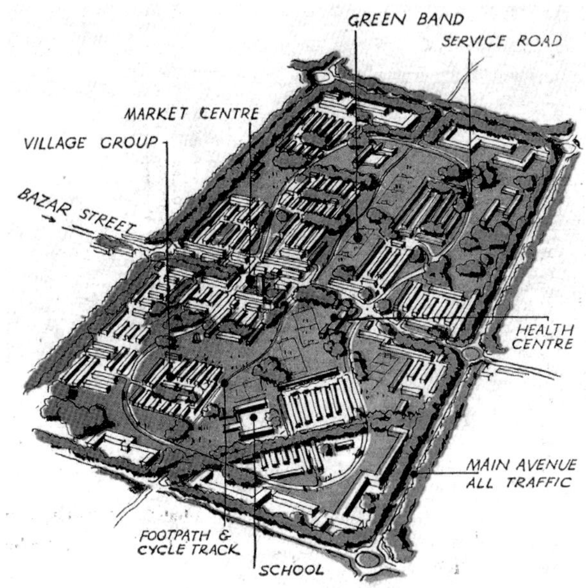

that anyone could use the space and go up the ramps, including the animals used for carrying materials for construction. We ignored these comments. The design was so overwhelming that it compelled us to study Chandigarh and discuss it amongst ourselves.

Arvind Talati, one of our schoolmates, got hold of the master plan of the city and made a presentation to a group of students at the school. He talked about the system of roads devised by Le Corbusier, which was hierarchical and designed to suit the traffic that they would take. We compared it to the plan prepared by Albert Mayer, who was initially appointed to prepare the master plan for the city, and found that both were similar versions of the grid plan, with sectors confined between roads, much like Jaipur, except that Le Corbusier introduced greenery as an integral part of the plan and softened the rigid road grids by scaling their widths and naming them differently. We found that existing towns in Punjab and other places in India had an informal order in which relationships between people and places developed over a long time. Chandigarh was a planned city with a formal order and relationships would therefore be different. All these discussions were over several rounds of tea under the magnificent gulmohur tree in Dileep's garden.

Following our newly awakened interest in Le Corbusier, we visited Chandigarh and Ahmedabad for the sole purpose of seeing buildings designed by him. During these trips, we would discuss how well the plan or choice of material or detail worked. We learnt more from these visits than in the design studio where we were designing fictitious projects on imaginary sites without a clue about how they would be built.

The group of which I was a part included Dileep Purohit, Shreekant Mandrekar (known to all as Maan), Raja Poredi, Kukki Mathur, Austin Lobo, Arvind Talati, Raphael David and Maneck Doongaji. We met often to visit

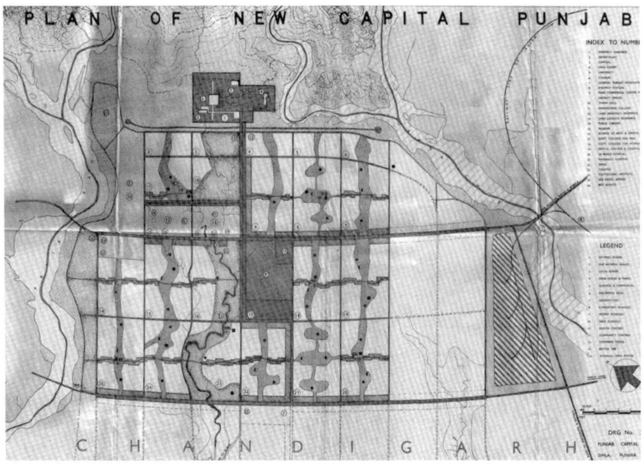

The master plan of Chandigarh had grids and a hierarchy of roads. It brings to mind Jaipur which was designed according to Vedic precepts using the nine-square mandala. Unlike Jaipur, however, the space within the Chandigarh grid is planned.

The High Court of Chandigarh, which Nehru described as "symbolic of the freedom of India unfettered by the traditions of the past".

buildings and talk about them, discuss our city and our future as professionals among other things. Some discussions stayed in our memory and looking at them, in retrospect and from a more mature perspective, we realised they had influenced our thinking to some extent.

One discussion stands out more than the others. It was at one of our tea sessions at Annapurna, the open-air cafeteria we could afford to frequent, that Austin Lobo made a statement that started a discussion which continued for a while. He said, "Modern architecture threw out the clutter of what preceded it. It was minimal and reduced everything to bare essentials." He showed plans and photographs of Mies van der Rohe's Farnsworth House in Illinois to support his statement. That building, he said, was the expression of a programme distilled to its essence by a process of analysis and elimination. It was, according to him, the epitome of modern architecture.

Looking at the plan and its details, the choice of materials, structural system and construction details, some of us were convinced that far from being an expression of a distilled programme, it appeared as though the programme was devised to justify a predetermined form. The client's brief was at best considered casually, the only reference to her requirements being the area of a building needed for a weekend getaway. It had a pristine quality in the way the space within 'the glass box' (the form of Farnsworth House) was defined by enclosed utility areas. The glass that wrapped the entire box brought the landscape inside. You became part of the landscape wherever you were in the house. In a way the house dissolved into the landscape, yet it was an immaculate object by itself. The entrance to the house was from a platform through a glass door to the space within, where everything was arranged as in a stage set. Nothing could

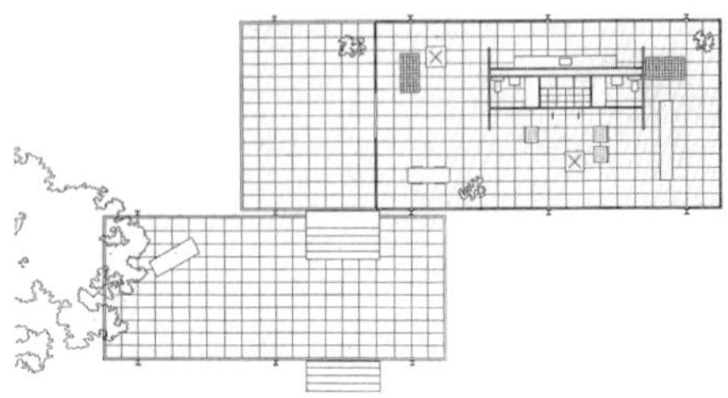

Plan of Farnsworth House

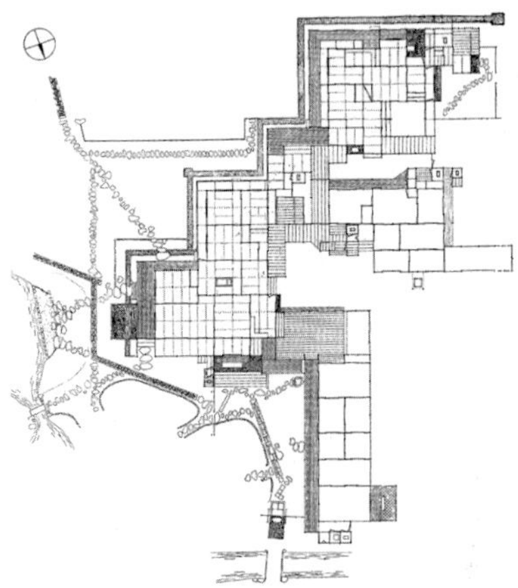

Plan of Katsura Imperial Villa

be shifted or rearranged. There was an obsessive concern for order, which included uniform light in the interior space, the only variation coming from curtains drawn, more for privacy than for modulating light.

We were not familiar with this compulsive order. We had learnt about order in classical architecture where columns were repeated and proportions worked out and applied. We found that constant repetition lead to stagnation and subsequent obsolescence. We saw the Improvement Trust's version of order, which came from maintaining street lines, arcades, levels of the first floor and roof cornice and specified heights. Within these parameters, variations were possible. We saw in Bora Bazar another kind of order which was not overtly visible. But Farnsworth House had order of a different nature. Here, all the elements fitted with one another in a way that did not permit variation even in the way space could be used. We concluded that the building was great to look at, walk through and enjoy seeing amidst its surroundings but not to live in. "There is no place in that order for a child to strew his playthings or go around on his tricycle," said Pravina Mehta, who was in the discussion group. It appeared to us that space was enclosed and proportioned as a work of art with little regard for the user.

Mies Van der Rohe backed his ideas with his famous words, "Less is More", implying a minimalist approach that meant getting the most out of very little. The philosophy pertained to architecture only, and it was limited to the use of materials and technology, both of which were necessary to express truth in the structure of a building. Some of us were interested in knowing if minimalism meant more than mere reduction of wants and whether it extended to a complete way of life. If that was so, did it show in architecture or other art forms?

Farnsworth House expressed minimalism through clarity in the organisation of space, use of materials and structural system. The minimalism here was a design tool unlike Katsura Villa which was an expression of Zen philosophy.

The Kobori Enshu-designed Katsura Imperial Villa in Kyoto provided us with some answers. In this beautiful seventeenth-century example of traditional Japanese architecture, a large house and pavilions are arranged in harmony with Nature. House and garden are inseparable, both following Nature, not competing with it. Possessions are few and they are stored discreetly in storage walls. What comes through clearly is the message that architecture is only a part of a larger vision of our world, in which peace and harmony are to be found through experience.

Like Farnsworth House, the buildings in the Katsura complex are modular, but differences in the derivation of the module are noticeable. In the former case, the module was used to arrive at a structural system, while in the latter, the module was derived from the dimensions of a floor mat. Within the house, sliding screens enabled the creation of a variety of spaces intended to be experienced more than seen. The programme for the house depended on the routine of daily life, much of which was ritualistic. The inside connected to the outside through sliding translucent paper screens, and light was shaded by wide overhanging eaves that covered a deck all round the house. The garden was experienced through framed views. The screen was seldom opened fully since the Japanese believe that you can experience the inner beauty of Nature only through glimpses of it. The view is never the same because only parts of the screen are opened at a time, and the experience is therefore different every time.

Katsura Imperial Villa showed an order of a different kind, one in which houses, Nature and the rituals of living are part of a complex culture in which minimalism is the underlying philosophy. This philosophy, central to the Japanese aesthetic, permeates its other arts as well – Haiku, a form of poetry, in just a few

Katsura Imperial Villa was the expression of a culture that is minimalist in all its aspects. Minimalism was a way of life for the Japanese.

sentences conveys images of the natural world while paintings like the 'The Great Wave of Kanagawa' by the eighteenth-century painter, Katsushika Hokusai, express the power and fury of the sea in a few brush strokes.

Farnsworth House and Katsura Imperial Villa, separated by three centuries, are both guided by the philosophy of minimalism. But while minimalism in the former was a design tool to achieve visual clarity, in the latter it was integral to its larger culture where the philosophy pervaded all aspects of life and found expression in art and architecture. Perhaps because of this, Farnsworth house had a sanitised clinical quality while Katsura was a total experience.

Teatime chats, first at school and then at Annapurna, were invigorating, but eventually words are poor substitutes for actually designing or seeing buildings both during their construction stage and after completion. It is a good way to understand how space within a building gets shaped.

Three Modern Buildings In Bombay

Three modern buildings that came up more or less at the same time in the 1950s set us off on a series of visits and discussions, both among ourselves and with professional architects. The buildings were Jehangir Art Gallery, the Tata Institute of Social Sciences and Stanvac House.

Jehangir Art Gallery

Jehangir Art Gallery, possibly the first permanent art gallery in the city, is located on the corner of Kala Ghoda, an important public space. It stands in the compound of the Prince of Wales Museum on its north-west edge. Designed by Durga Bajpai, the art gallery is an unusual building in more ways than one and raised more questions in our minds than any other building in the city.

We observed how the gallery followed the curve of the street for a part of the building and how the space behind the curve had been organised to accommodate an entrance and an auditorium. The entrance had a canopy, the profile of which was corrugated. There was some mention of the structural advantage of such a form. For us, it was unusual and we liked it.

The main gallery was rectangular and was naturally lighted and ventilated. On the east, the light came through a series of glass doors opening to the museum's garden. Direct sunlight was cut off by a deep overhanging weather shade, and subdued light washed the floor. On the west, there were windows at a high level which allowed the bright afternoon light to come in from a height. The quality of light in the afternoon was different from the one in the morning, softened as it was by an egg-crate ceiling. The overhang on the east came inside the building, which connected the inside with the outside. You could not miss this because it was in the lobby and you entered the main gallery through it.

The exterior of the building had yellow basalt stone-facing in panels. The stones were arranged to cast shadows, which everybody said was to reduce heat. Although the exterior was in stone, it was light in appearance unlike earlier stone buildings. This was because stone was used only in the panels.

Jehangir Art Gallery, the first of its kind in the city, occupied a vantage position in an important public space.

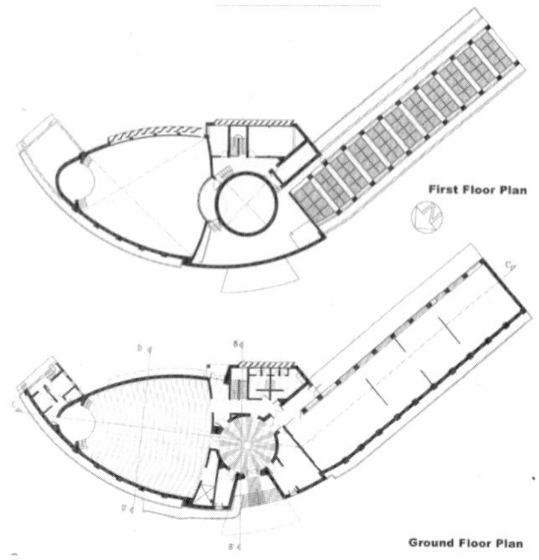

The building followed the curve of the street and the corrugated canopy over the entrance was unusual for its time.

Jehangir Art Gallery raised more questions and discussions among students and architects when it opened in 1952. The first debate concerned its location and its effect on the public space outside it. Architects and students held diametrically opposite views. While architects felt that the gallery marred the view of the museum and its dome, students like us thought it was located at a vantage position, one that gave an edge to an important public space. We did, however, feel that the visual connection between the circle and the museum was lost because the building did not provide any transparency. Had its entrance and rear been made of glass, one could have walked through the entrance hall of the gallery to the museum gardens, making the connection both physical and visual.

Older architects thought the building should have been designed in the style adopted by Wittet for the museum and built in Deccan trap stone since it was in the same compound and close to it. We rejected this view because the museum preceded the art gallery by several years. It was built in a traditional style, one that suited a technology that had become outdated. The new building was a refreshing change from the past and expressive of the present. But doubts about a new architecture in a square that had the city's iconic buildings still persisted in our minds. We felt more assured when Prof Bilimoria told us that these doubts were natural. "Our response to anything is always conditioned by what we already know," he said. "When something new and unusual turns up, we turn away from it because we are unsure of ourselves. We would rather stay safe with the known. That is why those who think differently have to struggle for acceptance and recognition." But time has a way of dealing with this phenomenon.

On the exterior, stone was used to cast shadows that helped reduce heat on the walls.

Windows at a high level and an eggcrate ceiling softened the light in the main gallery.

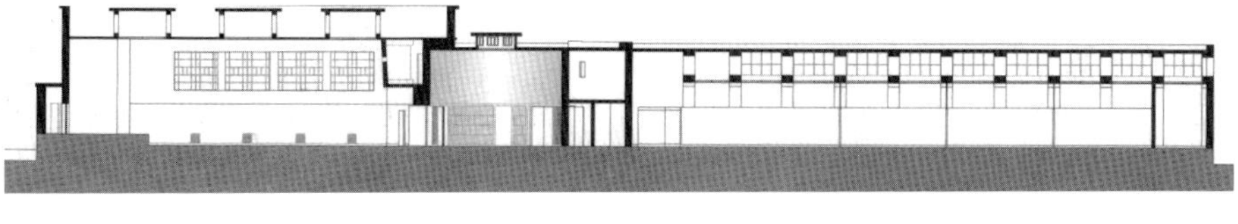

Tata Institute Of Social Sciences

The second building that impressed us greatly was the Tata Institute of Social Sciences (TISS) at Deonar. We went again and again to this beautiful campus set in the midst of trees and surrounded by hills though getting there in those days meant a long journey – taking a bus from Sion to Deonar with a wait at the Chunabhatti railway level-crossing.

At the TISS campus, we saw that buildings were designed to suit the slopes of the site and laid out informally – unlike the old universities and colleges where buildings are arranged around quadrangles or forecourts and formally and symmetrically planned with rooms or halls placed on either side of a central corridor or along an external verandah. The rooms in these are usually high, the windows narrow and tall and the exteriors built in dressed stone masonry. By contrast, the Durga Bajpai-designed TISS campus was closer to the vernacular architecture of the region, especially in its use of random rubble-masonry walls and sloped roofs covered with roofing tiles. But the resemblance ended there because the spaces within the building and the creative use of local materials and concrete made the campus modern in all respects.

The Academic Building had a flat concrete slab below a sloped tiled roof. The rooms were cool and well lit, as they had pivoting glazed windows that controlled air flow and let in adequate light. All concrete surfaces had been left exposed and unplastered – they were painted in bright colours while all the woodwork was coated with 'solignum', a wood preservative. Walking around the campus and seeing the way buildings were placed on the site, the free flow of space within buildings and the innovative use of

The Tata Institute of Social Sciences, built in the 1950s, is one of Bombay's earliest modern campuses.

common materials like stone and concrete reminded us of Alvar Aalto's work. Subsequently we learnt that Bajpai had worked with Aalto and the forms of his buildings were influenced by the Finnish architect and designer. His use of colour to offset the drab appearance of stone was borrowed from examples in India, including the painted brick-and-plaster superstructures of temples in South India.

We visited the Tata campus repeatedly because the discussions it spurred were always interesting. On one of those trips we saw a house behind the campus. It was a small structure, probably a weekend getaway, belonging to a Mr Tyebji and designed by one our professors, Vaman Gore. The walls of the house were made of rubble masonry in which every few courses were separated from those above by dressed stone slabs in much the way Frank Lloyd Wright built the walls of his houses. The house had a tiled roof supported on a wooden substructure which was designed with well-proportioned members and left visible. During discussions on modern architecture at school, we found that there was a constant reference to honesty in expressing the structure of a building. We argued among ourselves that if structural elements were to be shown, they would have to be designed efficiently and aesthetically, the beauty emerging from the way the structural members were arranged. Tyebji's house was interesting because we could test what we learnt about structural honesty. The building resembled TISS in its use of local materials and architectural language although it preceded it by several years.

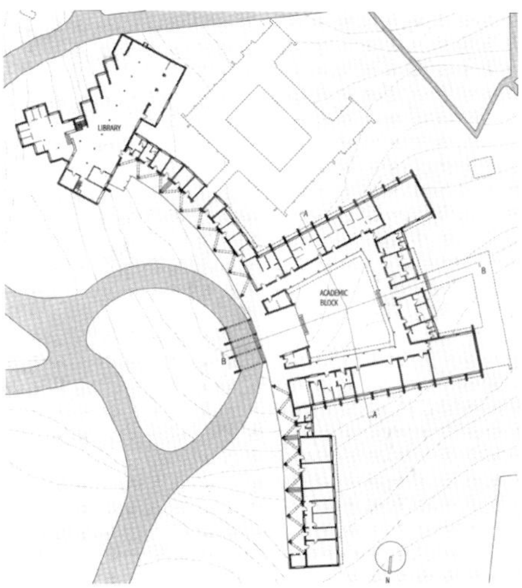

The architectural language of the buildings appears vernacular but spaces within are free and open, suitable for a modern campus.

Stone and concrete are creatively used to define a corridor that follows the contours of the site.

Stanvac House

The third building, Stanvac House, which was the India headquarters of the Standard-Vacuum Oil Company, was special for me because I worked on its details. The initial design for this building located at Churchgate bore a resemblance to the Burmah-Shell Company's Art Deco-styled 'Shell House' at Ballard Estate but it was rejected by the head office of Standard-Vacuum at New York. Standard-Vaccum wanted its buildings all over the world to reflect its global presence in the oil business by being modern in design. For its buildings in the tropics, the company insisted on using architectural features that would reduce energy consumption, especially for air-conditioning. The head office for its India operations was designed by Chauncey W Riley, whose clientele consisted of many oil companies. He planned the building and designed the sun control system after plotting the sun's path and its effect on the different faces of the building. His study aimed to reduce, if not eliminate altogether, direct heat loads on the walls and window openings and thereby reduce both the initial and running cost of air-conditioning. The final design had a combination of vertical and horizontal louvres.

The idea of sun-shading devices is very old. A chhajja, intended to keep out the rain and hot afternoon sun, was a part of every building in India from ancient times, and in the course of time became an important design element. Louvres are more recent. Antonine Raymond, in the Golconde dormitory for devotees at Pondicherry's Aurobindo Ashram, used moveable horizontal louvres to shade the light and allow the sea breeze to flow through the rooms. Le Corbusier used fixed louvres to soften the bright tropical light. He called these 'brise-soleil' and integrated them in the design of his buildings. Shading devices could be

The Standard-Vacuum Oil Company's head office in India was an early modern building that used louvres to reduce heat loads and air-conditioning costs.

The entrance to Stanvac House was designed by Chauncey W Riley who also prepared the base plans of the building and carried out studies to determine the position and angles of the louvres.

used for a variety of reasons. Chauncey Riley's mandate was to reduce heat loads, and he could design any shading device as long as the objective was met.

The plans, elevations and details of the entrance to Stanvac House were drawn by Riley and the structure was designed by John Ritchie and L Palfi, who were also the local architects. The construction, which was carried out between 1952 and 1954, was overseen by an engineer deputed by the company, whose job it was to get the building detailed, procure materials for construction and supervise actual work on site. He was assisted by a draftsman and site engineers. I was the draftsman who drew the details and saw them come up while still a student.

Riley's plan provided for open offices with no fixed elements except lifts and staircases. All internal divisions were created with moveable partitions made from wood studs and plywood. This was an inexpensive way of making partitions – prior to this, they were made with wood stiles and rails and infill panels, like joinery for doors. Generally everyone except managers worked in one space, and the supervisory staff was segregated by low barriers. The layout of offices in an American company differed from its British counterparts; it was less hierarchical.

What attracted everyone was the idea of louvres, which this building used as an important feature in its design, together with the concept of open offices, the quality of its construction and the organised manner of its execution. The mode of construction was not unusual because it was quite common for owners to supply materials and hire labour contractors for constructing a building. But identifying sources, negotiating prices and procuring and supplying materials to the site in time required a great

Stanvac House

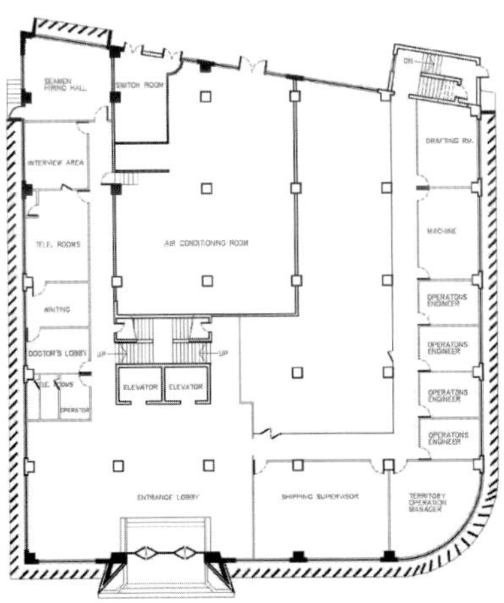

First-Floor Plan

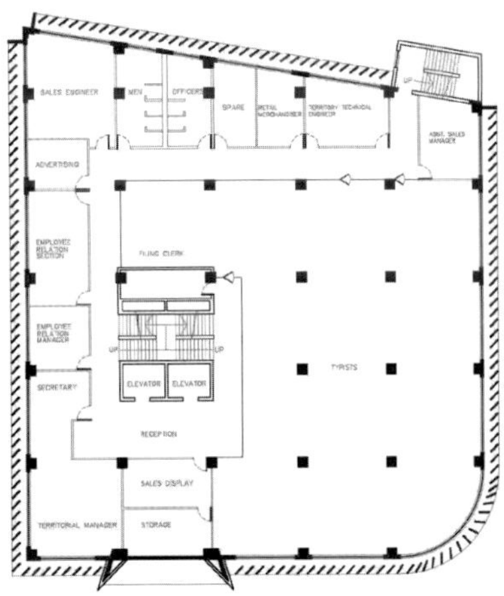

Second-Floor Plan

deal of organising. C B Plog, the engineer in charge of the project, could do this efficiently as he had the company's staff to assist him.

Projects where materials are supplied by the owner and work is executed by a labour contractor are not always successful. Very often, there is a mismatch between supply and work schedules. Where work has to be redone to rectify faulty workmanship, the owner loses more because he bears the cost of materials, both initially and later for the rectification. The labour contractor only loses his labour cost, which is much less. Moreover, a project done without a contractor requires a responsible engineer or a 'clerk of works' on site so that responsibility is fixed in case of failure.

Stanvac House or Petroleum House, as it is now known, was among the early examples of modern architecture that came up in the 1950s when we were students. It was such a contrast to the Mercantile Bank (now HSBC Bank), Bank of India and Industry House buildings next to it, all of which came up at more or less the same time but which were designed in the Art Deco or hybrid Indian style. The Stanvac building with its modern design showed the way forward.

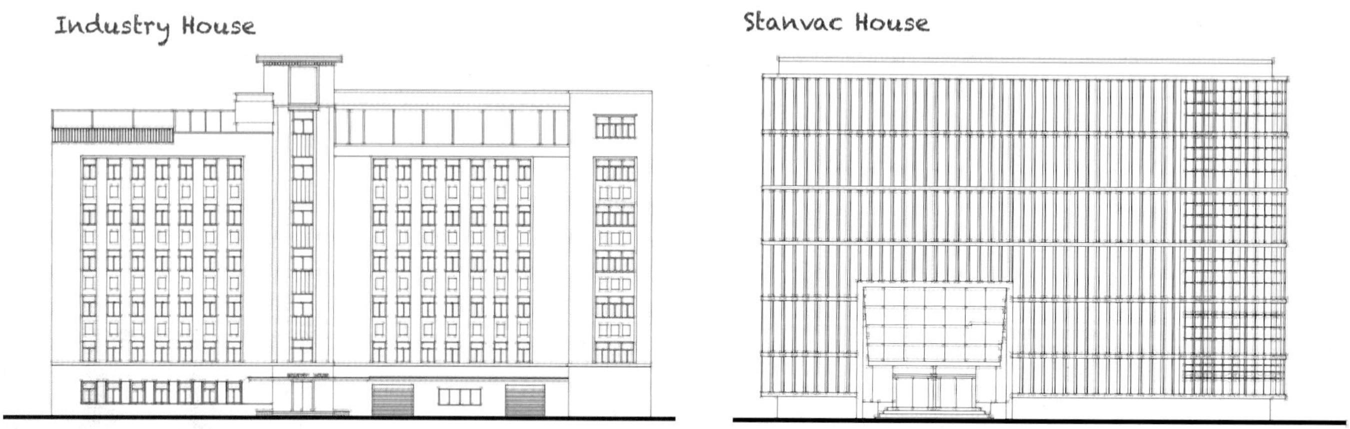

Industry House and Stanvac building are on adjoining plots and were built at the same time. One did not shed the past while the other showed a way to the future.

Learning About The Improvement Trust

Learning About The Improvement Trust

During my summer holidays and the occasional breaks that I took from school to pursue hands-on experience, I interned with engineers and architects. I first cut my teeth on projects in the office of H G Mahendra, who was the structural engineer for the well-known cinema houses New Empire and Liberty designed by architect Ridley Abbott. Like many of his generation, Mahendra's knowledge of civil engineering was vast and practical. He made all the drawings for his structures himself, as he believed that to design a structure the mere use of a slide rule (the calculator in use then) was not enough; one also needed to draw plans of the structure in order to understand how it would be built. He believed that a structure should look right visually.

Mahendra was proud that his drawings, unlike those of most engineers, contained the details of every structural element, leaving no leeway for confusion for the man on the site. When a detail was complex, he would circle it and write notes such as "Ask me on site" or "Show this to me before you construct". Sometimes his drawings would also detail the sequence of work if it was unusual. He drilled into me the idea that drawings were a means of communication that needed to be clear rather than attractive.

When my internship got over, Mahendra's parting advice to me was, "You need not know how to calculate bending moments but you must definitely develop a sense of structure, without which an architectural design is not complete." On a more philosophical note, he had this to say: "The reward that you get from doing a project, more than anything else, is the experience and the pleasure you get from it." That intense, rewarding summer internship gave me an invaluable glimpse into the world of brick and mortar.

In my next internship, I learned not just about buildings but about the city and its history as well – more of the latter in fact. G B Mhatre's office had three partners and a staff of 12. The partners designed and drew up the plans and elevations, after which the assistants developed working drawings. One of the partners, Akbar Parpia, was in charge of getting planning approvals from the relevant authorities. He got plans made to adhere to the municipal bye-laws, especially in respect to setbacks, height and other requirements. Assistants like me were called "improvers" and our job was to make drawings to a scale of eight feet to the inch.

It was from Parpia that I heard more about the Improvement Trust and the role of municipal laws in the making of the city. He was not a qualified lawyer but he came from a legal family and his exposure to property law, thus, was exceptionally wide. He was at his best when talking about the Bombay Improvement Trust, which was responsible for planning and improving the city, and the Bombay Municipal Corporation, which had to administer the city and collect taxes. It was these bodies that planned the city, laying out the sites for architects to build on. They made bye-laws specifying how much and how high you could build so that light and air and civic facilities were shared equitably. But these laws did not always exist, as Parpia showed us through the history of the Improvement Trust.

In the 1800s, British Bombay was restricted to the Fort area. The Fort and the docks on the east provided work for hordes of migrants from rural areas, who stayed in unplanned settlements north of the Fort walls, within three kilometres of their place of work. The British referred to these settlements as the 'Black Town', later toning this down to 'Native Town'. As in Bora Bazar and Parsi Bazar within the Fort, people in areas outside the Fort lived in densely packed tenements. There was little or no control on construction. Landlords were allowed to build as many rooms as they liked on very little land, not caring that migrants lived in sub-human conditions. The areas around the houses were filthy. Sanitary facilities were minimal and there were several outbreaks of plague as a result of this.

Even as the 'native town' continued to grow haphazardly, the Bombay Municipality drafted a set of bye-laws for construction in 1872 that were redrafted time and again over the next 31 years. Bringing in order was a big challenge – thus, the municipality divided Bombay, then limited to areas within the island city, into areas that were densely built and those that were less dense. They were called scheduled and non-scheduled areas and they had different sets of rules for development within them. In scheduled areas, open spaces around buildings were haphazard, so much so that in some cases, a building occupied the entire site. Owners of buildings were compelled by the new rules to provide 1.5-metre-wide house gullies for manual scavenging, which were later used to connect house drains to the city's sewers. Violations of these laws were not tolerated.

The event that dramatically changed the course of urban planning in the city was the plague of 1896. The outbreak began in the areas occupied by the 'natives', both within and outside the Fort. It was a threat to the British population too, and there was a time when, to escape infection, many Britishers and some 'natives' slept in tents on the maidans. Hundreds of lives were lost.

In response to the plague, the British set up the Bombay Improvement Trust in 1898 with members of the Indian Civil Service as well as engineers, architects and a host of specialists to execute projects. The trust was given extensive powers to clean up the city and develop new planned neighbourhoods.

How did the Improvement Trust go about its job? According to Parpia, it first realigned roads, demolishing parts of buildings. Next, it got building owners to create house gullies on the side to keep space between buildings and improve ventilation and sanitation. It then drafted a set of rules for development that determined the proportion of the building's footprint to its site, the maximum number of floors it could have and other design rules.

The most important design rule that the Trust introduced was what came to be known as the 63.5 degree light angle rule. The concept was developed in England for the redevelopment of blighted areas in London, Manchester and other industrial cities and subsequently imported to Bombay by J P Orr, the chairman of the Improvement Trust. At a meeting organised by the Bombay Sanitary Association in June 1912, he expounded the theory of light and air planes which set out a method of determining the distance between buildings relative to their heights. Planners in England found, through analysis and experience, that the open space in a plot, derived from an angle of 63.5 degrees, ensured adequate light and ventilation on the lowest floor. Without this rule, Orr emphasised, unsanitary conditions would continue to prevail. The distance between buildings were related to their heights and they were determined by front and rear light and air planes and angles.

The chairman was able to eventually convince the municipality to embed the 63.5 degree rule in the bye-law book. However, it could not be applied in scheduled areas where buildings were already closely built – in such areas, the requirement on minimum open spaces was reduced.

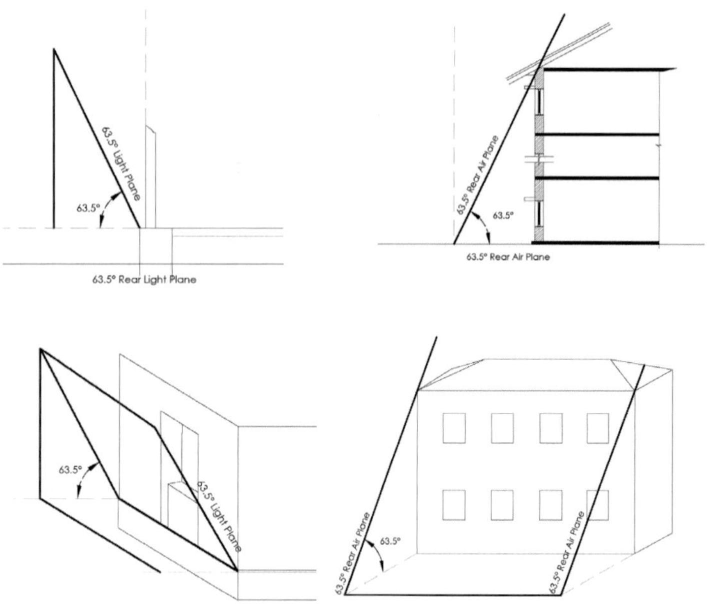

One reason for the frequent outbreaks of plague was a lack of light and ventilation in houses that were too close to one another. On account of this, the Improvement Trust later brought in the 63.5 degree angle rule which, put simply, meant that the distance between the building and the boundary of its site had to be half the height of the building. In all its lease deeds, the Trust insisted that 'heights of buildings should be governed by the municipal bye-laws and the 63.5 degree angle'.

Orr was a dynamic leader who conceptualised other important development schemes. He envisioned a broad road, which he called The Kingsway, running from Colaba in the south to Sion in the north. Implementing this idea was difficult because there were buildings in the way, properties that had to be acquired and road alignments that had to be changed. However, he was a determined and hard-headed administrator who had the backing of the government and acquisition laws to help him. Under colonial rule, this was aided by a political system dominated by the land-owning class. Many of the Improvement Trust's schemes displaced people, trampling on their rights. Orr's term in office saw rapid and competent development that benefited the city in the long term but its cost in human terms was high.

Parpia agreed with Orr's view that development often needs big bold moves. He gave the examples of Princess Street and Phirozeshah Mehta Road (PM Road), both of which were created by the Improvement Trust at great cost to the 'native' population, whose shops and houses were demolished to make way for those roads. The road projects had a sanitation objective – to bring the fresh sea breeze into the congested inner city. Buildings in Bora Bazar and Parsi Bazar were demolished to connect Ballard Estate to the Esplanade and the Esplanade to the sea through PM Road. Princess Street also served the purpose of connecting the market areas on the east to the Marine Lines railway station on the west, thus opening up commercial activity. Both roads were connectors but also corridors that allowed the sea breeze to flow through the city.

The eastern side of the city could have also done with some sea breeze. But the docks and warehouses had already been built, and demolishing them would have affected port activity and its economy, both of

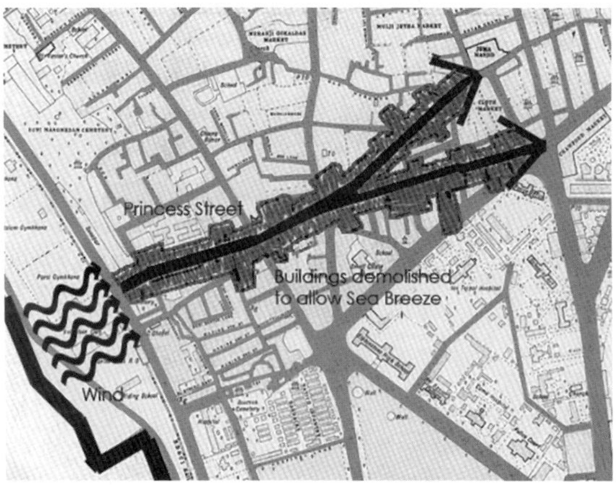

Buildings were demolished to make way for Princess Street. This was done to let fresh sea breeze into the inner city and improve sanitation.

A building was placed at the junction of two roads to deflect the sea breeze deeper into the inner areas.

which were vital for the city. On the other hand, demolishing houses to create Princess Street and PM Road would affect only the 'native' bazar. In the Improvement Trust's perception, the city was more important than displacing a few 'natives'.

The Improvement Trust demolished many existing buildings or altered them to comply with the light-and-air rule and built roads in some areas. But it soon outgrew the job of improving the city and wanted to play a bigger role in long-term development. To that end, it began acquiring land and developing housing estates. This was a more positive way of sanitising the city: through the development of new neighbourhoods, it showed how living conditions could be improved when built-up area and open spaces were balanced.

The Trust planned 91 schemes, of which 75 were executed. They varied in size from a single street to infill estates and greenfield projects like the Dadar-Matunga and Mahim schemes. While many infills were around existing villages, for the greenfield estates the Trust had to acquire land, a difficult task because compensation was always contested by land owners and often led to the Trust being drawn into elaborate arbitration. In the next step, the land was laid out with roads, house plots, parks and sites for civic amenities. The process of making a layout was also challenging because it meant balancing economic returns with social objectives, deciding on the number and sizes of plots, affordability and so on.

The Improvement Trust called the estates that it developed "planned interventions". The interventions were limited to providing planning inputs in specific localities and were not part of a uniform master plan

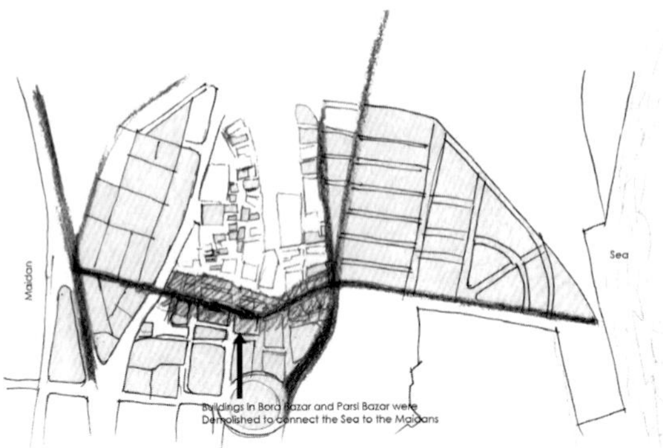

Sir Phirozeshah Mehta Road was built over the debris of buildings demolished to connect the sea on the east to the maidans on the west.

Sir P M Road became an important office district.

for the city. However, the rules for constructing a building were generally the same in all estates with some local variations.

Plots in the estates were leased out for long tenures through auctions. The latter, conducted by Bennett and Company for the Improvement Trust, were done one by one, not in lots, and bids were not necessarily the same for all sites in a scheme. In many auctions, it was architects who bid and bought land for their clients. They then designed the building and got it constructed. At that time, most architects were civil engineers who played the role of both architect and contractor. The architect as a professional employed to design and supervise a contractor's work with an unbiased view came later.

The lease rent for a site was six per cent of the capital value of the land, and a successful bidder paid six years' lease rent as a deposit till the building was constructed and certified for occupation. Lessees were allowed two years to complete construction, after which the Trust executed the lease agreement.

Land was good business. Plots changed hands before the building was constructed. Even letters accepting bids were traded. Parpia would joke that Indians as a people could make and complete a deal in the time between the departure of one local train and the arrival of the next one.

The size and number of plots in a scheme depended on the cost of acquiring land and developing it and the anticipated returns, all of which related to the clientele the scheme could attract. In Gamdevi and Agripada estates, sites cost more because they were bigger and lease rents higher. A conservancy lane between plots for tradesmen and garbage removal added to the cost of a plot.

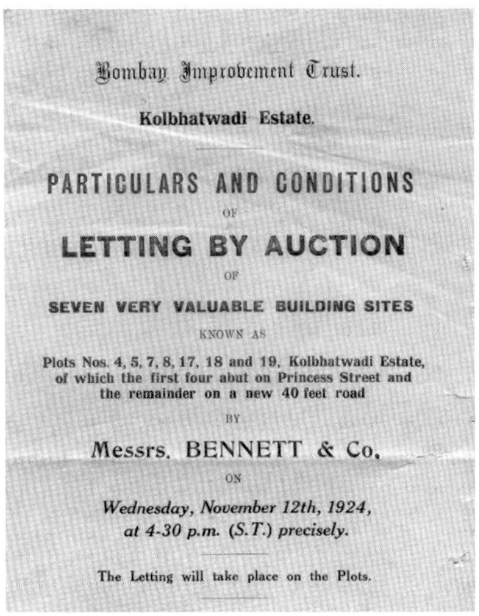
Bombay Improvement Trust.

Kolbhatwadi Estate.

PARTICULARS AND CONDITIONS

OF

LETTING BY AUCTION

OF

SEVEN VERY VALUABLE BUILDING SITES

KNOWN AS

Plots Nos. 4, 5, 7, 8, 17, 18 and 19, Kolbhatwadi Estate, of which the first four abut on Princess Street and the remainder on a new 40 feet road

BY

Messrs. BENNETT & Co.

ON

Wednesday, November 12th, 1924, at 4-30 p.m. (S.T.) precisely.

The Letting will take place on the Plots.

Plots in the schemes promoted by the Trust were offered for lease through regular auction houses.

The Improvement Trust planned 91 schemes but executed only 75 of them. They ranged from single-street improvements to infill estates and greenfield projects.

The buildings on the estates were either individual bungalows or large apartment buildings. In a way, this determined the economic and social profile of tenants who lived in the estates. Agripada, which stretched from Bellasis Road on the south to Jacob Circle on the north, and the railway lines on the west to Clare Road on the east, was one of the bigger estates. Though its land area was large, the actual development was only on a small area because the bulk of the land belonged to the Byculla Club, which, until 1948, was for the exclusive use of the British and European population. Till the mid-1940s, there was a sizable European population living in Agripada estate.

The Improvement Trust had a vision of how a planned settlement should look. Layouts and planning and building rules were intended to create a coherent visual fabric. To make sure that individual buildings did not become isolated entities, architects had to submit for approval the elevations of the building along with details of the entrance drawn to quarter- and half-scales. Approvals always came only after discussions with the chief architect of the Improvement Trust, who kept reminding the architects who submitted plans for approval: "Your building is only a part of the estate. The individual building is subsumed in the context."

The Trust did not insist on uniform facades, and the buildings in these layouts differed from one another in external appearance. However, they coalesced into one harmonious visual entity because they were not designed to be iconic, stand-alone buildings. Some architects felt that the volumes and setbacks imposed by the Improvement Trust were restrictive – architectural elements and features were limited to one-third of the length of the facade, for instance – but most were content with expressing their individuality subtly through design innovations within the permitted rules.

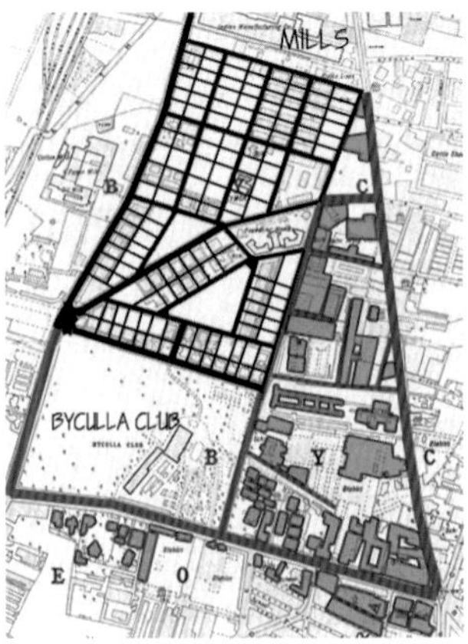

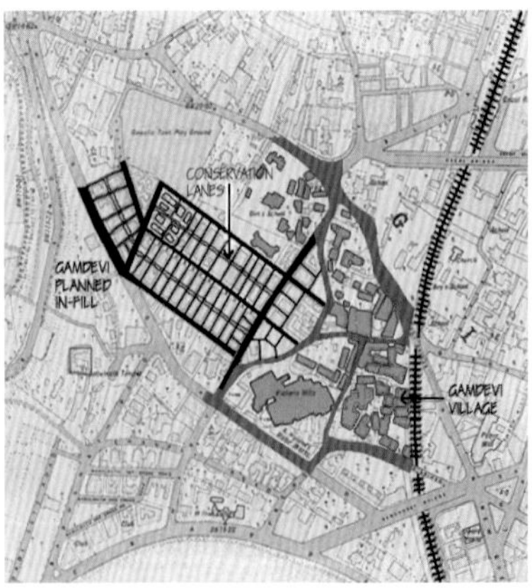

Gamdevi and Agripada were two major infill estate projects. Plot sizes were bigger to attract a clientele that could afford high rents. An estate defined the social profile of those who lived there.

Byculla Club till 1948 was for the exclusive use of the British and European population. Till the mid-1940s, there was a sizeable European population in Agripada.

Another design restriction to aid uniformity concerned the compound wall. The Trust's contention was that when standing on the street, the first thing one noticed about a given building was its compound wall. Just as uniform setbacks on the front kept buildings in a line, the compound wall maintained the street line, and its design, therefore, was also subject to rules laid down by the Trust: it had to be 1.5 metres high, with the lower part in either stone or brick masonry and the upper third done in grillework, either wrought iron or concrete. The grille could be in panels, but on corner sites it had to be continuous to enable visibility. Gates had to be of the same height as the wall but pillars could go higher. The grilles could be of any design but the height of the brick or stone base was constant in all compound walls – this gave the walls a unified appearance along a street. The design of the compound wall and gates also had to be approved by the architect of the Improvement Trust.

Over the years, building rules became more refined as shortcomings were rectified through amendments. Some rules were added to ensure that house owners maintained their properties well so that the estate as a whole had a well-kept look. Every house had to have a bin, whose garbage would be collected and transferred to bullock carts mounted with rectangular bins with roll-top covers. It was compulsory for the exterior walls of a building to be whitewashed or painted every three years. The base of the building had to be faced with dressed blue or yellow basalt stone. According to Parpia, all the conditions for construction and subsequent maintenance were included in the lease agreements with property owners.

During its tenure, the Improvement Trust made two other major design innovations – one was in the chawl window and the other in the norms for the arcade and elevations of buildings on major roads.

There were design rules for compound walls to aid uniformity.

In all layouts, buildings differed from one another in their external appearance but coalesced into harmonious entities. The rules of the Trust ensured this.

The chawl as a typology existed before the Improvement Trust but it was a crude example of housing. The rooms, accessed from a corridor, were narrow and deep and had only one external face, with the result that the light and ventilation were very poor. To mitigate this problem, the Improvement Trust chawls, which were otherwise planned like the generic ones in the city, were given an eight-and-a-half-feet window which commenced from the floor, allowing light to penetrate deep into the room. It had a transom at a level of three feet above the floor and another one at seven feet. The lower part of the window had vertical bars for safety and wood-panelled shutters that could be kept open at night to allow the breeze to reach the floor, where people slept. The upper part of the window had glass shutters that could be closed at night. There were no safety bars or grille for this portion. Above the glass shutters was a fanlight that could be opened if needed. The Improvement Trust did not alter the typology of the chawl, but by the ingenious design of the window made the tenement more liveable.

An important design rule emphasised by the Improvement Trust in all its major schemes was the ratio between built-up and open space. In its chawl schemes, distances between buildings were derived not only from the 63.5 degree angle but in many schemes additional space was left for social interaction. The light and air angle was accepted by all though some architects disputed the baseline. The official one was the ground level while the architects disputing this said that the sill level of the window should be treated as the ground line since light entered at that level. The sill was usually three feet above the floor. Using the sill level as the base would have helped reduce distances between buildings and thereby increase the number of dwelling units on a site. The Improvement Trust did not accept the argument that the sill level was more critical than the ground level. Not only was the sill lowered to floor level in the chawls

The chawl window was a major design innovation of the Trust. It was tall and started at the floor level. This facilitated a deeper penetration of light and provided adequate ventilation at the floor level where people slept.

it designed but the distance between buildings was increased. From the beginning, the Improvement Trust maintained that space outside and inside a building had to be matched, preferably with more space outside than inside.

The Trust employed an architect from England to advise it on all design matters, especially on facade and arcade designs, and approve plans submitted by architects. F G B Hawkins was the first to be appointed to this post. He did not contribute any meaningful design ideas and his tenure was full of controversy because he spent more time on private commissions than on official duty. After four years, he was succeeded by Professor Robert Cable, a former head of the department of architecture at the J J School of Art, who brought to the Trust some of his teaching and academic experience. During his term, he improved the design guidelines and rules and refined the rules concerning arcades.

Until Parpia asked us about arcades, we students had not really noticed that on important roads like Hornby Road, buildings were allowed to be built up to the front edge of their plot but had to provide arcades at the ground level for public use. Arcades formed a shaded walkway for pedestrians. The design of the arcade was specified by the Trust, including the centres of arches, their widths and springing levels. The external walls of most buildings at least till the level of the arcade had to be faced with coursed trap stone or yellow basalt Ashlar masonry. However, architects had some latitude in the choice of materials for the facade above the arcade.

Parpia showed us a set of building rules that was attached to the lease agreement for a building on plot 49/A in Sydenham Road Estate (now Mohammed Ali Road). The building was on a major road and had to

Arcades were an important urban design feature. The design of an arcade was specified in the lease agreement. Arcades provided shaded walkways and unified the exteriors of buildings on a street.

conform to facade controls in addition to the usual conditions imposed by the Improvement Trust. There was a drawing of the facade attached to the document, which also showed a section through the front wall. The level of the first floor was specified as "RL 112.50 THD". This was about 18 feet above road level. The cornice or chhajja at the roof level was specified as 44 feet above RL 112.50 THD, which was the level relative to the Town Hall Datum.

Town Hall Datum abbreviated as THD in documents, Parpia told us, was the first step in the flight of steps in front of the Town Hall. That was the datum line, and all heights in building were related to that. The first floor above the arcade, and the cornice level, which was above the top floor and below a sloped roof or parapet wall, had to compulsorily conform to the heights specified in the lease. Those two specifications created two uniform horizontal lines along the street. Between those two levels, however, the facade could vary even for adjacent buildings.

The documents for the building in Sydenham Estate showed pointed arches proportioned in the Ahmedabad style. The arches, their heights and the piers between them were all clearly drawn. But the document also stated: "The elevations of the building shall be Oriental in style of architecture. An illustration is attached to serve as a guide as to what is desired but it is not a type design necessarily to be followed." Many years later, I came across a book in which an office building in Helsinki designed by Alvar Aalto stood next to one by Eliel Saarinen, a Finnish architect of an earlier generation. Aalto maintained the important lines of the older building in his new one but his facade differed totally in the design and materials that he used. The facade of Saarinen's building had glass between stone masonry piers while

Building rules attached to lease deeds indicated the level of the floor above the arcade and the level of the cornice at the roof. These were relative to the Town Hall Datum. Lease documents also suggested the style of the elevation but architects could change it, provided the levels specified were maintained.

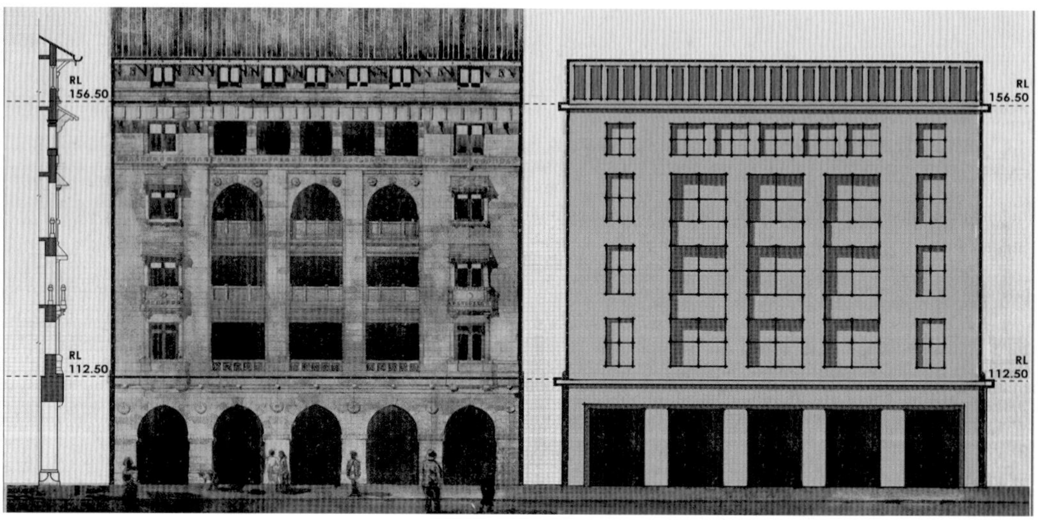

Aalto's had glass between metal mullions, spaced in harmony with those in the one next to it. It reminded me of the Improvement Trust, which maintained that buildings with different facades could co-exist in harmony if some levels were kept uniform.

Despite planned interventions in the form of estates like Gamdevi and Agripada, the built areas in the city did not decongest and the Trust had to look for virgin land to build larger precincts. The most successful of these was the Dadar-Matunga Estate Scheme V of 1899-1900. The scheme took over 44 years to develop but the Improvement Trust was associated with it only for the first 26 years – till 1926, when it merged with the Bombay Municipal Corporation for administrative reasons and also perhaps due to bureaucratic rivalry. For the next seven years, it only worked at tying up loose ends of incomplete projects. By 1933, it had lost its identity and from then the merged entity was called the Estates department of the Municipality.

Parpia lamented the end of the Improvement Trust's tenure, with whose end "the curtain came down on an era of development that made a city out of a haphazard collection of streets and buildings, insanitation and plagues". He made us reflect on the Trust's achievements which were significant. Apart from design concepts like the 63.5 degree light angle, the street arcade and the chawl window, the Trust was the first to show that different ideas and practices could be codified to give the city a coherent and workable form. Secondly, through the estates it developed, it showed that sanitation comes when there is planning on a larger scale and when individual house owners respect their neighbours' right to light and air. Thirdly, the estates helped the architectural profession grow because the Improvement Trust approved plans drawn up only by people qualified and licensed by the municipality. The municipality, till the 1970s, issued only

Buildings on D N Road followed design rules relating to arcades and cornice levels. The Improvement Trust insisted on approving the elevations to ensure that street lines and the continuity of arcades were maintained.

a surveyor's licence which was available to architects, civil engineers, surveyors and people with many years of practical experience. But only qualified architects and engineers could sign plans for approval. The Improvement Trust insisted that buildings constructed on its estates be supervised and certified by architects or engineers. As more buildings came up, the demand for architectural services grew. More architects went to college, got a degree and started practice.

Above all, before the Trust's planned estates appeared, the few architects who practised in the city were

2

refuse or give such consent being expressly reserved), apply to the plots as follows :—

(*a*) Each Plot shall be enclosed by a brick wall extending along the back and two sides, the height and design to be approved by the Engineer. Where the said walls are common to two Plots, their cost will be shared between the Tenants of such Plots as the Engineer, whose decision shall be final, shall determine.

(*b*) Nothing except the enclosing walls, as provided in the last preceding clause, is to be built on, nor is anything, except such reasonable weather shades as may be approved of by the ~~Board~~ Engineer, to be projected over any area beyond the boundary lines, delimiting the building area, marked on the plan attached to the agreement.

10. The level of the first floor shall be at R. L. ~~110~~ 112·50 T. H. D. (approximately 18 feet above the road level).

10*a*. The height of the main buildings shall be governed by the Municipal Bye-Laws and the 63½° Rule. Building of a single storey and upto the level of the first floor only may be erected on the portions hatched in white lines on the plan attached to the Agreement.

10*b*. A chajja or string course of design to be approved by the Engineer, shall be provided for the full length of the front of the building, the top of the said chajja or string course being 44 feet above the level of the first floor as fixed above. (R. L. 110.)

11. The footpath to the width of 16 feet along the entire length of the frontage of each plot where such frontage abuts on Sydenham Road shall be arcaded over at the expense of the Tenant in conformity with plans and specifications to be approved of by the Board and according to the following dimensions :—

Arches to be spaced at approximately 11 feet centres.
Arch opening to be 8 feet clear.
Height of springing of arches 9 feet below R. L. 110.
" " apex " " 4 " " "
" " plinth moulding 16 " " "
Arches to be struck on 5 feet radii.

12. The Arcade shall be of cut stone.

If the building is to be erected on a corner plot, stone facing to the ground-floor and the chajja or string course on the elevation fronting the wider street shall be continued on the elevation fronting the cross street to such depth as shall be fixed by the Engineer.

13. If the sanitary arrangements on the upper floors are placed in a position which necessitates the soil or waste-water pipes being laid along the roof of

An extract from a lease deed

only concerned with constructing stand-alone buildings with little regard for the city as a whole. The estates changed that view.

The Bombay Development Department (BDD) which followed the Improvement Trust took up schemes that were ambitious and very visible; however, the paradigm of development was merely a carryover of what the Improvement Trust had done in its short life. For 40 years after the Trust's closure, there were no new development ideas till the Development Control Rules of the 1960s introduced Floor Space Index (FSI), an abstract idea that changed the form of the city from a predictable to a negotiable one, and ultimately led to a steep decline. Architects who felt they were freed from prescribed footprints and volumes ultimately negotiated the bye-laws to build with little or no regard for the neighbourhood or the city. Old-timers who lamented the demise of the Improvement Trust and pointed out that Bombay began to slowly deteriorate in the absence of non-negotiable, public-spirited policies, were not far off the mark.

GO
INSTANT
Insurance in minutes
Star Union Dai-ichi

Marine Drive: Everyone's Icon

Marine Drive: Everyone's Icon

In the summer of 1956, I worked with Akbar Parpia once again. By that time he had parted ways professionally with G B Mhatre, and along with Khandu Parelkar and Vaman Gore, had set up an office called Parelkar Gore And Parpia. The firm had many projects, one of them an apartment building on Marine Drive on which I worked. Though the site was not on the sea face, the building design had to be approved by the Government Architect, who at that time was M K Jadhav. He insisted on discussing the plans and details with the designing architect before giving his approval.

At the meeting, Jadhav looked at the plans and elevations of the building carefully and asked questions about light and ventilation, stair positions and dimensions of the central light well. He also wanted to know how the building, which was on a corner plot, would turn the corner, which road the entrance would open on to and what the design of that entrance would be. He wanted to make sure that the stair tower did not ruin the skyline. I did not understand what he meant by skyline – the building would be surrounded by other buildings anyway so the top would not be noticed, I thought. I assumed his question was a matter of routine.

The definition of an 'iconic' building or place in Bombay can differ for different groups of people. For the English-educated, the Gateway of India is a symbol of the city while for the traditional Hindu it could be the steeped-in-myth-and-legend Banganga tank. For Muslims, the Haji Ali dargah, a mosque and tomb of a Muslim saint which was built in the fifteenth century, has great significance. All three, however, have one thing in common. They are along the sea, which means a lot to Bombay denizens.

At that time, the Princess Street flyover did not exist. There was a road from Marine Drive leading to Marine Lines Station. The site of our building was at the junction of that road and an inner one that was parallel to Marine Drive. Jadhav insisted that the elevation facing one road should be the same as the one facing the side street – a rule carried over from the Improvement Trust.

Corner plots on the sea face invariably had two entrances. The one at the junction of the roads lead to the stair hall, which was raised above the roof. In Parelkar's plan, the stair hall in the centre of the building was accessed not from the corner but from a side road. Jadhav suggested adding either a portico or a canopy to the main entry to make it stand out but Parelkar found it difficult to fit this into his design. After sketching different ideas, they agreed that a balcony should be set over the entrance, the design of which would have to be different from the other apartment balconies in the building. The drawings were amended and approvals were then given. But the plans had to be approved by the municipality as well because all buildings in the Back Bay Area needed permissions from both approving authorities.

Parelkar's freewheeling discussions with the Government Architect led me to believe that design rules were not written down in the form of bye-laws. Only a few important aspects like the alignment on the front, the height and the profile of the building were laid down. It was left to the individual architect to design the elevation of his building and the Government Architect would use his own judgement to evaluate the proposals that came to him for approval. This was not unlike the Improvement Trust's design norms for main roads, where buildings were kept in a line at the front and the height of two levels was specified but the other facade details were left to the building architect.

People gravitate to the sea for fresh air, and a spicy 'bhel' adds to the pleasure.

The sea is a vital part of life in Bombay. Chowpatty is where the major Ganpati immersions take place every year. Huge crowds bid farewell to Ganesha and pray for his return; their voices louder than the roar of the waves coming ashore.

Many years later, I realised that facade control (a term used in official parlance) around traffic circles meant that structures had to have uniform facades in order to maintain the visual identity of the circle. On important streets, one had to observe only a few rules because the individual building was merely a part of a larger group on a street, not a place needing identity.

I told my college friends what the Government Architect had said about the skyline, and we promptly went there to understand what it meant. We saw that from Nariman Point on the south to Chowpatty at the north end, the buildings on Marine Drive together formed a continuous curve with their roofs in one line without any jarring protrusions. The exceptions were buildings on corner sites where stair towers went above the roof level and were expressed as architectural features. The roofs being in a line added to the sweep of the road. The sweep of the buildings, the promenade and the sea wall were what made Marine Drive Bombay's most iconic image.

Uniformity in a roofline made sense on roads where there was an ensemble of buildings with a large enough foreground in front of them to see that line. The consistency of the roofline on Marine Drive did not come from a design compulsion – it happened because the plots and footprints of buildings on them were square and the setbacks on the front and the sides as also the heights were specified. This ensured uniformity. In a square plan, a staircase and light well in the centre made sense, as the floor could be divided into either two large flats or four smaller ones. A staircase in the centre with its tower above the roof would obviously not show on the front. Almost all the buildings on Marine Drive, except those on corner sites, were similar in plan. Little wonder then that the roofs of all the buildings were in a line.

The pillar commemorating the completion of Kennedy Sea Face - the British name for Girgaum Chowpatty.

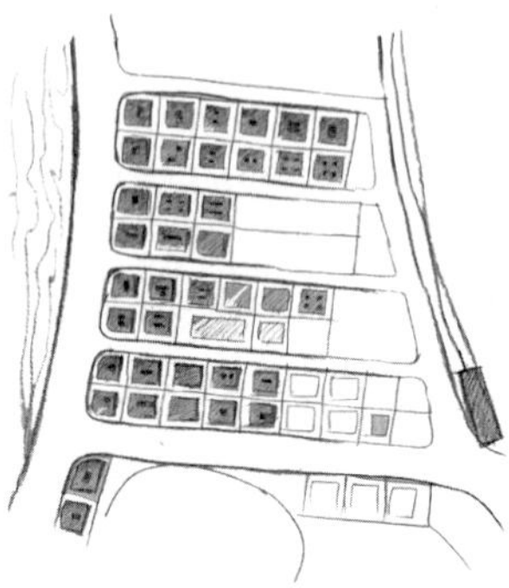

The sea wall defines the edge between land and sea.

The sweep of the buildings, the promenade and the sea wall is what Marine Drive is all about.

The row of buildings along Marine Drive form what I like to think of as the first of four parallel curved lines that make up the sweeping design of this celebrated space. The first line is formed by the row of buildings. The second line is the road in front of these buildings. The third line is the broad, paved promenade for walking along the sea. The fourth line is the hard edge of the sea wall. This ensemble gives Marine Drive its dramatic sweep and makes it the strongest image of Bombay.

My friends and I would walk along Marine Drive and Apollo Bunder, looking at every single building. We tried to find prominent features through which we could identify the architects who designed some of them. There were buildings designed by G B Mhatre and one, the Bombay Club, designed by Claude Batley. Mhatre's buildings were Art Deco in style but Batley had his own style, which was not Art Deco as some people thought. Many refer to the buildings of Marine Drive as being part of the Art Deco district of Bombay. Most of the buildings are not good Art Deco – at best they are passable or nondescript. Their effect comes from belonging to the group.

How Did The Back Bay Come About?

Marine Drive, also known by its sobriquet 'Queen's Necklace', is famous locally and even globally. Much less is known about the Back Bay Reclamation of which it is only a part. Marine Drive started as a road to connect Malabar Hill, where the wealthy and the ruling class lived, to Fort. The road from Malabar Hill's Walkeshwar, where the governor resided, to the Secretariat, which abutted Oval Maidan, was along the sea up to Chowpatty. Known as Kennedy Sea Face, this road was built in 1920. It made sense to extend it for

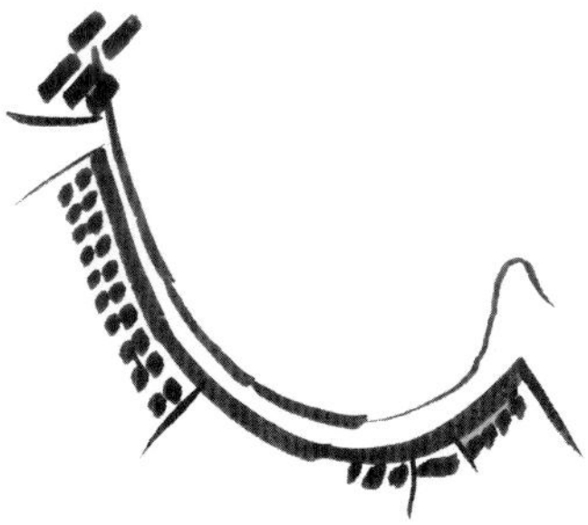

Marine Drive is uncluttered. It can be abstracted to a set of four curved and parallel lines, each expressing the sweep of the bay.

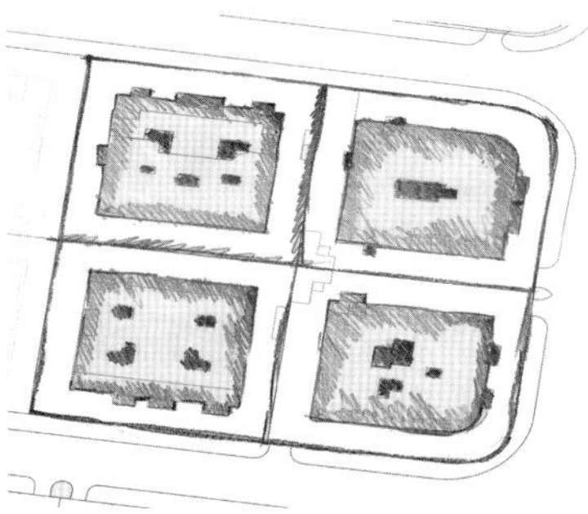

The uniform skyline on Marine Drive did not come out of a design compulsion. It happened because the plots and footprints of buildings were square and stairs were placed in the centre. The stair tower did not appear on the front. The exception was buildings on corner sites where the stair towers were allowed to break the skyline.

quick and easy access to Fort instead of diverting to Queen's Road on the east of the railway line. However, the cost of reclaiming land from the sea – which this extension would entail – for just a road would have been disproportionately high. It made better sense to extend the bay, reclaim more land from the sea and retain it by building a sea wall. The land could be for public use and residential sites for long lease.

The government entrusted the job to the Bombay Development Department, which had succeeded the Improvement Trust as the city's main developing authority. The BDD, predecessor of the present urban development department, had constructed the BDD chawls at Worli and other places before it was entrusted with the job of reclaiming land and developing it. The Back Bay Reclamation Scheme was its biggest project and it retained W R Davidge, a British planner, to prepare a master plan for this.

I found Davidge's plan in the library of the Indian Institute of Architects. The version I looked at had few details, but even the outline was enough to communicate its ambition. The plan was grand, covering 1,145 acres and focused on the area south of the axis connecting the Town Hall and the sea. It provided government offices with a grand forecourt – the Oval maidan – facing the Secretariat, University and the High Court. The Oval was to be a formal garden between these three buildings, which stood on the remains of the Fort wall and the new buildings proposed in Davidge's scheme. A boulevard ran through the full length of the precinct around the Oval and further south. The planning was formal, with tree-lined streets, parks for recreation and cultural activities. It did not provide for residential use in any meaningful way – instead, it included sites for educational and cultural buildings, government offices and other institutions of authority. The public spaces in the plan were big in scale as were the offices of the

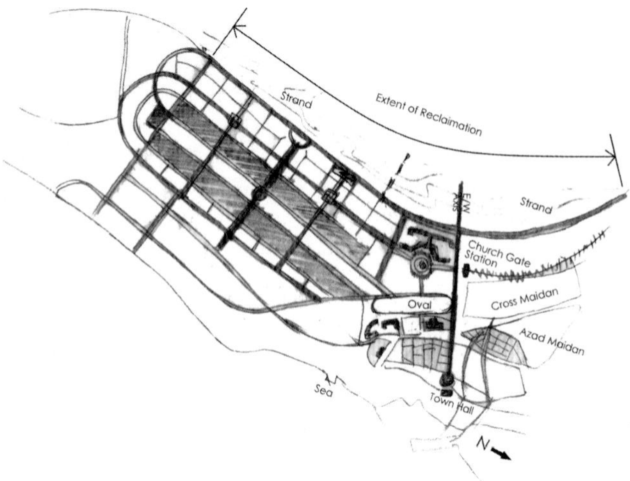

W R Davidge prepared the first master plan for Back Bay Reclamation. His was a grandiose plan that concentrated largely on the area south of the axis between the sea and the Town Hall.

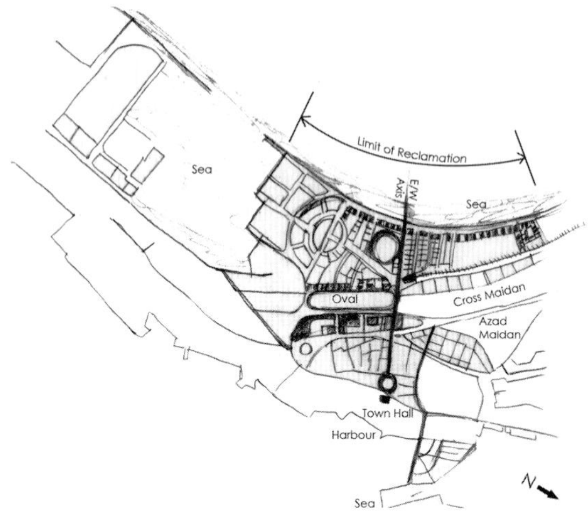

Davidge's plan was curtailed and revised. The new plan included development in the north of the axis. It was largely residential, and its layout, as Batley critiqued, "resembled a set of ill-fitting false teeth".

government. Davidge also planned a broad landscaped promenade called 'The Strand' for the length of the sea front that was included in his plan (north of the present Marine Drive). Buildings along the sea front were continuous, interrupted only by crossroads connecting the boulevard with The Strand at wide intervals. However, Davidge did not consider the sweep of the bay in his scheme.

The scheme was dogged by cost escalations and charges of corruption, which reduced the area from 1,145 acres to 552 acres. This led to Davidge's plan being set aside. An advisory committee was formed, which altered his plan from one that looked inwards to the city to one that opened to the sea and created a bay by extending Kennedy Sea Face (Chowpatty) to Nariman Point. A sea wall for the entire stretch defined the edge between land and sea. Claude Batley, who was interested in the city and wrote about it extensively, was not happy with many of these alterations. In a 1945 journal of the Indian Institute of Architects, he wrote: "The committee was appointed to take all the guts out of Davidge's scheme, which it did most effectively by seeing how many small rectangles it could contrive to draw over the area reclaimed." But he liked the idea of the promenade on the sea face. About this, he wrote, "If you have any doubt of its worthwhileness, watch the happy throngs of promenaders, of all sorts and conditions, drinking in the sea air morning and evening; an asset that has never been put down as of any tangible value in the profit-and-loss account of the scheme."

The revised plan focused on the area north of the Oval whereas Davidge's original design had focused on the south. In Davidge's plan, the gaps between buildings were set at wide intervals while in the revised plan they were at close intervals. Batley wrote that the buildings on the sea front resembled a set of

Promenaders at Marine Drive walk along and on the sea wall, sit on it and enjoy the sunset. Batley rued that planners never counted the sea and people's enjoyment of it as an asset in the profit-and-loss account of the scheme.

ill-fitting false teeth, a comment that was not quite fair, especially considering how the gaps between buildings let in sea breeze that benefited the inner city.

Unlike Davidge's plan, which provided for impressive public buildings, the revised plan was a commercial proposition that helped recoup some of the expenditure incurred in reclamation. In both the original and revised plans, the proportion of open space was relatively high compared to the built-up area, which added to the value of land in the precinct. Land was apportioned rationally, with half the area being used for residences and the remainder being shared by commercial premises, roads, the promenade and recreation grounds. The combined areas of these recreation grounds made for a large percentage of the total open area of the city. Railway lines separated the inner city and the sea front, and there was no connection except a footbridge at Marine Lines Station and outside Charni Road Station on its southern edge.

The Back Bay scheme generated some ideas and controversies. Batley published an alternative plan in a 1945 issue of the Journal of the Indian Institute of Architects. Nobody contradicted him as he was an important figure but neither did his views get much attention.

In the 1950s, a rather unusual proposal concerning a public utility kicked off a lot of criticism. A commercial firm offered to fund and build a footbridge at the Chowpatty end of Marine Drive which would connect Mafatlal Baths and Roxy Cinema on Queen's Road. The condition attached to the offer was that the sponsors would have the right to use the sides of the bridge as an advertising site for a fixed number of

A commercial firm offered to build at its own cost a foot bridge over the railway lines at the Chowpatty end of Marine Drive if it was given advertising rights on the sides of the bridge. The offer was unprecedented and triggered much debate in the municipality but was subsequently agreed to.

years. This was a total departure from the rules of the municipality, which owned all advertising sites in the public domain and leased them annually to individual advertisers; moreover, construction of a public building or utility was solely the prerogative of the government. Those who wished to donate towards such constructions could at most deposit their contributions with the government or the Municipal Fund and leave construction to the PWD or municipality.

The proposal generated a lot of debate within the municipality and featured in the newspapers. Questions were raised about the propriety of an individual funding and building a public facility and getting advertising rights in return. There were questions about legal and financial obligations, and everyone had doubts about the design of the bridge. In spite of all this, the municipality went ahead because the proposal was commercially attractive.

The bridge was by no means attractive in design but it made immense sense for advertisers, whose hoardings on it were visible to cars and pedestrians from a long distance away. Despite its mediocre design, it was like a gateway that opened up the sweep of Marine Drive and its buildings, and also linked two different worlds: the rich zooming by in their cars on the one hand and the middle class pouring into the railway station to catch a train on the other. Both images express very differently lived realities, but there is a common thread: a desire to better one's life, which, essentially, is the character of Bombay.

Walking on the promenade towards Nariman Point now, the skyline and buildings do not look the same as they did when I was in college. Until the 1960s, the controls were faithfully followed. Later, deviations

The bridge linked two different worlds. From atop it, the image of cars speeding by evokes the idea of a city with well-to-do people driving to their place of work to add to their wealth.

At a railway station on the other side, the chaotic image of people rushing into and out of trains depicts a different reality - of a city crowded with people trying to keep themselves alive.

slipped in, as controls were relaxed due to exigencies, arising when owners with either political or bureaucratic backing pressed the administration for concessions. These were dealt with on a case-to-case basis which was discretionary and often lead to misfeasance. A building named Firdaus was the first to deviate from the established skyline when a penthouse with a sloping roof was permitted. Bombay Club was replaced by a hotel called Natraj that was later rebuilt and called Intercontinental. The facades of some buildings were changed totally. But Marine Drive could take in all these changes because it is itself such a strong statement.

The alternative plan suggested by Batley in the Indian Institute of Architects journal retained the "ill-fitting false teeth" of buildings on the sea front. But behind them, he put ten-storeyed buildings built around landscaped open courts. He argued that buildings behind those on the sea front should also enjoy the view and the breeze. He supported the idea of using the external courtyards of buildings as a community space that could be used for a variety of purposes, including sleeping out on nights when the weather was very warm. Batley said: "At least fifty per cent of our useless little short cross streets could be paved and utilised as extra sleeping spaces at night and safer places for the children of the neighbourhood to use during the day; further, not a single of our public gardens should be barred at night against the more sensible of our people who prefer the open air to the airless hovels to which they are otherwise condemned. However ideal these open spaces may be for the dry months, they are of little use in the monsoon, which is one reason I have always advocated street arcades for Bombay. There are also other possible ways out. One is roofing over our traffic roundabouts so that they may be used by our licensed hawkers and their patrons during the day and add to the conveniences of pavement sleepers during the night."

Soona Mahal at Marine Drive is one of the few buildings that have an Art Deco facade. Yet, everyone refers to Marine Drive as an 'Art Deco district'.

Batley may have critiqued the Back Bay Reclamation Plan but he was not a mere armchair critic and came up with an alternative. He also suggested that cross streets that had little or no traffic could be used as sleeping spaces at night when the weather was very hot.

For the European population residing in Bombay during the nineteenth century, sleeping outdoors in tents was not an unusual idea; what was then known as the Esplanade (the Oval and Cooperage maidans) was often used for this purpose. Sleeping outdoors made great sense in a city whose sultry weather had earned it the classification of a 'fan city' by the British administration, which categorised places where its military or civil service officials were posted as 'fan stations' or 'non-fan stations' depending on the weather. Officials posted in fan stations were paid an allowance to hire a punkah-puller.

A punkah, the Hindi word for 'fan', was the standard contraption used to cool rooms in fan stations. Made of cloth or cane matting stretched on a wood frame, this huge manual fan was hung from the ceiling by ropes and worked by a cord which passed through a fanlight above the door to a punkah-puller outside who operated it. Interestingly, the classification of fan and non-fan stations continued after buildings were electrified and even in post-independence India.

Batley's suggestion to make use of public streets for sleeping was not taken seriously. But Charles Correa in 1968 coincidentally came up with a somewhat similar plan which involved modifying the sidewalks on the main roads to accommodate both hawkers and pavement sleepers. He explained his design, saying, "In the crowded centres of Indian cities, pavements are used intensively: during the day they are crowded with hawkers so that pedestrians are forced on to the road, blocking traffic lanes. As evening falls, the hawkers gather their possessions and go home to be replaced by people unfolding their bedding for a night's rest. These night people are not pavement dwellers (who are another group altogether) but mostly domestic servants and office boys who have to share a room in their places of work where they keep

Batley's suggestion about sleeping outdoors was not uncommon, as many Britishers used to sleep in tents on the Oval and Cooperage maidans during sultry weather and plague outbreaks.

Places with hot weather were classified as 'fan stations' and officials posted here were paid an allowance to hire a 'punkah puller'.

The half-naked punkah puller sweated to keep his overclad masters cool.

their belongings and use city pavements for sleeping. This allows them to economise on their expenses. Furthermore, on hot, sultry nights, sleeping outdoors is a more attractive proposition than the crowded airless room: that they have to do so under unhygienic conditions with the public walking right amongst (and over) them is truly reprehensible."

Correa's plan provided a line of platforms two metres wide and 60 centimetres high, with water taps at intervals of approximately 30 metres. The platforms "during the day would be used by hawkers – thus clearing the pavements and arcades for pedestrians (the platforms would also act as a safety barrier between pedestrian and vehicular traffic). In the evening, the taps would be turned on and the pavements washed clean by municipal sweepers. They would then provide convenient *otla*s for people to sleep out of the path of any pedestrian walking home at night".

Both Batley and Correa showed that public space can be used for many purposes and shared in different ways. In most Indian towns, people live their lives as much outside their houses as inside them. Open spaces are, therefore, integral to city life. Traditionally, the hierarchy of open space is defined. The courtyard within the house is private; the *otla* in front is available for anyone to take shelter. The street belongs to the community that uses it daily – it is where people meet and speak to one another. The large space outside belongs to all and is inviolate. It is sometimes articulated through architectural elements like water bodies with steps around them that are used for social interaction.

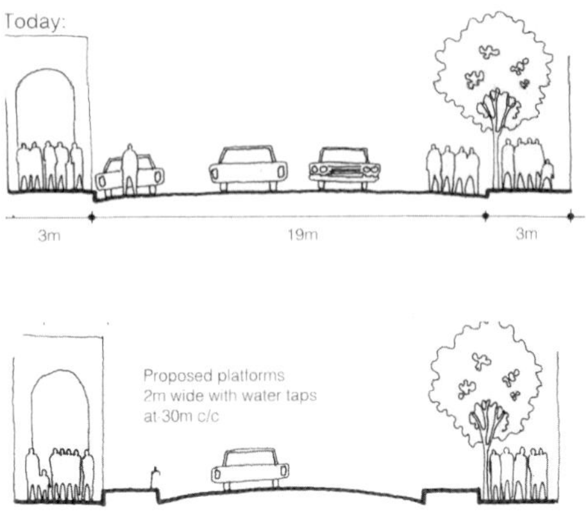

This is how a pavement is used.

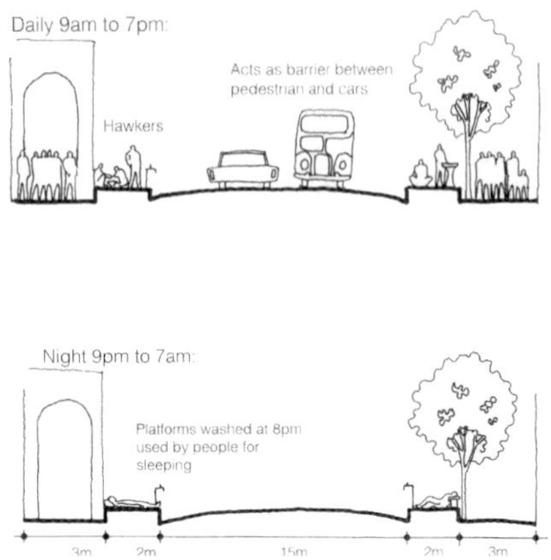

This is how Correa's plan modified it.

Charles Correa drew a plan that modified pavements of main roads to facilitate the poor people who slept there. Batley mooted an idea but Correa made a feasible proposal. Both showed that public space could be used and shared in different ways depending on the time of day.

In a city, public space is usually the street corner (the *naka*), the marketplace and the chowk. These are used for daily social interaction; the larger spaces are used for big gatherings during festivals or political rallies or protests. It is only in the public domain where citizens, who otherwise group themselves into castes and communities, forget their individual identities and share the same space. Built form and open spaces determine the character of a precinct and also differentiate one precinct from another. In Dadar-Matunga, buildings and people complement each other without one dominating the other. The scale of the neighbourhood brings them together unlike Back Bay where the buildings are big and tall and streets have fast-moving traffic. There, buildings dominate and people don't count. The scale makes all the difference.

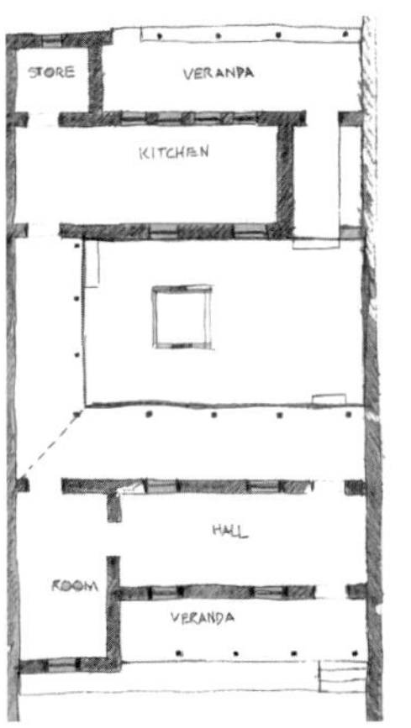

Open space is integral to built space. It is defined by its use. The courtyard in the house is private.

In a village, the otla or verandah is semi-public; anyone can take shelter in it.

In the city, it is the naka, marketplace or chowk that belong to everyone.

The large open spaces like the chowk or the village water body are public. Steps around the water body are where people, especially women, exchange news.

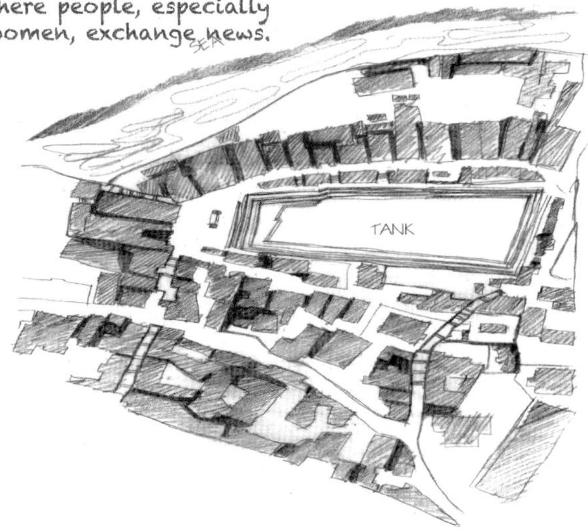

Art Deco Phase

Art Deco Phase

Art Deco emerged as a trendy architectural style in Bombay during the 1930s and 1940s. There are many reasons ascribed to its popularity. The wealthy were fascinated by its flamboyance while others saw it as a symbol of aspiration and upward mobility. Art Deco designers paid a lot of attention to the aesthetics of an object, especially its shape and profile, and buildings were thus beautified with many surface embellishments and abstract motifs. In earlier decades, these decorative elements in the design were restricted by the limitations imposed by the materials that were used to construct the building and the prevailing style of architecture. Now, new technologies meant that the architectwas freed from the inhibitions of the past and could choose from a variety of shapes, materials and forms. He could create his own style by choosing crowning features like turrets, stylised 'chhatris' and other elements – anything as long as the building attracted attention. It did not matter if the elevation or facade did not reflect what lay behind it.

One of my summer internships was with G B Mhatre, a professor at the J J School of Architecture and the architect who designed many of the Art Deco buildings in the Oval and Marine Drive sub-precincts. At

Art Deco was the name given to a style that included in its sweep several things from furniture to light fixtures to surface decorations to articles of daily use. It was most widely seen in the facades of buildings on the Oval and Marine Drive

school and in office, he always insisted that design was a matter of good proportion and refined detail, a belief that was visible in all his buildings. Mhatre was often asked to design only the facade or elevation of a building – this was when I first realised that the elevation of a building and its plan could be treated as two different things, not necessarily done by the same person. This differed from what we had learnt at school. The dichotomy was not uncommon in Bombay's Art Deco buildings, most of which were designed by two different architects.

Many of the older buildings in Hindu Colony and other places also had two different people involved in the design – an engineer playing the lead role and an architect designing the elevation, especially its details. But in these buildings, all the elements in the external elevation were germane to the design. Nothing was added on for effect. A balcony, for instance, was an extension of living space and used as such. The structure and size of these older buildings were determined by the engineer but they were also shaped by the architect, who was trained to bring beauty to a utilitarian object and among whose tasks was the designing and detailing of balcony railings, leadlights, brackets, weather shades over windows, joinery, staircase details and so on. Essentially, designing a building was an integral process though there were two disciplines working on it. In contrast, most Art Deco buildings had elements on the facade that were there only for effect.

Mhatre's buildings, however, were an exception. When we studied the Art Deco buildings in the city, we found that there was a mismatch in most of them between the inside arrangement of spaces and the external expression. Not in his. Moreover, even in buildings where he was retained only to draw up

Art Deco buildings had crowning features. They were either like turrets or stylised Indian 'chhatris'.

Art Deco motifs were often derived from objects or abstract ideas.

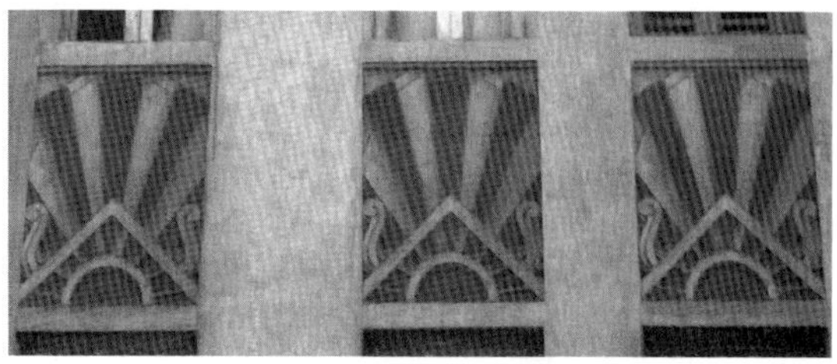

elevations, he enlarged the scope of his work by also designing the entrance foyer, staircase and lift front. However, most of the buildings that he designed at the Oval, including Sunshine, Moonlight, Sohrab Mansion, Queen's Court and Empress Court, were not signed off by him since they were commissioned to other architects, and he remained in the background.

Mhatre used RCC technology and new materials for creating and finishing interior spaces. Although he may not have been aware of the term Art Deco and the theories behind the movement, his buildings were truly Art Deco in form and detail, from the entrance hall to the doors of the individual flats, the lift front and doors, the staircase and the ceiling. His buildings were rich in detail unlike many others at the Oval that had Art Deco facades and nondescript interiors. He understood Art Deco as a complete design process, not merely as a style for the facade of a building.

Mhatre's output was prolific and outstanding for its time. Unlike many artists, he did not pursue a single stream of design inquiry. His work covered a wide range of ideas from the traditional to the modern. He believed that style meant elegance and mattered in everything, whether in the design of buildings or furniture or tapestry or even clothes. In the design studio at school, he would constantly repeat one mantra: "A design is only worth the paper it is drawn on unless you know how it is built."

In his own practice, Mhatre demonstrated this in the skilful way he used materials like wood, marble mosaic, chrome and many of the new materials that Art Deco brought – he once showed us a monastery he had renovated at Walkeshwar, where he had combined these materials with great finesse in the head

Empress Court, designed by G B Mhatre, stands out for its proportions and elegance of details.

Mhatre designed a building in its entirety – from the staircase and the entrance to the lifts to the individual flat.

Verandah railings were a special feature in Art Deco buildings.

monk's quarters. His prowess as a designer got him work from Poonegar and Billimoria and several other prominent firms but it took many years for him to get independent commissions, mainly because he lacked social skills and contacts. He was known in the design community for his skill, yet he did not have a public face. Batley, somewhat apologetically, called him a 'shadow architect', a sobriquet that haunted him all his life.

Since Art Deco buildings are predominant at the Oval and Marine Drive, I spent days wandering around that area looking at buildings. I would also read about those that were featured in magazines and debate with friends on whether the buildings had any merit other than belonging to a style. Although everyone pays more attention to Marine Drive, it is the Oval, which was once a riding track, that is important for its row of Art Deco buildings. These buildings, together with those on the sea face, make Bombay one of the few places in the world with such a large collection of Art Deco buildings in a single precinct.

Why was the Art Deco phase in Bombay's growth considered important? Initially, the style was a fashion import popular with one section of society. It was a transition between the architecture of the colonial period and that of the modern era, although as a design style it endured for a longer period in other countries. The style extended to furniture, kitchenware, items of daily use and styling of motor cars but it was most noticeable in buildings. Most people recognise Art Deco architecture by the features in the facades of buildings. Among these were stair towers, motifs derived from objects or abstract symbols and expressed in surface embellishments, mouldings and features seen in ships like porthole windows, deck railings and observation towers. These nautical elements indirectly reminded the onlooker that ocean

Art Deco buildings in Bombay and Miami are similar. Waldorf Towers in Miami resembles the one to the left in Bombay. Both came up at the same time.

Nautical features like porthole windows were reminders of the elegance and luxury of ocean liners, which were associated with a chic lifestyle.

liners coming from the West were the epitome of elegance and high living – something to aspire to. Art Deco was promoted as 'style' and everyone was convinced that it was a symbol of upward mobility and progress.

In the Art Deco aesthetic, everything in a building had to be tastefully, meaning decoratively, designed. This included the lettering for its name which was positioned prominently and formed an important design feature on the facade. Weather shades over windows or openings which, curiously, writers on Art Deco architecture in the West called 'eyebrows', were included as important elements in the design. In India, the 'eyebrow' or chhajja is an age-old device to provide shade and protection to an opening, and its shape and proportions were conditioned by the materials with which it was built. In the Art Deco period, chhajjas were built with RCC, which allowed architects to design them in a variety of shapes and sizes. Art Deco buildings in Bombay have chhajjas in abundance unlike their counterparts in the western world whose 'eyebrows' lack the same exuberance.

After studying Mhatre's work and that of other architects, we found that Art Deco as a style proliferated more because of local factors than the direct influence of western countries. What were these local compulsions? The primary one perhaps was that the estates developed initially by the Improvement Trust and later the Bombay Development Department had lease terms which demanded that buildings be completed within two years of land allotment. This could be achieved only by switching from load-bearing masonry construction to RCC technology, which lent itself to speedier building. RCC was also suitable for the multi-storeyed apartment or office buildings which, due to high lease rents, became the most

'Chhajjas', referred to as "eyebrows" by western writers, have been an essential part of Indian buildings from the beginning. With the coming of RCC (reinforced cement concrete), chhajjas began to be designed in a variety of shapes and sizes.

Architectural lettering was an important component of Art Deco design.

preferred typology. Besides, property owners wanted their buildings to look like those abroad so that they could attract a clientele that could pay high rents.

For architects in Bombay, both the typology of the high-rise and the technology of RCC were new, and the architectural language they were familiar with did not match either. It meant finding a new language. Art Deco as a style filled the lacuna since it was a product of modern construction technology and new materials while being decorative in appearance. The other influential movement in modern architecture of that time, known as the International Style, did not appeal to Bombay architects who, used as they were to embellishing facades, found its buildings stark and barren. Art Deco rejected the barrenness of the International Style and presented an alternative that was more acceptable to the Indian aesthetic.

While architects and theoreticians were arguing about Art Deco as a new art form, cement-based products and technology, especially RCC, were quietly changing ground realities. RCC technology permitted greater freedom in dealing with interior spaces, and facades were now free from the constraints of the earlier load-bearing wall construction systems. Lifts enabled easy access to upper floors, and internal walls became lighter and thinner. RCC made cantilevers possible, and chhajjas and balconies could be shaped at will. For architects, the new-found freedom was both exciting and scary – exciting because new technology opened up many possibilities and scary because there were no precedents to fall back on.

While both the Art Deco and Modern movements let architects design freely without the burden of tradition, apprehensions about the new aesthetic remained. It was left to Batley, who had influence over

ACC Ltd promoted cement and RCC for the construction of modern buildings. The cement company published brochures featuring designs for a variety of buildings.

architects then, to exhort fellow architects to accept change and move away from old ways. He said this after attending an exhibition, organised by the Indian Institute of Architects in 1937, which displayed the interiors of rooms using Art Deco-style furniture. The use of new materials like metal and streamlined styling shocked architects, who were unsure about the effect this could have on architecture.

The exhibition also triggered a debate about the role of design in objects of daily use like crockery, cutlery, furniture and light fittings. Votaries of Art Deco said the style was a conscious attempt to bring beauty into everyday life; it was a symbol of elegance and lifestyle, usually of the rich, but also expressed the aspirations of those not as wealthy. The modernists, however, disparaged this form which emphasised craftsmanship and exclusivity rather than mass production and whose products were, therefore, expensive. Art Deco, they said, emphasised only the superficial qualities of a product to the exclusion of the total design process, which ought to include function, optimum use of materials and efficient production methods. They argued for removing all barriers between crafts and arts to bring about integrated design that could be used for improved industrial products and mass-produced articles for daily use. They extended their design ideas to a wide range of building types from factories to housing for workers – however, they could do this more easily in Europe than in India since they used improved RCC and steel technology. In India it took time for architects to become familiar with it.

At this time, Associated Cement Companies (ACC), a pioneer in cement-manufacturing in India, was also promoting the use of cement in building construction. The company actively advocated RCC technology and showed that framed structures were more suitable for multi-storeyed buildings than load-bearing

'60 Designs for your new home' – a brochure from ACC.

'80 Designs' published in 1950 was a sequel to '60 Designs'.

An exhibition of furniture and interiors designed in the Art Deco style exposed architects to new ideas of design.

masonry walls which buildings in the inner city were constructed with. Architects and property owners were reluctant to accept a system where loads were carried on "thin sticks that go for pillars". ACC, therefore, had to push hard for the new system.

As part of its marketing strategy, the company published a series of coloured brochures titled *40 Designs* in 1944, followed by *60 Designs* in 1946. Encouraged by the popularity of these, it followed with *80 Designs* in 1950. The brochures contained designs for a variety of buildings, almost all of which had flat roofs in RCC. Architects in the city were commissioned to make plans and coloured perspective views. The brochures also had articles on Modern Architecture written to propagate the new technology using cement and RCC. ACC also published *The Indian Concrete Journal*, which contained articles on concrete technology and details of projects, both completed and under construction.

These publications influenced contractors, structural engineers and students of architecture. *80 Designs* was a favourite reference for us at school, the only other one being the *Journal of the Royal Institute of British Architects*. The JJ school collection was an apology for a library, and British and American magazines were too expensive for us to afford. Initially, we referred to these brochures to learn rendering techniques. Later, we studied the designs and read the articles. You could, in a way, say that ACC promoted modern architecture in Bombay.

RCC brought in its train some division of responsibility within the civil engineering profession. Some engineers specialised in structural designing and restricted their role to designing the structure only but

A public building and a house featured in '80 Designs'.

several of their brethren portrayed themselves as engineer-cum-architects or contractors. Till the 1940s, most people considered engineers to be more competent to get a building constructed than architects whose forte was seen to be only beautifying the exterior and providing architectural details for interior elements like joinery, grillework and flooring. That perception remained for a long time. Little wonder then that almost all the buildings on the Oval were commissioned to the engineer-cum-architect firms, most of whom drew the initial plans and then used an architect to design the facade and the architectural details of the insides.

In larger projects, the architect was brought in from the start and was given credit for his work. In such cases, he was called a 'consulting architect'. An engineering firm like Poonegar and Bilimoria understood the role of an architect. They retained Mhatre to design and detail the building in all respects and even oversee the execution of architectural details on site. Drawing up contracts, appointing contractors, and checking and certifying work was done by the firm. The division of responsibilities worked very well, and the collaboration between Mhatre and Poonegar and Bilimoria continued for 15 years.

Just as RCC structures freed interior space and gave the designer freedom to make openings of any size, plastered surfaces gave him the opportunity to experiment with a variety of textures, mouldings, motifs and shapes which could not be easily done in stone. Along with the new technology came a wide range of materials – larger-sized glass sheets, for instance, and decorative metal work and chromium-plated fittings to enrich interiors. The exteriors, on the other hand, were finished with plaster and either painted or rendered – a design condition imposed by the Bombay Development Department for all buildings on

Art Deco buildings were plastered on the exterior. The architect had the opportunity to experiment with a variety of textures, mouldings and shapes.

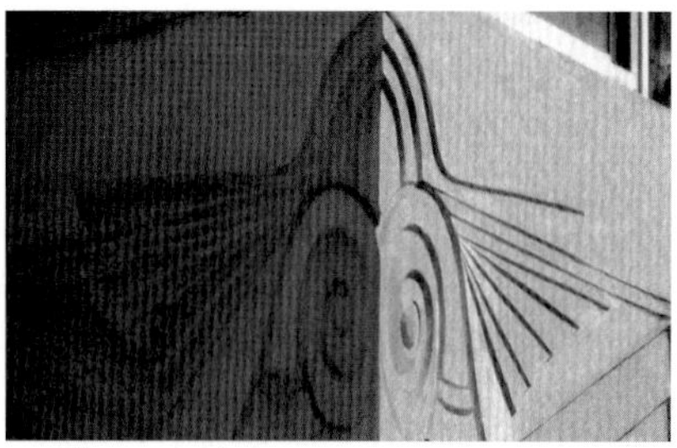

Surface embellishment extended to the corners of buildings as well.

Verandah parapets had decorative features. Art Deco architects accepted embellishment of the facade as an important element of design unlike the modernists who frowned on anything that was not strictly functional.

Marine Drive and the Oval. Renderings using coloured cement called 'colourcrete' or 'stonecrete' were very popular – in this, walls were coated with a layer of coloured cement mixed with fine stone or marble chips that was finely chiselled to give a textured finish.

One of the innovative materials that came in at this time was marble mosaic tiles for flooring. Italian Jewish émigrés such as Mario Levi, Christiano Francorsi, and others who came to India during the World War II exodus from Europe, brought with them the technology for manufacturing tiles and laying and polishing them. The technology for doing this in situ was traditionally known to Indian masons – after all, Red Oxide floors have existed all over India for over a century – but making precast tiles, laying and mechanically polishing them was an unknown technology. The in situ way, where cement floors finished with Red Oxide and mosaic floors were polished by hand, involved a lot of labour. The new technology brought in machines to reduce manual labour and get the same effect. The pre-polished tile samples, in a variety of colours and designs, helped architects visualise the finished floor unlike the in situ mosaic, which kept clients in the dark until the work was over. The flooring in stair halls and foyers, too, was laid with a lot of attention to colour and pattern; likewise, the front walls of lift shafts were finished with marble mosaic and their panel joints emphasised with chrome-finished metal strips.

Mhatre's skill and refinement of Art Deco details was well known. In many cases, tiles would be specially made to suit his design. He also used 'colourcrete' for the exterior, mostly for the base of the building, as he believed that the latter, like the plinth in traditional buildings, was the most important element and had to be emphasised. Knowing that the base was the most vulnerable to wear and tear, he preferred to use dark shades of colourcrete which concealed dirt better.

Marble mosaic tiles for flooring added colour and livened up interiors. They were laid in patterns that combined tiles of different designs.

Mosaic tiles were also used in stair treads, risers and mid-landings. The technology for making and laying mosaic tiles was brought in by Italian Jewish émigrés in the 1930s.

How did architects come to terms with the new technology and materials, clients' aspirations and their own sensibilities? Buildings crowned with pitched roofs gave way to flat concrete terraces, as the former, which were more expensive and took longer to construct, began to be shunned by builders. Wood, the main structural component of a roof, not only cost more but also required skilled carpenters whose wages were higher than the shuttering carpenters used in RCC construction. Roof tiles needed frequent maintenance and owners of buildings complained about the recurring annual cost. The RCC roof slab was more permanent, required little upkeep and rendered a terrace available for use.

The flat profile of a building's roof was associated with modernity, and architects took to it immediately. But they had to find an alternative architectural language to express the new typology and technology. Architects of the generation trained in the 'Beaux Arts' system of art education at the Sir J J School of Art, where the aesthetic (decorative) aspect of architecture was given prime importance, found Art Deco appealing, as it helped them cope with emerging modernism.

Owners and architects considered embellishing the elevation or facade of a building as essential. Invariably, drawings and details for this would not be ready when tenders were invited, and all tenders or estimates would, therefore, provide a lump sum amount for 'elevation features'. This was prevalent even when I started practice in the '50s. Clients accepted a provision for such items in the tender without question, as beautifying the facade was a must.

The price for elevation features could not be easily arrived at, as the labour component would typically be higher than the cost of the materials. The price would always be negotiated and a contractor, usually

Art Deco was easy to adapt and change. It was suitable for almost all buildings

Art Deco was not limited to buildings in South Bombay. It was present in buildings in the suburbs as well.

enthused about beautifying the building, would execute the item even if it fetched him less money. Interestingly, smaller contractors, especially those who were artisans-turned-contractors, took some pride in their work and prevailed on architects to embellish the facades. That is, perhaps, also one of the reasons why Art Deco was so readily accepted by clients, architects and contractors.

Some authors say Art Deco's proliferation was influenced by the cinemas – Regal, Metro, Eros and later New Empire and Liberty. Their rich Art Deco interiors were symbols of luxury, and the style was adopted by the rich in the design of their houses, furniture, furnishings and artefacts, down to their ashtrays. Kamdar, the well-known furniture-maker and interior contractor, and his German designer, Messerschmidt, had a field day during this time. But beyond the elite, Art Deco was a language that was easy to adapt, change and build with – the style, with numerous variations, propagated itself by sheer repetition without any external stimulus, like the banyan tree which perpetuates itself by sprouting rootlets.

Art Deco is most visible in the group of buildings at the Oval and Marine Drive but its influence can also be seen in smaller apartment buildings in the Parsi and Hindu Colonies at Dadar and bungalows in the suburbs. My neighbourhood, Matunga, is full of such examples, including Aurora, a cinema house built in 1940. This cinema, designed by architects Marathe and Kulkarni in the Art Deco style, could have had a greater influence on other buildings if it had got the attention it deserved. But since it was located in Matunga, it was dismissed as a suburban cinema. Likewise, Strand, a small cinema hall in Colaba, designed by A B Schwarz, a Czech architect practising in Bombay, did not get the recognition it deserved though it was a good example of Art Deco in both exterior and interior design.

A cinema at Matunga designed in the Art Deco style did not get the attention it deserved only because of its location and its suburban clientele.

The collection of Art Deco buildings at the Oval and Marine Drive, for which 'world heritage site' status is being sought, is cited as an important phase in the city's history only because the buildings are in one location and built within a short time frame. The individual buildings, some of which do not deserve a second look, as well as the good ones, might have been ignored if they were located elsewhere. Office buildings in the Fort and Churchgate areas of the city as well as residential buildings in other parts of the city, though good examples of the Art Deco style, do not come under the scanner of conservationists because they are looked at as isolated constructions.

To look at Art Deco as an important phase in the city's history only because the style was imported for the design of elite houses or important public buildings or apartment buildings would be facile. It has to be seen in the context of the city's overall development and the typology, technology and sensibilities of the time. The Art Deco phase in Bombay's architectural history tapered off from the early 1950s. As an architectural language, its novelty wore off. Newer designs were only repetitions of what preceded them, as most architects began to find the style unfulfilling. Ideas coming out of modern architecture began to seem more interesting.

Two Office Districts

Two Office Districts

During my time at architecture school, an architect named George Wittet was spoken of frequently and with reverence. His fame came from designing the Gateway of India, the Prince of Wales Museum and other buildings that became landmarks in the city. He was cited for his skill in adapting different architectural styles to modern building requirements. In the specialised history class at school, we studied his buildings in Ballard Estate. Initially, we looked at the buildings alone without seeing them as part of the larger estate which Wittet had also designed. But we soon realised that as with Marine Drive, the individual buildings in Ballard Estate were not as important as the precinct.

Ballard Estate was built between 1918 and 1924. Fifty years later, another office district was built on the western side of the island. Nariman Point was supposed to be Back Bay's crowning glory, the culmination of the sweep of Marine Drive. The differences and similarities between the two office districts are arresting.

Both districts were developed on reclaimed land. Ballard Estate came up on land reclaimed with the material that was excavated to deepen the Alexandra Dock basin on the eastern waterfront. The fact that

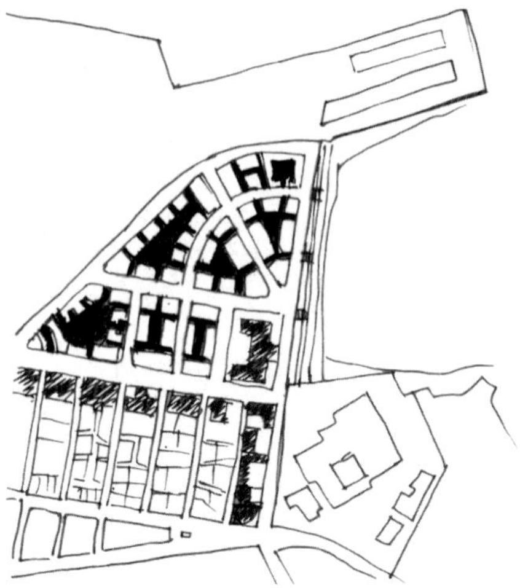

Ballard Estate was developed as an office district on land reclaimed from the sea. It was built in 1924 by the Bombay Port Trust.

Nariman Point, a similar office district, was also built on reclaimed land in the 1960s. It is the culmination of the sweep of Marine Drive.

it added jobs at the southern end of the city, increasing the number of commuters coming in every day on the trains, was ignored because locational convenience outweighed concerns about pressure on the transport system; besides, overcrowding on local trains was not yet a big problem. Planners then argued that it did not matter if trains or buses were overcrowded as long as there were jobs to be had.

The land for Nariman Point on the western tip was reclaimed in the 1960s. By this time, both government and civil society showed more concern about the expanding office area in South Bombay that would only add to congestion and overload the transport system. Planners suggested creating a commercial district by reclaiming land between Bandra and Kurla and giving a push to the development of New Bombay, the plan for which had been accepted by the government but put on hold.

The state government did not act on these concerns, possibly because of a lack of political will and bureaucratic lethargy. When the Nariman Point scheme was announced, reclamation was not fully complete, yet plots, including those that were still underwater, were sold to bidders. This was a political decision taken to raise funds for the coming elections. Land and dealing in it is always on the agenda of governments and political parties because it is the most important resource of a city.

Planners had a vision for both precincts. George Wittet imagined Ballard Estate as a replica of a late nineteenth-century London office district, and laid out the precinct and set the building guidelines to suit that image. The result was a unified form with a harmonious blend of built and open spaces. Buildings were uniform in height and the skyline did not vary.

George Wittet wanted Ballard Estate to resemble a London office district. Footprints of buildings and their heights were set out with few guidelines for the exterior design of buildings. Important junctions were emphasised with architectural elements like this war memorial.

Development in Nariman Point was based on FSI, a ratio between built area and land area, which resulted in high-rise office blocks. Planners visualised the district as a symbol of the commercial might of the city.

Nariman Point's planners, on the other hand, were driven by the image of buildings in the US, not UK. They wanted the space to be a twentieth-century office district like Manhattan with stand-alone high-rise office towers. They wanted it to be a symbol of the commercial might of Bombay, the financial capital of the country. To get this effect, they used an abstract idea called FSI, where the ratio between plot area and built-up area was specified. In Nariman Point, the ratio appeared to be designed in such a way as to generate isolated high-rise buildings with no specified footprints or heights.

The typologies in the two districts differed. Yet, both achieved similar built-up areas and fulfilled the same commercial requirements relative to the areas of their sites. Ballard Estate was community-based in the sense that spaces between buildings were shared. These were used for a variety of purposes, including office staff parties and parking and for connecting buildings. In Nariman Point, open spaces are within the compounds of individual buildings and used mainly for parking.

Ballard Estate was the first planned office precinct in Bombay and also the most successful. Students of architecture have studied it and written theses on it. Our class conducted a study on how spaces in the estate were used at different times of the day and how those spaces could be kept lively at all times. These were design ideas debated at schools by students year after year. As a student, I loved walking around Ballard Estate, studying the area and the buildings designed by George Wittet. I also spent months working in the area, enjoying, like many other office-goers, lunch breaks at the garden on the southern edge of the estate. At the time, I was working in Standard-Vaccum Oil Company, making drawings for their headquarters building at Churchgate. On Sundays, boats offered pleasure cruises around the harbour, which was reason enough to visit Ballard Estate again with friends.

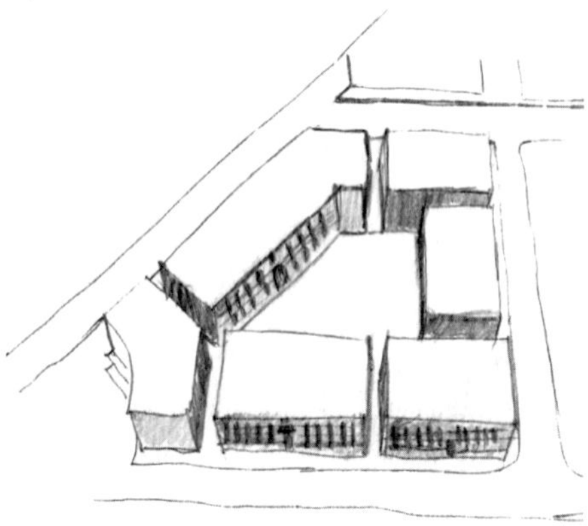

Footprints and heights of buildings in Ballard Estate were specified. Rear open spaces were merged to form a large space that could be used for several purposes.

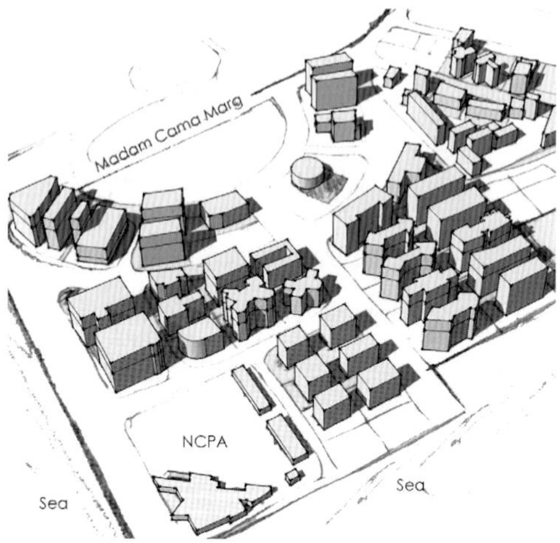

Office blocks in Nariman Point were designed as stand-alone office towers that stood on individual plots without specified footprints. The area around a building belonged to it and there was no community space that could be shared.

The entrance to the area from Mint Road culminated at the defunct Mole Station (the latter fell out of use in the 1960s) at Ballard Pier, where we frequently went to bid farewell to our fellow students when they sailed abroad to study or to welcome the few who returned. The road from Mint Road went past a terraced garden and curved to end at Mole Station in a way that was similar to Marine Drive. The garden actually retained the earth filling of the reclamation. It was a firm but soft edge unlike the hard edge of the sea wall at Marine Drive.

My friend Arun Ranade, who had done research on the city, gave me some information about the design of Ballard Estate. Wittet was consulting architect to the Government of Bombay when he did the entire layout and design of the estate. It was the first comprehensively planned office precinct where the land for buildings and the space around them was balanced. Forty-one per cent of the area is occupied by buildings and the rest by gardens, roads and paved alleyways. Alleyways were created by the combined rear setbacks of buildings. The total built-up area is 126,000 square metres – which means an FSI of 1.8 for the precinct. It is dense, yet has more open space mainly because the setbacks of individual buildings are merged into the general open space of the precinct. It is at a human scale that you can relate to easily; you can walk around the precinct without being intimidated by cars or buildings.

The estate, named after Col J A Ballard, the first chairman of the Bombay Port Trust, was meant for port-related offices, but other companies also found the location convenient. The district was meant to be exclusive in use. The lease terms for all the plots specified that the sites could be developed only for offices though some exceptions were permitted. A lessee could build a residence or hotel or shop, provided

Wittet did not set out design rules or guidelines for the facades of buildings at Ballard Estate. The only 'rule' was that the external walls of all buildings had to be done in stone in order to give a unified appearance to the whole estate. The buildings that he designed, though differing in their elevations, were faced in basalt stone.

these were of 'first-class' quality and approved by the Port Trust. Shops, if approved, would have to be on the ground floor. Lease deeds also specified some design conditions. For instance, the entrance door to a building could not open on to the road, which was public property. Steps leading to the door would have to be within the limits of the site – not spilling on to the pavement – and a canopy over the entrance door could not project beyond 1.2 metres or be placed lower than 4.8 metres. The position of the building on the site, and its height and footprint were specified.

Wittet insisted that the exterior walls of Ballard Estate's buildings be faced with yellow basalt stone. It was said that he imposed uniformity in design by insisting that all buildings be designed in the European Renaissance style. But this is not true. In an article titled 'An Architect's Ramble', published in the journal of the Bombay Architectural Students Association, he wrote: "I was asked to make a type design for Ballard Estate. I did not like the idea of 'type design' – but a certain degree of harmony must always be preferable to a series of discords, and on this principle, regular horizontal lines were settled and good proportions of solids and voids were fixed and materials to be employed were specified. Otherwise the types allowed considerable latitude to the individual designer, the real object being prevention of erection of buildings which might be offensive to the eye." The guidelines were similar to those set up by the Improvement Trust, especially in the rules relating to horizontal lines.

Nariman Point, unlike Ballard Estate, was developed with FSI as a planning tool – an abstract idea that compelled architects to respond to numbers more than anything else. As one might then expect, the built form turned out to be unpredictable. The FSI was 4.0 for an individual plot. The reason given for such a high

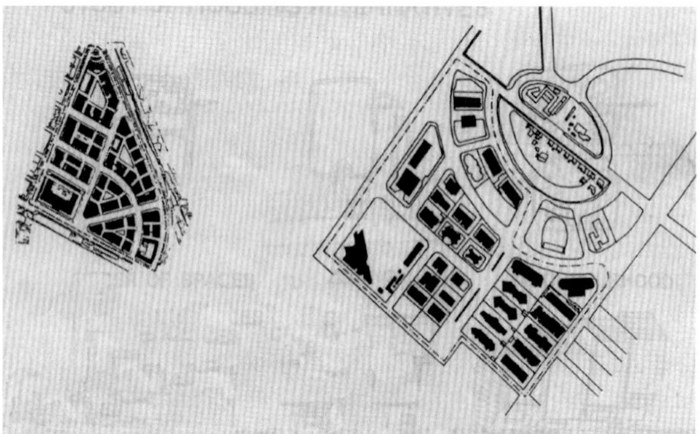

	Nariman Pt	Ballard Estate
Total Area (sqm)	2,57,735	70,000
Built Up Area (sqm)	5,67,017	1,26,000
Plot Area	63.3%	55.2%
Foothpath Area	5.9%	15.1%
Road Area	30.9%	29.7%
Plinth Area	20.4%	35.9%
Global F.S.I(2/1)	2.2	1.8

The typologies of buildings in Ballard Estate and Nariman Point were different. Despite consuming similar FSI, Ballard Estate's buildings were low-rise while Nariman Point had towers. The decision to go high was made before looking at alternatives.

FSI was that a lower one would not attract buyers. Planners, obsessed with a vision of skyscrapers, did not stop to question if the city's infrastructure could support such tall buildings. The fire brigade did not have equipment suitable for high-rises nor were hydrant lines laid or even commissioned before the first lot of buildings was constructed. Fire rules and standards were not drawn up for many years due to inexperience in setting out norms for fire safety.

The issue of what should be the most appropriate height for buildings is a recurring one for Bombay. The debate has mostly centred on the relationship between FSI and heights, with the common perception being that higher FSI implies taller buildings. A study by the Kamla Raheja Vidyanidhi Institute of Architecture, which I was a part of as a guide, compared Ballard Estate and Nariman Point. Both contain office blocks built with different development parameters. Ballard Estate had rules that specified footprints and heights of buildings and setbacks on the site. Footprints were large, occupying 73 per cent of the site area, and buildings were four storeys high. Yet the FSI came to 4.3 on the individual site and the global FSI (the ratio of built-up to land on the entire precinct) was 1.8 on the total area of the estate, which was 70,000 square metres. In Nariman Point, buildings had to have 20 floors to fulfill an FSI of 4.5. The global FSI was 2.2 on a site area of 2,57,735 square metres.

The typologies of buildings in the two office districts were different even though the built-up areas and FSI were comparable – Ballard Estate can accommodate as much density in its low-rise buildings as Nariman Point with its high-rise ones. The comparison shows that plot sizes, shapes and design rules determine the form of a precinct. To predetermine a form without looking at alternatives and their suitability on a city scale is short-sighted. In Nariman Point, the decision to go high was made even before the layout was drawn up: a conclusion about heights and FSI was reached before the proposition was even examined and alternatives explored.

In a larger way, the decision to build Nariman Point – one made for quick political gain – affected the city in the long term. The commercial development of Nariman Point added to the congestion in South Bombay and strained public transport further. It also set the development of New Bombay – a town that intended to take the pressure off the island city – back by at least 15 years.

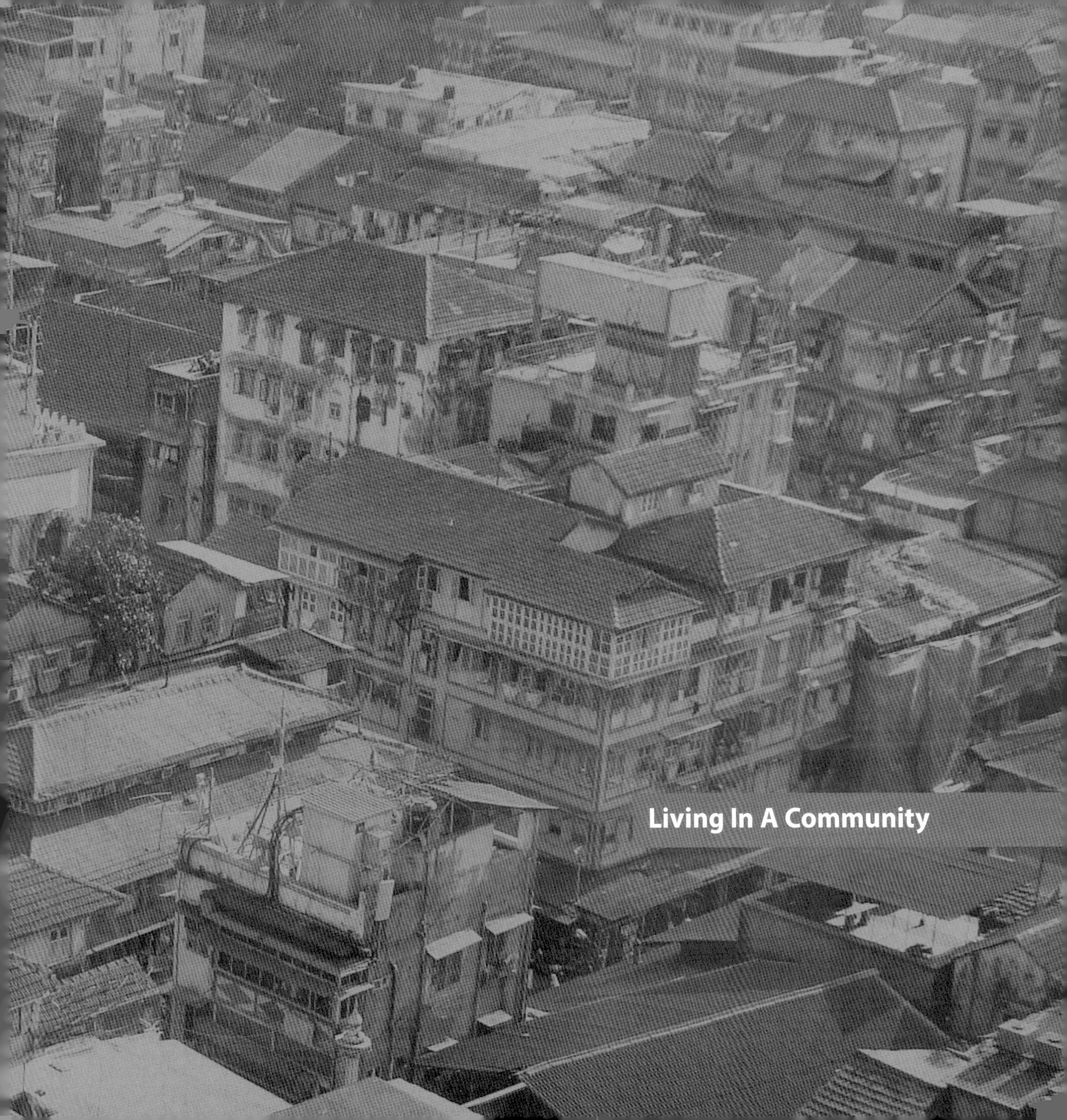

Living In A Community

Living In A Community

A city may be known for its iconic buildings and spaces but these do not necessarily reflect its worth. If this was the case, Agra, with its Taj Mahal and other stunning monuments, would have been a great city – which it is not by any stretch. What makes a city truly great is the urban fabric – the shops, homes, public spaces, places of leisure and schools that it contains within it. All these make up the true index of its quality.

An important component of the urban fabric is the kind and variety of housing that is available to citizens. While I have always lived in apartment buildings in Bombay, many of my friends have inhabited other types of houses which emerged at different times in the history of the city: Arun Ranade lives in a chawl at Girgaum, Jehangir Choksi lived at Cusrow Baug, a housing enclave for Parsis, while J B Fernandes, an architect associated with Ridley Abbot (the designer of New Empire and Liberty cinemas), lived at Khotachiwadi, a gaothan or urban village in Girgaum.

The diversity of houses in a city adds to its richness and is an important part of what makes it unique. Bombay is a palimpsest in which the imprints of successive housing typologies and their individual histories overlap. These housing types did not evolve in a sequence – most emerged independent of one

A city's fabric comprises interwoven elements like streets and houses, shops and marketplaces, railway stations and parks. Its texture is closely woven in areas of high density and more loosely in less populated ones.

another and concurrently. Of them, the apartment building is the newest form as also the one that has changed the most. The one that has changed the least is the oldest, the urban village or gaothan.

The Gaothan

At one time, housing in Bombay used to be community-based. Groups with a commonality of customs, culture or religion opted to share living space, which gave them a sense of belonging and security. This was especially the case with gaothans, whose unchanged character can partly be explained by the fact that their inhabitants have lived there for generations and also because many of these belong to a single religion or sub-community. In a gaothan, families live in one- or two-storeyed houses built with plastered brick walls, wooden floors, sloped roofs done in timber and tiles and elaborately decorated eaves boards. A gaothan, however, is more than a collection of picturesque houses. For the architect, it is about place, density and a typology of low-rise housing.

Gaothans are hamlets inhabited by descendants of the original residents of Bombay – agriculturists, toddy tappers, fishermen and others who lived on the original seven islands that the modern city grew out of. The Portuguese, who took over these islands, transformed the haphazard hamlets into a recognisable form – one reason why gaothans in Bombay are more orderly than the typical Indian village. Houses and roads here were laid out around the village square and the church, and the houses themselves were influenced by Portuguese design.

Khotachiwadi is an urban village in the heart of Girgaum which is one of the densest localities of Bombay. Houses in Khotachiwadi are two-storeyed with tiled roofs and colourful eaves boards. They resemble those in Goa and other Portugese colonies.

In a way, the term 'village' is a misnomer, as the gaothan is more urban than rural – the scale and typology of the houses here are nothing like those in the rest of the city. Over the years, gaothans have been absorbed into the city – some through redevelopment and some because the areas around them got developed – but a few like Khotachiwadi, Matharpacady and Ranwar have survived in their original form despite the steep land prices and development around them.

Most gaothans have a sizeable population of East Indians, who were among the original residents of the islands of Bombay who converted to Christianity during Portuguese rule and petitioned Queen Victoria to grant them status as 'East Indians' to differentiate them from Goans. That status, along with their English skills, gave them an advantage in getting jobs with the East India Company.

There are also non-Christian gaothans like the one at Chembur which my friend Anil Nagrath took me to. Residents here are Hindus from the Pathare Kshatriya Pachkalshi community, who are mainly occupied in the building trade. This gaothan has community spaces, a temple and a large common well which is also a meeting place for the women of the village. The houses are similar to those in the Christian gaothans but the houses are not influenced by European design. The nine-acre gaothan has 2,700 persons living in it – this is dense, but not as dense as the city's chawl tenements.

As newly minted architects in the 1950s, my colleagues and I often pondered on the relevance of urban villages in the city. Their existence seemed incompatible with rising land prices. In a city growing as fast as Bombay, gaothans seem to be in a time warp. Buildings in them requiring reconstruction have little

Ranwar, a gaothan in Bandra, is a Christian-dominated enclave that has retained its character despite the rise in land prices and rapid development around it.

space for adding area. The plot sizes are too small for financially viable apartment buildings. The prices of apartments nearby are higher, a disparity that seems unfair to gaothan property-owners.

Should gaothans be preserved? The answer may depend on whom you put the question to. Young people in gaothans are in the same dilemma that young chawl-dwellers face when they have to choose between living in a community and living on their own. Many residents, especially the young, want more space and would rather live in apartments, especially in high-rises. In the gaothan, there are concerns about fire safety and a lack of parking space for their new cars.

But the gaothan and its homes are exclusive and valuable in their own way. They add a rich layer to the city, which is worth preserving. They show us that housing is not only about building types but also about what surrounds the house and about how the home relates to the city. Conserving the urban village is not so much about preserving 'exotic' relics of history for our nostalgia – it also has to do with conserving a place with its unique scale, density, pedestrian streets and social cohesiveness. What the gaothan lacks is fire safety and easy access for emergencies, which do need to be provided for. The rules for redeveloping deteriorated buildings or extending them also have to be tailored to each gaothan since each has its own special character.

The biggest deterrent to conservation is the Development Plan, the rules of which are imposed uniformly all over the city, regardless of the nature of a space. An abstract idea like FSI (the ratio of built-up area to plot area which determines the permitted size of a building) does not work in a gaothan because certain

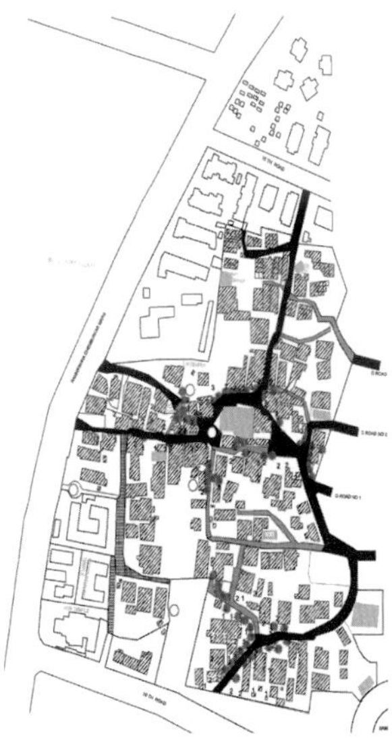

Chembur Gaothan is similar to other gaothans but the typology of houses and spaces within the village are different. They are suited to the culture of its Hindu inhabitants.

Houses in Chembur Gaothan, which at first sight resemble those in Khotachiwadi or Ranwar, actually differ in their plan and usage.

factors here differ from the rest of the city – for instance, the relationship of built-up area and heights of buildings to street widths and lengths, the proximity of houses, the density and the needs of the gaothan's residents. The gaothan is a compact and complete urban form that requires a separate set of rules for redevelopment. The task of formulating these is within the competence of conservationists who have until now restricted themselves to only restoring individual buildings.

The Wadi/Baug

Another early community housing type is the wadi or baug built by trusts and communities up to the late 1940s. Baugs consist of groups of chawls or apartment buildings within an enclave. The best examples of these gated colonies are those built by the Parsi community, including Cusrow Baug in Colaba where my school classmate, Jehangir Choksi, lived.

Parsi baugs were usually designed by architects – Cusrow Baug was designed by Claude Batley – and the living space in their apartments was generally larger than in most community-based housing. Most of the apartment buildings in Cusrow Baug had two bedrooms in addition to a living-room and kitchen. There were also three-bedroom apartments. Buildings were laid out so that the rear opened on to a courtyard in which children could play. Like all baugs, this one too had a large open space for recreation and social gatherings. In addition, there were buildings for community use like an agiary (fire temple), a community hall, a library and a gymnasium.

Apartment blocks in Cusrow Baug were laid out along the perimeter and looked inwards onto a large common open space that was meant for recreation.

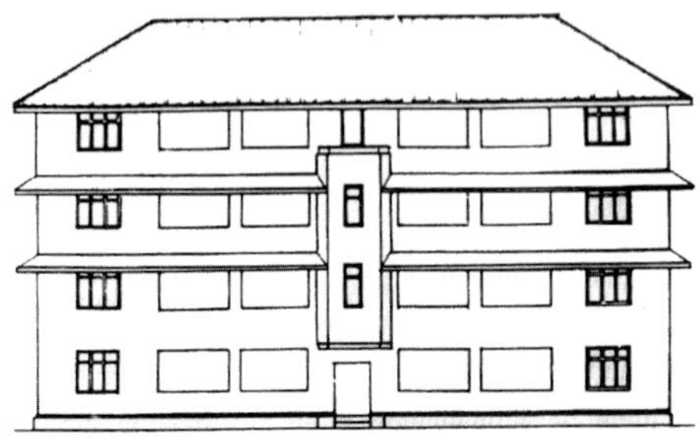

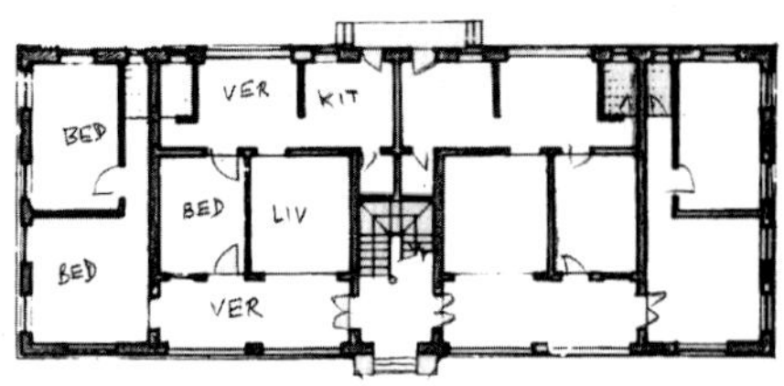

Apartments were intended for middle-class Parsis. Their accommodation standards were superior to others in the city.

Batley designed Cusrow Baug just like a housing estate in England, down to the size of the flats, the plan and design of the exteriors and the layout of the estate. The only Indian element was the verandah in every flat. He laid out the buildings along the perimeter of the site so that they formed a protective barrier and opened on to the space within the site. Vienna's Karl Marx Hof, a public housing scheme and a key example of socialist architecture, which was built between 1927 and 1930, was similarly designed.

Cusrow Baug has a three-storeyed building that stretches across the entire front of the site. With a high-arched entrance in the centre, it is like a long wall behind which lies the world of the baug. The front setback of the building at the edge of the site has been innovatively used to earn some additional rent – it has a platform which is used by the shops facing the main road. When I worked in Colaba in the 1960s, I would often stop for tea at a restaurant called Faletti's, which operated from this platform.

The charitable trusts that ran the baugs provided better housing for the lower- and middle-class members of the Parsi community than did other communities. Though the typology of the houses was similar – mostly two-roomed tenements – they were independent units with their own toilets. In comparison, the gated colonies of other communities were not quite as good. These other colonies, which were known as wadis, had smaller plots, and the buildings on them were therefore spaced more closely. Bhatiawadi, or Halai Bhatia Mahajan Wadi in Kalbadevi, contained chawls, a temple and marriage hall. There was a high wall with a gate that was kept closed at night.

Cusrow Baug resembled Karl Marx Hof, a housing estate in Vienna where apartment blocks were similarly arranged to enclose a central open space.

The entrance to Cusrow Baug is through a four-storeyed building that accommodates shops. Above the entrance is a hall that can be used as a gymnasium or library. The setback of the building is ingeniously used as an extension to the shops.

The Chawl

The predominant kind of building in the wadis, as well as in most parts of the inner city, was the chawl – the most visible and longest-lasting form of community-based housing in Bombay. Chawls started as dormitory accommodation for migrant workers in the late nineteenth century and were later used for family living without any alteration to the arrangement of rooms or their sizes. Initially, chawl tenements were built near places of work. Textile mill owners built chawls within the mill compounds to keep essential and permanent staff on the premises so that they would report for work on time and be available during emergencies. The mills also employed casual labour called 'badlis' to fill in for absent workers. Badli workers preferred to stay near the mills so that they could reach early for the day's employment, and chawls with rooms for rent thus came up around the mills. The area was called Girangaon, a Marathi word that means 'village of mills'.

The chawl is possibly the earliest instance of a modular system of housing. The basic module is a hundred-square-feet room, in which every dimension is ten feet. This was derived from the standard, economical lengths of timber used in the floor, the roof as well as supporting posts. Dwelling units were strung along an access corridor or verandah. Each dwelling unit was two rooms deep so as to make the ratio of paying areas to the non-paying ones more favourable to the landlord. One of the two rooms was used for cooking and was provided with a washing place in a corner that doubled as a bathing space.

There were other community-based housing enclaves like Halai Bhatia Mahajan Wadi at Kalbadevi where chawls, a temple and marriage hall were within an enclosed area. A high gate allowed entry only to persons living in the wadi.

Bhatiawadi is a gated enclave that houses members of the Bhatia community. The typology of housing is the chawl.

A two-module tenement provided a living space of 40 square feet per person. When it was used as a workers' dormitory, the living space reduced to 20 sq feet per person. Landlords were more concerned with cutting costs and getting the maximum returns for their investment than providing better living conditions for their tenants. The living space increased to 48 sq feet per person after a municipal bye-law in 1946 increased the area of a tenement to 240 square feet. The revision, then as in earlier times, was arbitrary and not backed by studies of the actual requirements of a family. The chawl tenement was smaller than its counterpart in the gaothan mainly because the design differed. The design of the chawl was based on affordability and shared sanitary facilities. Tenements had to be small to be affordable, and the toilet block, due to poor municipal sanitation, had to be isolated and shared.

The plan of a chawl is generic. Rooms are accessed from a central corridor or an open verandah. The single-loaded corridor or verandah (a corridor with rooms only on one side) was the preferred design since windows on both the front and rear ends of the tenements enabled cross-ventilation.

Chawls were mostly occupied by lower- and middle-income groups in Central and South Bombay. The chawl, in some localities, was the predominant typology of housing, and the people who lived there brought a distinct character to the area. Girgaum has an ethos different from that of Parel-Lalbaug, though people in both localities live in the same type of housing. The chawl also has to be seen not just as a typology of housing but as part of a larger picture that included social relationships and cultural ties. Spaces around and between the buildings were used as community places, especially during festivals. The community provided emotional security, and its unwritten code of behaviour was implicitly observed.

Spaces between and around chawl buildings in a compound were used by residents for various purposes, including the celebration of festivals and hosting of social events.

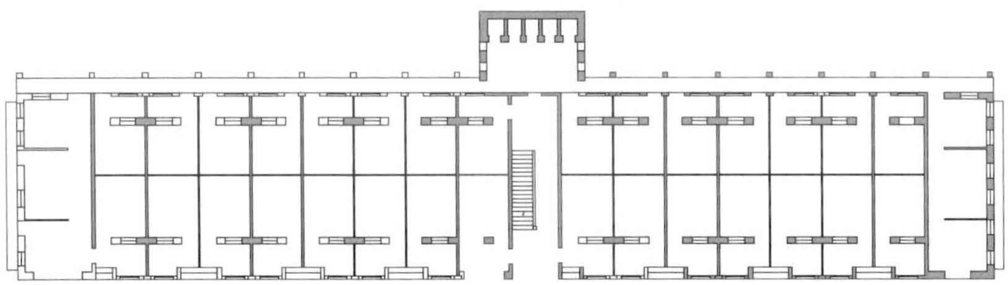

Tenements in a chawl were accessed either from a central corridor or, more often, from a verandah. The verandah was preferred since windows on the front and rear ends of the tenement provided cross-ventilation. In many chawls, like Anand Bhavan at Cadell Road, the ground floor had shops on the street side. The owners of these shops lived in the rooms behind.

Chawl committees would supervise the maintenance of common areas and matters concerning residents; on the recreation front, many chawls had kabbadi teams and would hold tournaments with other chawls between the months of March and August every year. Chawls, like wadis, were usually occupied by people belonging to the same caste, language or religious group.

People who lived in chawls were ingenious in the way they made optimum use of their meagre space. Invariably they built lofts which were used for storage. Rooms that were under a sloping roof had high ceilings, and on these floors the loft doubled as a sleeping area. In most chawls, the access corridor was wide, and occupants used portions of this to store water in drums or keep shoe racks. I have seen women in Hasnabad Chawl at Dongri use the central corridor for cooking and storing water, thereby freeing up the living space in their rooms. Cooking the day's meals and exchanging gossip thus became a community activity.

Most chawl tenements had inter-connecting doors that were often kept open after the men went off to work. The women and children would be in and out of their neighbours' houses. Barriers were seldom rigid between families in adjoining tenements or between the dwelling unit and the corridor outside it since the front doors would be closed only at night. Similarly, common areas like the chowk or wider parts of the entrance were used either by a tailor or dhobi for ironing clothes.

Most chawls were built by contractors, who never consulted architects in designing the building. They replicated earlier constructions with some minor adjustments for the new site. Architects, too, were

Chawl verandahs were usually wide and occupants used the extra width to store water, dry clothes or keep shoe shelves – anything that helped increase usable area in their own tenements.

Common areas, especially the stair hall on the ground floor, were wide. Sometimes these would be given to a tailor or dhobi, who would provide their services to chawl residents along with their regular customers.

reluctant to design chawls. Claude Batley, in his report on housing for Greater Bombay, deprecated this form of housing because the small rooms resulted in overcrowding and insanitary conditions. Chawls were generally built with load-bearing brick masonry walls over stone plinths, internal walls with wooden posts and infill walls in brick, wooden joists and stone slab floors (known in local parlance as *laadi* and *coba*) and flat or tiled sloping roofs. The buildings generally had three floors, although some in the dense scheduled areas were five floors high with shops on the ground floor.

Over time, the chawl lost its usefulness as a typology of urban housing because of its inherent limitations. Only minor variations were possible in the interior layout because of structural restrictions. Private toilets, opted for by those reluctant to use the common WCs of the chawl, further reduced the limited living space. As family incomes improved, the younger generation, which could afford to pay higher rents or repay large loan instalments for ownership housing, opted to move into apartments as much for convenience as improved status and upward mobility. Privacy also became an issue as the joint family gave way to the modern nuclear family which was less enthusiastic about relatively intrusive communal living. However, most retained their social connections with the chawls they left.

As tenements emptied out from the 1970s, families that stayed back often took the vacant rooms. My friend Arun Ranade, for example, merged his room with the one next door to create a two-module, four-room tenement in his Girgaum chawl. He could have added a bathroom in order to make it a proper apartment but chose not to, as, having grown up in the chawl, he was not averse to a common toilet. Adaptive reuse

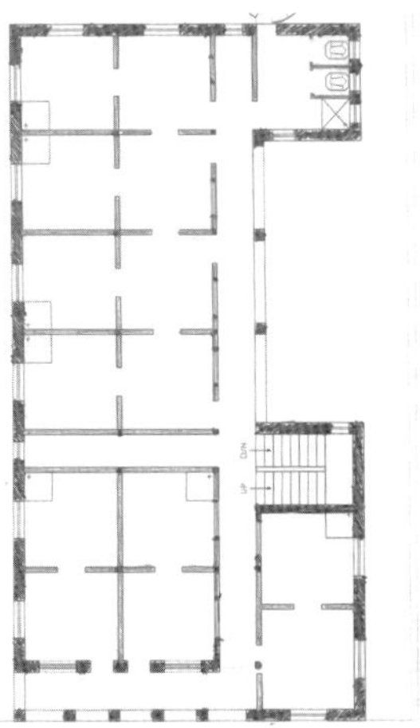

Samarth Sadan is a small chawl in Girgaum. Since there are few tenements on each floor there is better privacy. Tenements are airy and well lighted. An unusual feature is a dead end corridor between two sets of tenements. Whatever may have been the reason, it certainly helps ventilate the staircase.

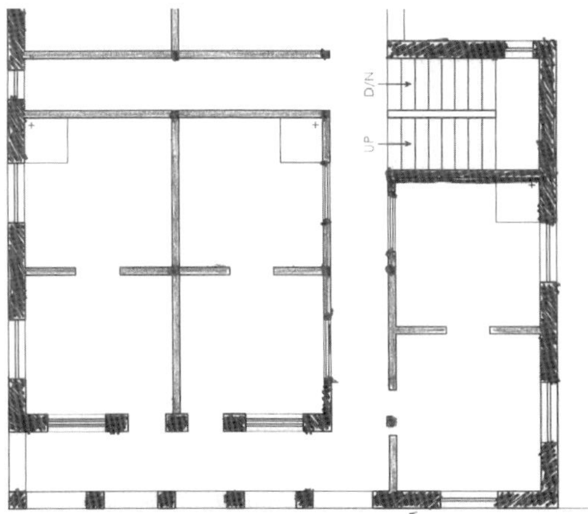

Two tenements in the same chawl are combined to make an apartment. Being modular, the chawl typology permitted flexibility and tenements could be combined easily.

of space in a chawl, however, was more the exception than the rule. In most chawls, rooms that were converted to apartments still did not give the occupants privacy since the windows still opened on to the main corridor.

Writers and film-makers have romanticised the chawl and the social amity between its residents. There is certainly a human side to life in a chawl although this may be scarce compensation for poor living conditions – small spaces, shared toilets and a lack of privacy. People rented chawl rooms because they had no affordable alternative, and, having been thrown together, had to coexist peacefully. But the emotional support system that developed in this space over the years benefited everyone, especially children and elders. In a chawl, security comes from a sense of belonging to a social group that shares space. That is one reason some families choose to return to the chawl – as Vinodini Gajaria and her husband, our long-time friends, did. The couple grew up in Bhatiawadi and continued to live there for many years after they were married. In the 1960s, they moved out to a flat in Walkeshwar but found themselves missing the company and support of their chawl friends. Vinodini could not leave her children alone in the apartment; in the chawl, there were always neighbours to look after them. A year after moving out of their chawl, they moved back in.

The typology of the chawl slowly became obsolete, and no new chawls were built after the 1940s. Landlords found the low rents incommensurate with rising property values while tenants, on their part, were either unable or unwilling to pay higher rents. In many cases, rents were in arrears, and landlords lost interest in either maintaining or redeveloping their properties, especially after the Bombay Rent Act, which froze rents at 1940 levels and gave tenants immunity against being evicted.

Had the government allowed rents to be based on current land values, they would have become disproportionately high for the accommodation and facilities provided. Tenants paying these higher rents would have demanded self-contained flats, and the chawl would have naturally given way to the apartment block much sooner than it actually did. In a way, therefore, the Rent Act, by disallowing the dishousing of tenants and thereby the demolition of buildings, saved the chawl typology from vanishing from the cityscape altogether.

The Apartment

The Apartment

Bombay was the first Indian city to see the emergence of the apartment building, an indicator of both the city's early embrace of modernity and its long-standing space crunch. Multi-storey buildings helped contain the urban sprawl, and the apartment evolved over the years, both as a housing typology and an agent of social change.

The chawl and its predecessor, the gaothan house, were community-based housing where people shared space and facilities and were dependent on one another. The decline of these in the mid-twentieth century and the ascendance of the apartment block reflected a major shift in the way people lived in Bombay. Apartments give people privacy, sometimes a feeling of security, and always an anonymity that helps them shed their caste or community identity and the restrictions that these often entail. Unlike the chawl and the gaothan, which seemed to fit the needs of a particular time, the apartment has continually changed and evolved.

Early Buildings

The apartment block comprises independent dwelling units, with their own bathrooms, grouped together in one building. Before the Improvement Trust developed planned infills and precincts, most dwellings were free-standing two-storeyed structures where the owner usually stayed on the ground floor and leased the first floor to one or two tenants. Toilets were always detached from the house and located on the ground, often at the back of the plot.

It is difficult to trace the origin of the apartment block in Bombay since individual buildings came up at different locations and in different forms. Flats in early apartment blocks had toilets at one end so that they could be cleaned manually, a practice carried over from the chawl. The early apartments resembled the chawls in appearance, but there were differences in the access to the individual flat and the arrangement of rooms. The similarity with the chawl came mainly from the construction materials and methods.

The technology adopted for constructing these early buildings was labour-intensive and time-consuming. It was, however, affordable since the cost of labour was low and prices of materials did not fluctuate. Contractors absorbed any increase in the cost of materials, which, in a working season, rarely exceeded two per cent. Work was carried out in a predetermined sequence and included jobs like wetting surfaces that required 'curing'. This was done by members of the water-carrying tribe known as *bhisti*, who were, incidentally, paid a higher wage than unskilled labour. In early Public Works Department (PWD) practice, the *bhisti*, who traditionally carried water in a goatskin bag, also fetched drinking water from wells and other sources in addition to that put to use on construction sites. This job has now become extinct in the building industry.

The general construction practice codified by the British in PWD handbooks was conservative and placed a high value on safety in design and construction – one reason why buildings from that era weathered better than present-day ones. Early apartment buildings were designed by civil engineers who also called themselves architects. Until the Architects Registration Act came in 1972, practitioners in the city were licensed by the Bombay Municipal Corporation as 'surveyors', a term that covered architects, engineers, surveyors and qualified draftsmen. However, only qualified architects or engineers among the holders of surveyors' licences could sign plans for approval. The nameplates and letterheads of architects before the 1970s invariably read 'Architect and Surveyor' although most architects had only a rudimentary knowledge of surveying.

Apartments After RCC

As technology improved, the apartment building changed. The introduction of RCC technology in the 1930s changed the building structure, while improved plumbing and sanitation technology also had its influence on design. Individual flats in some localities became larger and layouts changed. Toilets were no longer placed at one end of the apartment – they could now be anywhere within the flat, provided

Early apartment buildings were built by civil engineers who used brick walls, timber floors and balconies in their designs.

Before RCC came in, buildings were built with traditional, labour-intensive construction methods. This included 'curing' surfaces, for which a 'bhisti' or water-carrier was employed. This trade is now extinct.

they abutted an external wall and were stacked over one another in the building. RCC floors were more waterproof than the earlier joist-and-stone floors, which made it possible to attach toilets to bedrooms. The use of sweepers to clean toilets reduced although spiral staircases were sometimes still provided for domestic servants and tradesmen to access a flat from the rear of the building.

The apartment block by definition is generic: standardised dwelling units stacked next to and over one another, with each apartment layout varying slightly. The principal differences lie in the design of the entrance, stair and lift hall and verandah or balcony fronts. Despite the limitations of the apartment template, some architects like Claude Batley and G B Mhatre were creative and unique in their apartment designs, especially in the way their buildings were sited, proportioned and detailed. Batley's apartments suited a western style of living, although he remained faithful to traditional Indian elements like verandahs, chhajjas and mouldings. Like Walter George, the Delhi-based British architect who was part of the team that designed New Delhi, he believed that flush surfaces (large unbroken plastered surfaces of walls) were best avoided since every building material moved and cracked in the Indian climate. Cracks, caused mainly by shrinkage, could be contained if large areas were broken by courses that reduced the area of a single surface. Batley also felt that stone was a better material for external walls than brick and plaster since it weathered better. Invariably, he crowned his buildings with pitched or sloping roofs, which, he insisted, were the best protection against Bombay's heavy monsoon.

Batley believed that building typologies should emerge from understanding a client's way of living, and he followed that principle in his own practice. In the house he built for well-known Indian industrialist Kasturbhai Lalbhai on Carmichael Road, he located the kitchen at a level lower than the living and dining

Claude Batley insisted that pitched roofs were the best protection against Bombay's heavy monsoon. He demonstrated this in the design of 'Sealand' at Cuffe Parade.

In the Art Deco phase of Bombay's development, architects often rounded the edges of balconies and even rooms.

room to accommodate Lalbhai's traditional lifestyle in which the kitchen was not supposed to be next to the dining area. The decision to accommodate this belief by locating the kitchen at a lower level was shaped by the fact that construction techniques had already advanced considerably.

Mhatre was known for his Art Deco buildings at the Oval and Marine Drive but those are not necessarily the best examples of his work. His later buildings, Marble Arch on Pedder Road and Sanghi House on Nepean Sea Road, were outstanding when they were built in the 1940s and remain so today. Both buildings are especially interesting in their site placement and entry way. Marble Arch is curved so that both sides are seen as you approach it from Pedder Road. The building is not set back from the road uniformly. The logic of its orientation becomes clearer when you see that Marble Arch was part of a group of buildings set around an open space. The adjoining buildings, KumKum, Ark Royal and Windcliff, also designed by Mhatre, were part of the ensemble. Marble Arch was modern in the layout of its rooms and their proportions and details, though the rounded end of the living room shows a trace of Art Deco.

Sanghi House, earlier known simply as 94 Nepean Sea Road, was designed to have its front edge parallel to the road – however, this feature had to be discarded when an abandoned well was discovered on the plot. The owner, a Parsi lady, insisted that the building could not be constructed over a well even though the well was not in use. So Mhatre cut out the corner and curved the front end. Sanghi House is modern in concept, and yet some of its details are Art Deco.

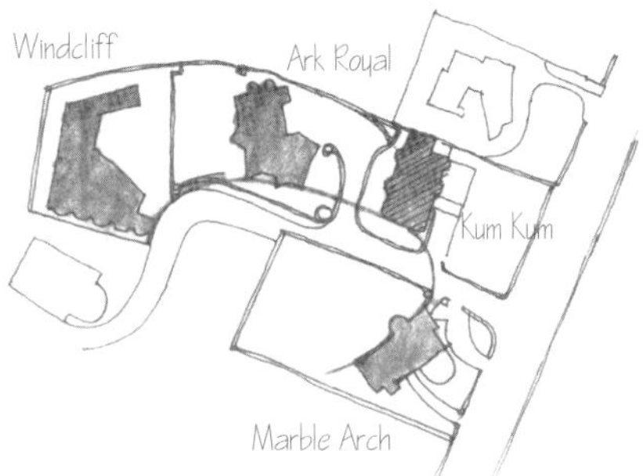

G B Mhatre sited his buildings skilfully. This site on Pedder Road shows buildings in an arc to form an ensemble of which Marble Arch is a prominent component. Kum Kum, Ark Royal and Windcliff, all designed by Mhatre, are the others. Marble Arch curves away from the road, which is intriguing. It makes sense when seen as part of a larger group of buildings that encircle a central space.

Sanghi House, though on a middle site, has a cutaway corner to enable a corner entry. Two faces of the building can be seen from the road.

However interesting these buildings might be, Mhatre did not make any fundamental change in the typology of the apartment. Nor did any other architect of that time attempt to find an alternative to the conventional apartment block. Claude Batley deviated slightly from the standard apartment layout when he made duplex units – in the manner of London terrace houses – in buildings like Gold Croft and White House on Gamadia Road. In White House, all the flats were on two levels connected by an internal staircase. Batley did this because the footprint of the building was small, and two large flats on one level were not possible. But duplex apartments remained rare and buildings which had both conventional flats as well as duplexes were even rarer until Darshan Apartments was built in the early 1950s.

Darshan Apartments

Darshan Apartments on Mount Pleasant Road designed by Gautam and Gira Sarabhai was one of the early modern buildings in the city. As students, we were taken to see its construction and were shown the plans. This was the first building in Bombay to be raised on stilts – an idea initiated by Le Corbusier. 'The free plan', as it was known, advocated the separation of the building's walls and its supporting structure, and left the ground space for car parking – though we learnt much later that the area under Le Corbusier's buildings was seldom used for parking cars. The 'pilotis', as he called those spaces, was used to visually connect the building to the spaces around it. In Darshan Apartments, the ground level was used as a play area and extended to a deck over a car park. The upper floors contained an ingenious mix of one- and two-level flats. The interlock of apartments was skilfully done and was not seen on the facade. The kitchens and servants' rooms on the south were arranged for efficient and economical utility lines and

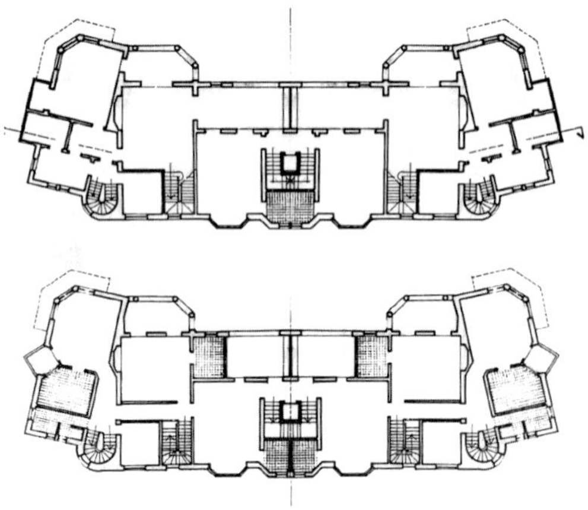

Gold Croft, designed by Claude Batley, was among the early buildings that had duplex apartments.

were on the less private side of the site. The main rooms on the north opened on to a landscaped garden. The arrangement and proportion of spaces were functional and rational, and so were the choice and use of materials, which were inexpensive.

Darshan Apartments reflected some of the ideas of the modern movement. It was the first building to have concrete surfaces that were exposed and not covered with plaster (a feature seen later in Stanvac House and the Tata Institute of Social Sciences in Bombay as well as buildings designed by Le Corbusier at Chandigarh). Its floors were paved with broken stone or tile laid in an uneven pattern, a concept popularly known as crazy-paving. Lift wells were faced with rough stone slabs laid one over the other. There was a noticeable absence of chhajjas or other weather-protecting devices on some of the facades – a deviation from conventional design practice in India and a point of debate in our architecture school. The argument in favour of this deviation was that the building was oriented with its longer sides facing north and south, and the main rooms facing north would not suffer from the rigours of the climate. Hence, on the north side, rooms were fully glazed with large folding and sliding windows. The south side, which bears the brunt of the monsoons and heat in summer, had the service and utility areas of the apartment. On this side, there were verandahs and louvres.

Darshan Apartments is minimalistic in its details. For students like us, who were outgrowing the Beaux Arts system of education in our school of architecture, it was a good example of the ideas of the modern movement. It showed that a good building comes not from facade-making but from clarity in identifying the requirements and the design solution that follows. Darshan Apartments set a new trend in apartment design, though its imitations did not always achieve the same level of finesse or quality.

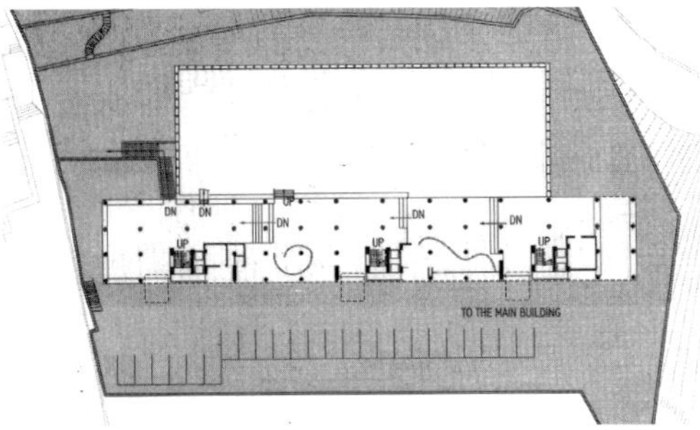

Darshan Apartments on Mount Pleasant Road was the earliest instance of a building raised on stilts. Le Corbusier defined the modern house as one where the main living floor rested on free standing columns with space being used for parking. But in this building it is used as a children's play area. You can see through the building at the ground level.

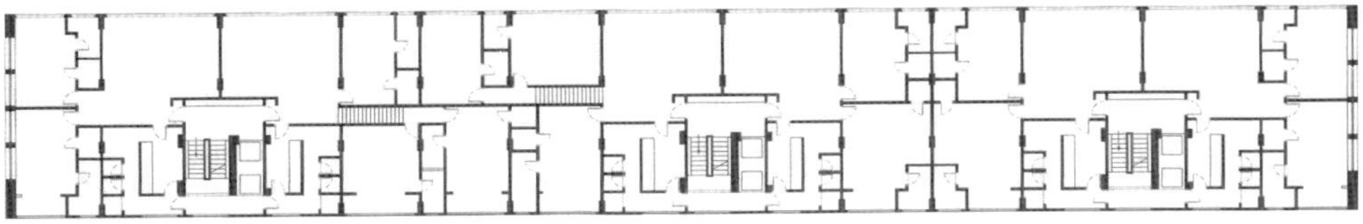

Most flats on the upper floors are on one level, but a few are planned in two levels. The interlock of flats is not visible on the outside.

Kanchanjunga

Till Kanchanjunga was built in the 1970s, the only deviation from the generic plan of apartment buildings and the arrangement of rooms within the flat was the two-level duplex apartment.

Kanchanjunga on Pedder Road designed by Charles Correa radically altered the apartment typology both in plan and section. The elevation, different from all others, was a consequence of that. The design is not the result of the usual 'problem-solving' approach taken in most projects. The idea underlying the design of the building is expressed in a diagrammatic section showing dwelling units interlocked one above the other. It is a continuation of ideas developed from observation of previous practices in dealing with the climate. The ideas used in the design of the building were, possibly, incubated in the architect's mind long before he was commissioned for the project.

The building is positioned such that two of its sides are visible when one approaches it from either end of Pedder Road. The building, square on plan and four times as high as its footprint, was the first tower block containing multi-level three- and four-bedroom apartments to which a fifth or even sixth bedroom could be added. A central stair and lift core provides access to two apartments on a floor. Though its footprint is small, a skilful use of levels accommodates the large area of the flat. A conventional flat for the same area would need a larger footprint and the arrangement of rooms within the envelope invariably requires corridors. Flats in Kanchanjunga are compact, circulation spaces being restricted to the internal staircase connecting the different levels.

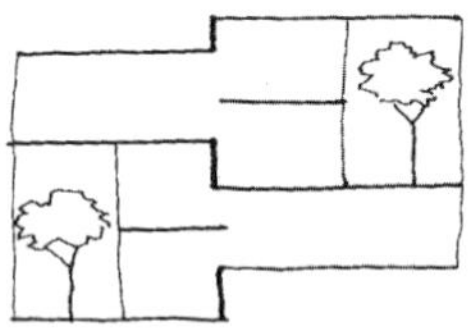

A diagram showing the interlock of apartments. This was the genesis of the design of Kanchanjunga.

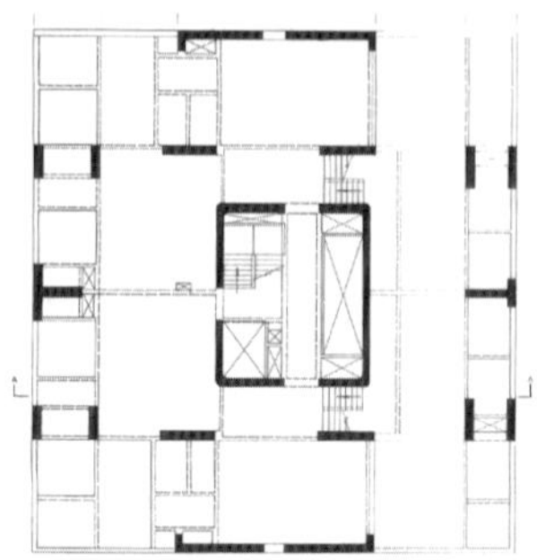

The structure of the building allows the corners to be cantilevered.

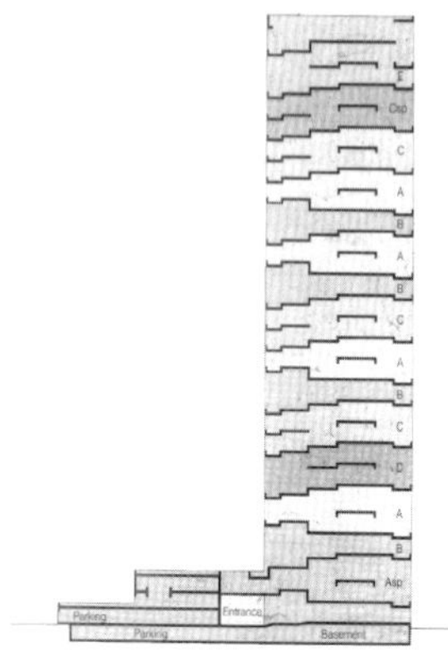

The cross-section of the building shows the advantage of placing rooms at different levels. Doing so reduces the footprint of the flats.

The clarity in the structural design, also visible, helps articulate the spaces within the envelope. The structural plan is a cross, at the centre of which is a staircase and lift core that was built first using a 'slip form' method of construction. On the north and south ends of the building are shear walls while the east and west ends have columns. The shear walls and columns along with the core leave the corners free. These are cantilevered and house either rooms with step-out balconies or covered terraces. The terraces are like large outdoor living spaces on to which rooms on the upper level of the flat overlook. The ingenious use of levels make the facade different from the usual one of the generic apartment building which has projecting balconies repeated floor over floor like half-open drawers in a chest. The tower with residential apartments rises above a base containing shops and other amenities. Kanchanjunga, because of its design, is a landmark in the city.

Batley, Mhatre, Gira and Gautam Sarabhai, Charles Correa and a few others designed for individuals who developed their properties for leasing to a select clientele. Both owners and architects, being aware that buildings are an important part of the city's fabric, ensured quality in design and construction. By the late 1960s, landowners stopped developing properties for leasing and sold out to developers for whom neither the city nor its fabric mattered.

Developer-Driven Buildings

Housing typologies alter over time for natural reasons such as changing family structures, living patterns and incomes as well as for artificial reasons like changes imposed by planning rules. Of all the housing

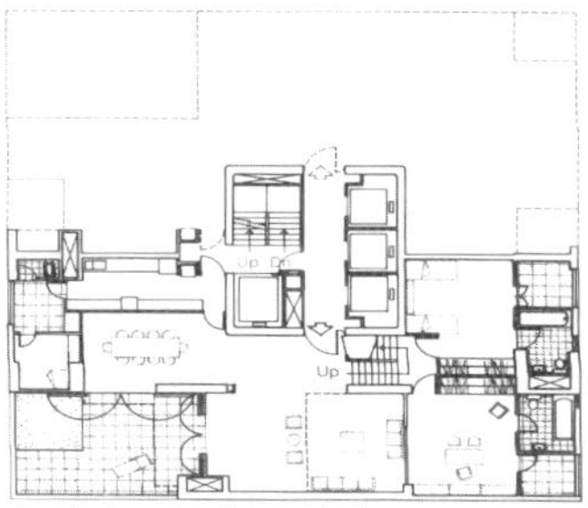
Four-bedroom Unit - Entrance level

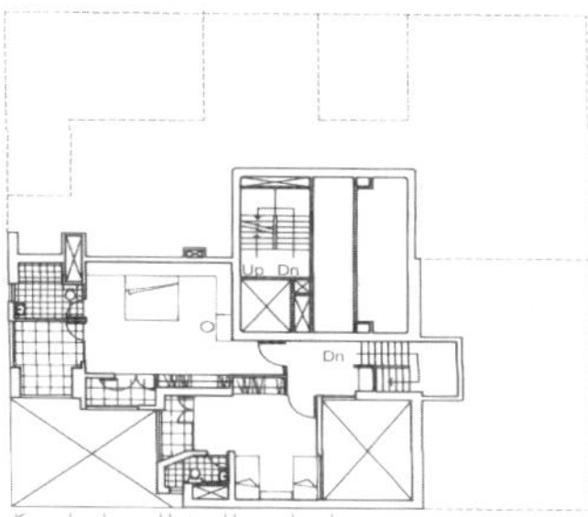
Four-bedroom Unit - Upper level

Multi-level flats are accessed directly from a staircase. They are open on three sides and are designed to provide adequate cross-ventilation.

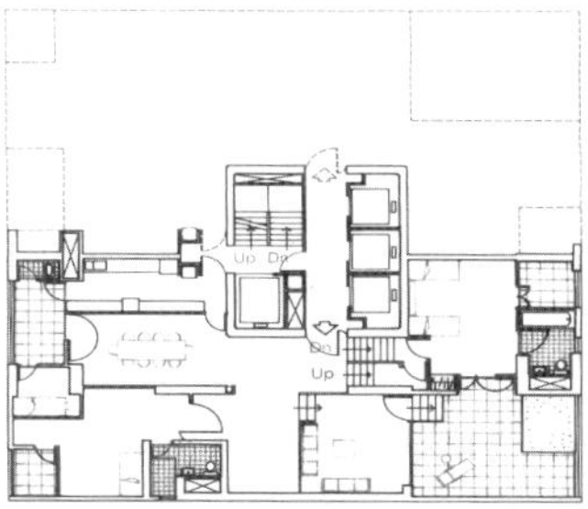
Three-bedroom Unit - Entrance level

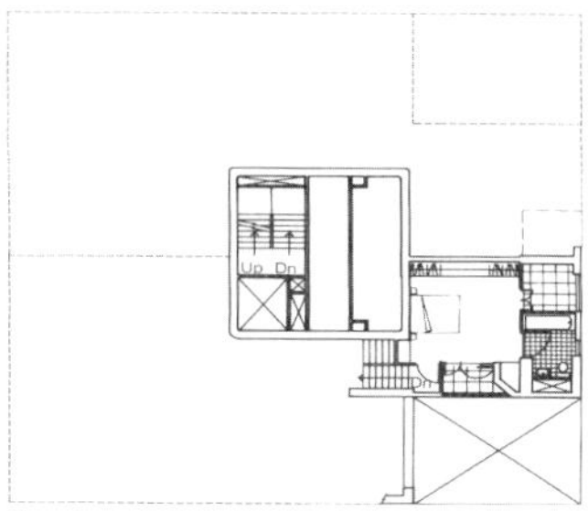
Three-bedroom Unit - Upper level

The verandah has been proportioned to serve as an outdoor living space.

typologies in Bombay, the apartment has transformed the most – on account of both these reasons. Initially, the changes came about because customers and architects wanted flats that suited newer times and technologies but later they were increasingly prompted by new development rules, especially the introduction in 1967 of the concept of FSI or the ratio of built-up area to plot area.

By the 1960s, the major promoters of apartment buildings in Bombay were profit-driven developers, for whom the rule of FSI was a measure of commercial opportunity. It opened up various possibilities of extracting the maximum saleable area even if it meant manipulating the interpretation and calculation of FSI. This ratio became an important guiding factor in the design of an apartment building. The total built-up area possible on a site indicated the monetary worth of the property because land was now worth only what could be built on it. A building on a site had, therefore, to fetch maximum returns while design and construction standards had to take a back seat.

The design of apartments commissioned by the developer stayed largely the same, though with some key differences. One difference was a general reduction in dimensions and areas of rooms and floor heights. Builders also economised on staircases, insisting that architects provide access to as many flats as possible from a single staircase, and minimised other common areas like corridors and lobbies. This was done to increase saleable area.

Until the 1950s, apartments were built by individual landlords in order to be rented out to tenants. Land and building costs were not big factors in determining rents. In developer-built housing, the relationship

When the FSI in the island city was increased to 1.33, additional floors were added to existing buildings. In some, the additions blended with the original buildings, while in most they were incongruous.

between land and construction costs had a bigger role to play in determining the sale price of flats. After the Emergency in the 1970s, a steep rise in land prices distorted the relation between land and construction costs. Builders convinced themselves that land was scarce and that construction was only profitable if the saleable area was maximised and sold at high prices. High-rise buildings that had to satisfy the requirements of Building Codes for lifts, escape stairs and routes, specialised plumbing, fire safety and electrical systems came at a high cost. Construction and delays in approvals further added to the price of the flat.

From the late 1980s, buyers who were spending huge amounts for apartments became more demanding. To satisfy them, builders started spending money on embellishing facades and on finishing common areas like foyers, stairs and lift fronts with expensive materials. This was a return to the 1930s and '40s, when buildings were commissioned to civil engineers who retained architects to design the facades, staircases and entrance halls. Mhatre started his career providing architectural inputs for buildings built by engineers. But while the facades that Mhatre designed were modern and appropriate for his time, by the 1990s architects were simply grafting styles of the past, such as Neo-Classical, on to the facades rather than trying to find their own language to express their present. It was a 'copy and paste' approach to design. The mismatch between exteriors designed in past styles and interiors planned for modern use did not bother either architects or developers. As for the customers, they seemed to love it.

The relationship between the architect and the developer in contemporary housing projects is different from a conventional architect-client one. The developer, who has little attachment to a building and

Buyers of flats demanded that buildings be designed with 'attractive elevations'. Builders got facades designed by architects who specialised in churning them out without paying any attention to what lay behind them. Neither builders nor architects were bothered whether the elevation and the plan matched as long as buyers liked it.

promotes it solely as a business proposition, hires an architect to make floor plans, which he vets to ascertain their profitability. He then passes the project on to another architect who specialises in accommodating the maze of rules and procedures of the approving authorities. The first architect is commissioned to detail the elevations and interiors of the common areas. In most projects, a well-known architect is appointed to design the elevation of the building to attract a clientele that is willing to pay a premium for the architect. The role of the architect in most developer-driven projects has returned to one of a beautifier of buildings – a throwback to the Beaux Arts approach that the modernists threw out half a century ago.

The High-Rise Debate

The buildings on Marine Drive and the Oval were seen as special in their time partly because they had six floors – higher than most buildings then, although similar heights existed in Mohammed Ali Road before the Back Bay scheme was completed. Buildings on Marine Drive were governed by the 63.5-degree rule – this was the angle that determined heights and distances between buildings. Generally, this meant that the distance between buildings was half their height. The urban infrastructure – road widths, fire services and communications – could cope with the density of people and cars housed in buildings of this height.

In the 1960s, the FSI for the island city was increased from 1 to 1.33, enabling developers to add more floors to their buildings. The high-rise building went from six storeys to seven storeys or 23 metres (76 feet) high. When the notion of scarcity of land for housing took root and land prices began to rise, especially after the Urban Land Ceiling Act was introduced in 1976, it was thought that the only way to meet the housing

needs of the city was to increase the buildable area. This meant higher FSI and taller buildings, which developers have since maintained is the only way to make a project viable. High-rises were once again redefined in the late 1970s as buildings over 70 metres (230 feet) or about 23 storeys.

As buildings grow taller, the key issue becomes not light but fire safety. Any building higher than 24 metres (78 feet) needs its own fire-fighting systems. The early Fire Safety Codes were based mostly on empirical rules and on equipment that was available to the city's fire services department. With improved equipment and experience gathered over the years, the code adopted by the municipality was amended but it was invariably based on ease of implementation and efficient use of equipment. The code had little to say about physical infrastructure required for high-rises like location of fire stations, road widths and distances between buildings.

Today, buildings are considered high-rise if they are more than 30 storeys or 96 metres high. They are radically different from older buildings not only in design but also in structure, construction and services.

The world over, tall buildings have been found to be less efficient because in such buildings the area of the core and the thickness of the structural components and utilities, like the lifts and staircases, affect the floor area efficiency ie the ratio between the net and gross areas. In buildings with small 'floor plates' (areas on each floor), the space occupied by the structural and utility elements is disproportionately high compared to the rentable or saleable areas. It is only when the floor plates are large that the high-rise tower block becomes viable. In addition, the scale, complexity and magnitude of such a building involve

The high-rise apartment block has come to stay. Architects and builders are vying with each other to go higher. There is ample built area for those who can afford it but not for the majority of Bombay's citizens who are starved for decent and affordable housing.

the services of several specialists. An architect is not the sole driver of the project here – technology has the edge over architectural design because safety measures and the services required to meet these outweigh any design considerations.

The space requirements of a high-rise apartment building in India are different from those of the western world. The density of occupants is higher and so is the load on services. The average size of a family is four, to which is added domestic servants, drivers and a few part-time service providers, all of whom use the lifts, staircases, power and water. In addition, municipal rules insist on cars being parked within the premises, and the calculation is usually for up to three cars per apartment. Thus, for every square metre of living space, an equal or larger area is required to support it. Safety standards require automated fire-fighting systems, escape staircases and refuge floors that are often misused as community spaces. Automated systems for fire-fighting, lifts and security require sophisticated, expensive instrumentation. An important difference between a six-storey block and a high-rise is the exterior skin. Wind forces above a certain height compel mechanical climate-conditioning since windows cannot be kept open. The exterior has to be designed to withstand wind forces, given an arrangement for cleaning and replacing glass and maintenance of exterior panels. The shape and design of the facade is important because its energy efficiency, life cycle and sustainability determine its cost.

Has the high-rise apartment building typology provided a suitable answer to the housing needs of the city? Many people, including politicians, planners, developers and architects, have argued that higher FSI and tall buildings are the only way to reduce shortage of housing, given the scarcity of land, and cite dense

The tower block has given way to the megastructure housing over a thousand residents. It is truly the 'urban beehive'.

Asian cities like Shanghai or Singapore as examples. The principle of the skyscraper is reducing ground cover and using air space instead.

But the idea that high-rises are a housing solution is just convenient fiction repeated by investors and speculators in the real estate market. While high-rise buildings have provided more built-up area to the city, they are unaffordable to most of the population, even the middle class. Not only is the high-rise building inherently expensive to construct and maintain but developers are generally interested in clusters of blocks on larger sites that can charge even more because of extra amenities like a health club, swimming pool, landscaped garden and so on. These high-end 'gated communities' have elaborate security systems and sophisticated surveillance. A vendor or courier cannot ring the doorbell of an apartment without going through an elaborate gate pass system, nor can a resident stand in the verandah, look at the street and call out to a hawker. This version of the apartment typology disconnects people from their association with the street and life on and around it. Heights isolate occupants from their surroundings. Isolation could also lead to alienation from society and is unsuitable for an average family with children and elders.

In recent years, the apartment block has gone even bigger – it is now a megastructure. This typology could be more appropriately called an 'urban beehive' where people live in isolation without even knowing their neighbours. A megastructure, on an average, houses over 1,500 residents, is over 45 floors high and has a maintenance staff of over 100. The cost of living in a megastructure is very high, which, added to the initial price, puts the apartment out of reach of all but the very wealthy. The justification trotted out for the megastructure is the old argument that scarcity of land and hence high prices force buildings to be built with smaller footprints and greater heights. However, the fact is that the distortion in real estate values is not so much an issue of deficit as of skewed and inequitable distribution of the city's main resource – land.

You Can Judge A City By How Its Poor Live

You Can Judge A City By How Its Poor Live

The difference between the poor man in Bombay and his counterpart in, say, Patna or Bhubaneswar is that while the Bombay man can probably earn enough to feed himself, he cannot afford a roof over his head. He has, perforce, to live in a slum – or *zopadpatti* in local parlance – with little real hope of graduating to better housing.

In Bombay, shanties huddled closely together in unhygienic surroundings are relatively recent. But slummy living conditions, as in overcrowded and ill-ventilated tenements, are as old as the city. Although the state and city governments have made several half-hearted efforts to house the poor over the decades, they have largely failed. Meanwhile, the number of people forced to live in the slums is increasing – thanks to the consistent rise in land values and rents, even skilled and educated migrants who earn well and own a personal vehicle or air-conditioner have joined the ranks of the poor as far as housing is concerned. A greater percentage of people (now around 50%) live in huts and various forms of makeshift shelter scattered all over the city than in the past 40 years. Modern high-rises may dot the cityscape, but there has

Shanties on the fringe of the city were the only form of housing the poor could afford. The government, after failing to evict slum dwellers, started providing minimum infrastructure in the 1970s by way of 'kaccha' roads, electricity and water.

been no real advance in the technology or supply of affordable housing. It is Bombay's biggest failure; the quality of a city is measured, after all, not by its iconic buildings or skyscrapers but by how its poor live.

This failure was inevitable because housing the poor has never been a priority. Most architects do not concern themselves with the design of low-income or public housing except when government housing authorities announce design competitions. That was also the case when I was a student. Although the college curriculum in the 1950s did not include designing housing for the working class, our school canteen debates often revolved around this issue – we talked about everything from the socialist ideals of inclusiveness to modern architecture's emphasis on utility and the rational and honest use of space and materials. We were especially inspired by the social housing efforts in Europe of that time – including workers' housing in pre-war Berlin, Le Corbusier's work at Pessac, a housing estate for industrial workers in Vienna called Karl Marx Hof which, even today, is an outstanding example of public housing, and most importantly, Hasan Fathy's sensitive adaptation of traditional forms of Egyptian architecture for housing the poor. These projects convinced us students that affordable housing could be helped by good architecture, and we set out to find out more about local low-cost housing in the city.

'Pucca kaccha' housing is an ingenious type of incremental housing. A 'kaccha' structure is first built using posts of cheap wood and second-hand iron sheets for roofing and enclosure. This is later replaced with brick walls, and over time one or even two floors are added that are used to either increase the owner's living area or leased out. Barring the structure which is 'pucca', everything else is 'kaccha'.

Early History

When the East India Company first lured villagers to settle in Bombay by promising jobs and a better life, it made sure that the demand for jobs was more than the supply to ensure a constant supply of cheap labour. Most people wanting jobs lived near their places of work, as they could not afford to commute. Chawls built by the companies were the only type of housing that was affordable to working-class migrants of that time, with single-room tenements of 100 sq ft (9.30 sq metres) often housing ten people. Migrants put up with these abominable living conditions for the sake of their incomes and the other advantages of city life – anonymity, escape from the rigid caste barriers in the villages, and the opportunity to go up in life.

Chawls, however uncomfortable, were not unlivable, as they provided a pucca roof, a shared toilet and civic utilities. The situation changed after the Rent Control Act was enacted in 1947 and landlords stopped building small tenements, forcing people to live in slums and squat on footpaths. Housing for those at the lower end of the food chain does not interest practising architects and developers, who see it as a social obligation, the onus of which rests on the government. The government and its agencies have, by default, become the chief providers of housing for the majority of poor people.

The first public housing projects were undertaken almost a century ago (between 1923 and 1927) by the Bombay Improvement Trust and later the Bombay Development Department. Operating as they did

Till the 1960s, few, if any, squatted on the footpath. Those who did were compelled to do so because there was no affordable housing available near their place of work. By the '70s, many families lived on footpaths in makeshift houses made of recycled materials. When the fear of eviction receded, some footpath dwellers even added a loft to increase their living space.

decades ago, they did not have to face some of the challenges that are inherent in housing for the poor in the present day, the most significant of which is perhaps the lack of land.

Most land in Bombay is privately owned because the British government encouraged individual land ownership for revenue, and the acquisition of such land or vacant land by the government is a difficult and slow process. Private developers, who build only with the aim of making humongous profits, corner most of the land in the market, with the result that present land use is skewed in favour of upmarket housing which more often than not caters more to an investing clientele than actual users. Housing boards that build tenements for the poor are concerned with social demand, not market forces. This is essentially the difference between public and private housing, and lack of adequate land is a setback in fulfilling a social obligation.

Another difficulty lies in figuring out the size of a social group in a housing unit. As Lewis Mumford, the noted writer on cities and urbanism, wrote in his book 'What Is A City?', "It is important to express size always as a function of the social relationship to be served." Planners invariably depend on numbers, economic viability and administrative yardsticks since social needs and relationships cannot be quantified and incorporated in building programmes. In 1953, as students, we met Maxwell Fry who, along with Jane Drew, was involved in designing public housing in Chandigarh. He told us that public housing was about designing the most efficient dwelling unit and repeating it in numbers that made for a close community. When numbers are large, the community becomes unmanageable and, beyond a point, almost inhuman. Architects, he added, were best suited to judge the size of a community because they are involved with people all the time.

A third difficulty is the lack of a rational basis for deciding living space rate per person. The chawl typology was perhaps the first attempt at calculating this because a room was based on a modular unit of 100 square feet, two of which made a tenement. The municipal bye-laws in 1938 mandated an increase in the area of a single-room tenement from 100 square feet to 180 square feet and a double-room tenement to 240 square feet. This excluded the shared toilet and verandah. There have been other revisions from time to time but these have been arbitrary. No one studied how much space a family actually needed to live in without overcrowding. This would have helped arrive at a living space rate per person and a more rational basis for deciding the size of a tenement. But planners were more concerned with the size of the dwelling unit and its cost than with living space rate. For instance, a tenement in a chawl had a clear living area of 240 square feet since residents had a shared toilet. In buildings built by the housing authorities, a tenement had the same area but it included a toilet, thereby reducing the living space. Yet, this was overlooked while planning housing schemes.

First Major Public Housing Project

The typology of the chawl formed the basis of the city's first major public housing project, the Bombay Development Department's 1920s project to build 50,000 tenements in the island city. There were some positive features in the project. The BDD's approach involved standardisation and the use of technology suitable for repetition. This was different from the Improvement Trust whose schemes had only standard sizes but did not adapt technology and management systems suitable for repetitive housing.

The BDD chawls at Worli, the first to come up, used the modular concept of the traditional chawl in respect of arrangement of rooms and common facilities and access to individual tenements but differed slightly in room sizes. A fixed number of tenements formed a building unit, and these were laid out in rows. The space between units was based on the principle of the 63.5 degree light angle. That was sufficient for community functions and festivals especially since buildings were not separated by compound walls. Buildings were constructed with RCC frames, walls were in concrete block masonry, and precast concrete elements like *jaali*s and stair treads were used. The window, an important component in a tenement, followed the design innovated by the Improvement Trust. The plan provided ten tenements on either side of a three-metre-wide central corridor. The plan arrangement lent itself to different uses. Some buildings were used as a medical centre, a primary school, and a maternity ward and hospice.

But the project also faced many of the problems that have plagued public housing across the world – chiefly, greater concern with cost and economies of scale in the production of the buildings than in the

This street in Dharavi has semi-permanent houses. Its occupants are not poor but they live in a slum area because there is no affordable alternative.

design of the tenements and their surroundings. The Worli project left no land for schools and community facilities, forcing residents to use facilities in the neighbouring areas. The BDD chawls were criticised by many when they were built, including Claude Batley, who said it was lucky that only a third of the original planned number got built "since they were judged uninhabitable by those for whom they were intended but curiously enough were never consulted either before or during construction". The BDD projects were efficiently executed, using a set procedure of tendering, supervision of work on site and financial control, but were otherwise inadequate in meeting the needs of the people they housed.

The lack of sanitary affordable housing was recognised in the Greater Bombay Plan first drawn up in 1948. Also known as the Modak-Mayer Plan, it said, "The most pressing part of the problem is relief to low- and medium-income workers from frightfully overcrowded, ill-lighted and unsanitary homes." The report even suggested prohibiting "for a certain period the construction of luxury homes and all other construction not urgently needed in order to permit maximum volume of low-rent housing".

The Housing Panel Report

In June 1945, Claude Batley, representing the Indian Institute of Architects, became a member of a housing panel appointed by the Government of Bombay tasked to recommend standards for public housing in the Greater Bombay Scheme. His ideas featured prominently in the panel's report which made comprehensive suggestions on the design of individual units as well as neighbourhoods and the city. The report recommended that tenements be two-roomed with a minimum floor space of 250 square feet (23 sq metres) for a family of four, excluding the verandah and WC. In addition, it suggested a common washing place for every four tenements and a partially covered terrace for sleeping in every building. This idea was an important one because a roof over the terrace floor provides shade that cools the floors below, protects the building from the heavy monsoon rains and can be an excellent covered place to sleep through the year. A decade later, Le Corbusier used a similar idea in the High Court at Chandigarh, where a huge parasol roof provided shade to the floors below.

Another suggestion of the report was the provision of a variety of housing: bigger tenements for bigger families, ranging from 360 square feet to 420 square feet (33.50 to 39 sq metres), hostels for single men, women, boys and girls, and night shelters for the homeless. Colonies or units could range from 100 to 1000 tenements with no more than eight tenements of 350 square feet (33.50 square metres) on each floor of a building served by a single staircase and no more than eight tenements of the larger size on each floor in a block or building. The report also specified that the ratio of built-up space to open space in a plot should be 1:2 in the city within a radius of four miles (6.50 km) of Crawford Market and 1:3 beyond that radius and in the suburbs as well. Each unit of 1000 tenements would have to be provided with social amenities located within easy access, including a primary school, a welfare centre, a dispensary and maternity and child welfare centre, a reading room, a consumer cooperative society and playgrounds. It was recommended that a group of five such units, containing 25,000 to 30,000 persons, should also have a market and enough land for a secondary school, post-office and other public buildings.

With the Worli BDD chawl project in mind, the panel, especially Batley, recommended that both residential and public buildings should be designed with an eye for beauty, individuality and appropriateness, and that competitions could be held for design solutions. The panel also emphasised that "care will have to be taken to avoid segregation of the poor and working-class people in isolated zones of their own and that adequate transport facilities should be provided. As far as possible, residential housing for the poor should be within easy reach of their places of work and not more than a mile (1.60 km) from the nearest railway station."

This recommendation was the most important one since it envisaged mixed communities that reduced the stratification of society. Localities in the inner areas of the city contained mixed-income groups but this happened because of incremental growth and not by plan. The Housing Panel suggested that new developments should consciously plan for mixed communities. Unfortunately, none of these ideals are alive in city housing today – the gated high-rises of the present day show that the stratification of society the Housing Panel was worried about has now become a reality.

In 1948, acting on the panel's recommendation, the government set up the Bombay Housing Board. This later merged with the Maharashtra Housing and Area Development Authority (MHADA). The Board

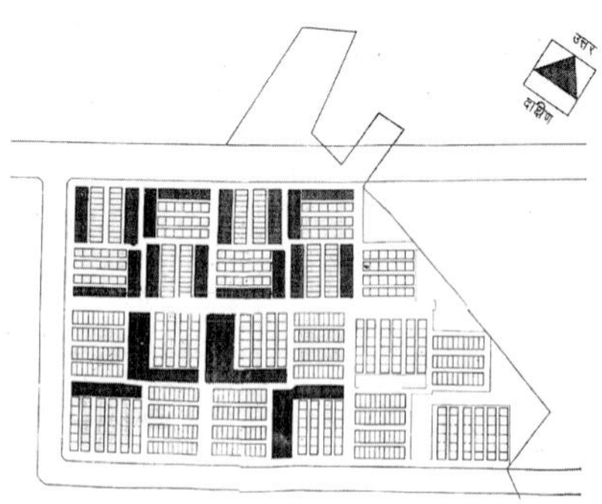

The Maharashtra Housing and Area Development Authority took on the social responsibility of providing affordable houses for the lower income groups. The schemes included 'Sites and Services', in which developed sites were given to individuals to build on.

Houses developed in 'Sites and Services' schemes.

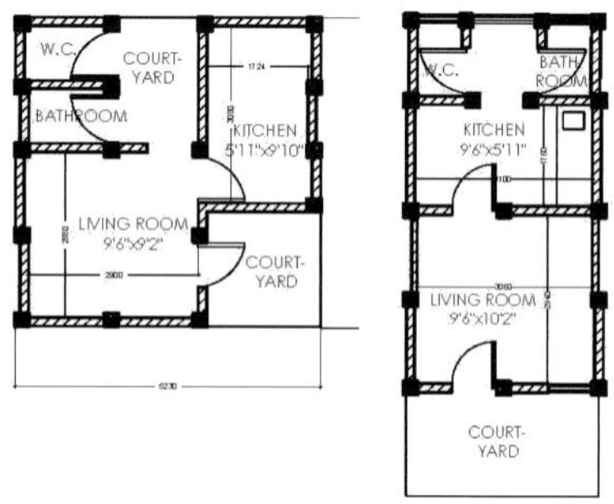

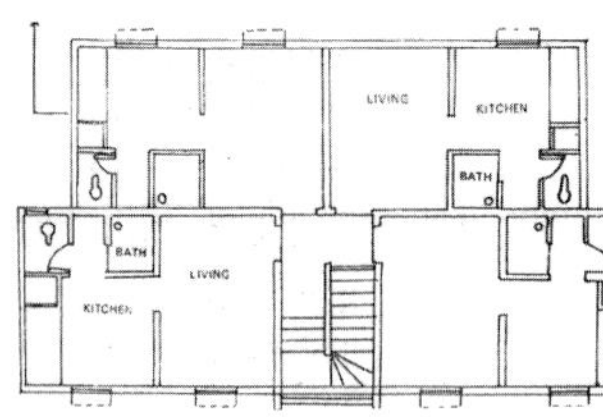

MHADA also built apartments that were affordable since they were not built for profit.

adopted most of the panel's recommendations and also drew from the experience of the Improvement Trust and the Bombay Development Department. The Housing Board built a number of colonies for different income groups wherever it could acquire land. There was an element of cross-subsidy whereby the price of a flat for the higher income groups subsidised the dwelling unit of the lower income group. The Board offered a number of design options, ranging from 'sites and services' (a supply of minimally developed sites for individuals to build on) to apartments accessed from a corridor to those grouped around a staircase. All of them were walk-up apartments and did not have lifts. There were also layouts with individual plots on which small houses could be built to designs that allowed for incremental growth.

In projects of this nature the entire estate is more important than the individual unit, but the Housing Board limited its design to a prototype unit that could be repeated without bothering to explore the option of constructing high-density housing with low-rise, individually owned sites and houses. Had it developed an estate using this model, it might have shown how people could build their own houses or add to what the Housing Board gave them as a start.

In addition to the mediocre model, poor delivery systems and procedural delays resulted in a huge backlog in housing meant for the middle- and low-income groups. Moreover, inadequate supervision of construction work led to the quality of the completed buildings being poor. The housing projects taken up by the Housing Board and other public agencies fell short in other ways as well. Planners attempted to find a common solution for all housing needs, irrespective of site conditions. This was a literal interpretation of standardisation, resulting in a mindless repetition of designs. Planners decided on the

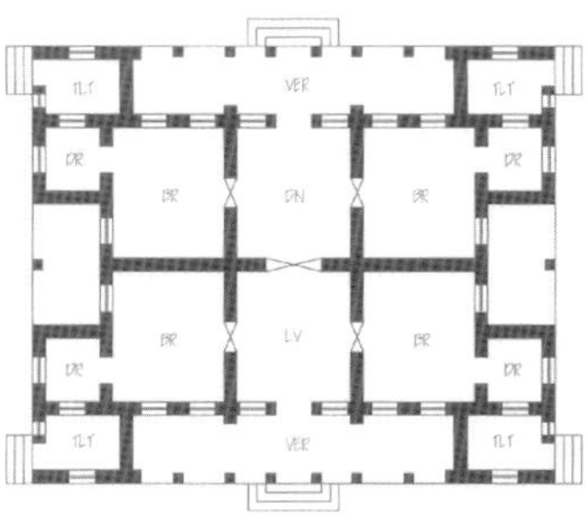

Housing Board planners used standard plans regardless of site conditions or user requirements. Though the idea of standardisation was inherited from the PWD in British times, type designs were sometimes modified within limits by individual engineers to suit local conditions. This rest house at Ghataprabha in Karnataka, for instance, was an imaginative deviation from the standard design. This kind of ingenuity was rare in latter-day engineers.

location of housing areas, allocation of land and area of dwelling units based on standard plans with little regard for ground realities.

This approach continued when the City and Industrial Development Corporation of Maharashtra (CIDCO), a public sector undertaking, was entrusted with planning New Bombay in the 1970s. Planners there deliberated long and hard on the kind and size of housing for the poor, and finally decided to make the total built-up area of each unit 12.5 square metres (134 square feet), which included the shared area of a bath and a toilet. That was 12 square metres (130 square feet) less than the minimum recommended by the Modak Committee. The living space rate was lowered from 5 square metres to 2.20 square metres per head (54 to 24 square feet). The argument, based perhaps on precedents in Hongkong and other places, was that an apartment of 12.5 square metres was all that an average family could afford to rent after providing for food, clothing and living expenses. This decision, based on an arithmetical derivation, did not take into account the space physically required for a family to live in. The decision to base the area of a dwelling unit on economic calculations rather than practical, humane ones resulted in occupants later making unauthorised additions to their homes. A post-occupation audit of housing schemes, if done, would have revealed the mismatch between the needs of the user and the accommodation provided as well as the extent of modifications made by occupants. However, in the projects executed later, the area of a dwelling unit increased to 18 square metres which was still lower than what the area of a dwelling unit in a chawl was.

Policies on public housing that are based more on planning and economic demands than social and human needs tend to fail because they derive the footprints of buildings from overall FSI calculations and

C O M P A R A T I V E S T A T E M E N T

		Alt.I (G + I)	Alt. IA (G + I)	Alt. II (G + 2)	Alt. IIA (G + 2)	Alt.III (G + 4)	Alt. IIIA (G + 4)	Alt. IV (G + 5)	Alt. IVA (G + 5)	Alt. V (G + 7)	Alt. VA (G + 7)	Alt. VI (G + 11)	Alt. VI(G+11
1.	Area of Plot (sft)	43,200	43,200	43,200	43,200	43,200	43,200	43,200	43,200	43,200	43,200	43,200	43,200
2.	Number of tenements in the plot	192	192	252	252	320	320	384	384	384	384	384	384
3.	F. S. I.	0.92	0.92	1.36	1.36	1.49	1.49	1.80	1.80	1.83	1.83	1.82	1.82
4.	Gross area per tenement (sft)	211	211	201	201	198.50	198.50	198.50	198.50	198.50	198.50	198.50	198.50

A study I did for CIDCO showed that for a constant area of land the number of tenements in buildings above a certain height stayed the same—because as buildings went higher, distances between them increased and the number of buildings on a site reduced. This disproved the notion that more people can be accommodated if buildings go higher.

the space around buildings as the minimum required for light and ventilation. They do not consider the spaces immediately outside the houses as extensions of covered living space. In multi-storeyed buildings, living space extends to a verandah, which is why tenements on the ground floor of such buildings need to be bigger so that there is no disparity in size. As a public undertaking, CIDCO was more concerned about the cost of a dwelling unit and optimum returns on the cost of land since this was quantifiable and could, therefore, be priced.

In 1971, CIDCO commissioned me to do a study comparing the cost of buildings of different heights, each housing tenements of 18 square metres. My study comparing buildings between two and 12 storeys revealed some interesting results with implications for both low-rise housing and the high-rise solution. The study showed that the cost of tenements was relatively low in buildings of up to six floors, provided they did not have a lift. As buildings went higher, the cost of the structure increased which, in addition to lifts and fire-fighting services, made tenements more expensive. The cost of a dwelling unit also depended on the foundation needed for prevailing soil conditions.

The relationship of the building cost to the cost of the land and the number of tenements was another eye-opener: for a given area of land, the number of tenements in a six-storeyed building was the same as in the twelve-storeyed one because the increased height of buildings required greater distance between them. Buildings lower than six storeys had fewer tenements but the space around them could be used. In low-rise developments, the individual tenement's share of land cost is higher but the construction cost is lower.

In a high-rise building, since the numbers are more, a tenement's share of land cost is less but the building costs more to construct. The popular contention that you need to go up to save on land stood

Precast doubly curved concrete shells were used for the floor and roof in a mass housing scheme at Ambala.

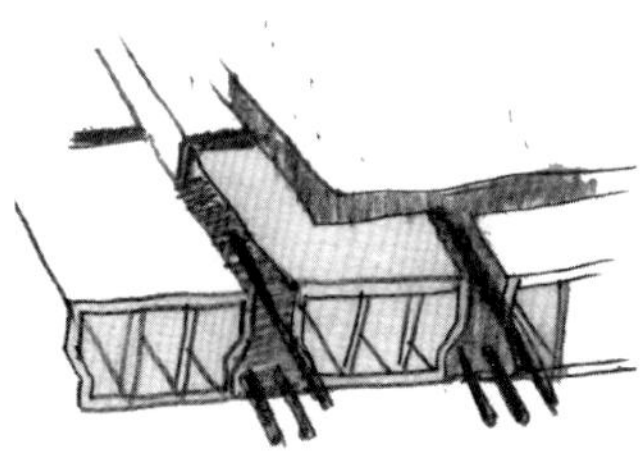

There were also alternative methods of making concrete slabs with fillers.

exposed in this study because the number of dwelling units stayed constant beyond a certain point. I also understood from this study that housing is not only about the design of individual buildings but about the relationships between heights, density and land. Those who argue for high-rises to house low-income groups see the relationship between land and building only as a cost-sharing one, failing to note that people in that income group live in a community and use land around the house as an extension of their living space.

Technology For Mass Housing

If design is one challenge in mass affordable housing, another significant one is figuring out the technology and management systems to implement such large-scale projects. This too was a matter of interest and debate among architects in the 1960s and 1970s, in large part due to the innovation that was happening on this front during these decades. Among the most famous innovators was Laurie Baker, a British architect who worked in India and experimented with affordable and environmentally sustainable housing, using local materials and skills. Baker, who was influenced by Mahatma Gandhi, believed in using material economically while maximising its potential; he also believed that it was possible for people to build their own houses without involving a contractor.

Another interesting project of low-cost housing happened at Ambala in 1958 in which the Army built houses. Called Operation Amar, it involved the construction of about 1000 tenements using precast doubly curved shells as floor and roof elements.

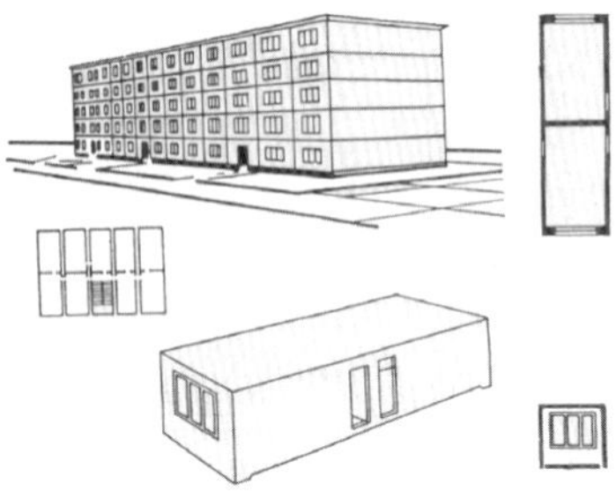

In Russia, completely preformed dwelling units in precast concrete were assembled on site using a gantry crane. This reduced construction time on site but did not result in good housing. A system using a gantry crane for assembling units meant putting buildings in single rows one behind the other because the crane's efficiency depends on the distance it travels.

The shell was designed by the Central Building Research Institute in Rourkee. The design of the tenements was unique because it eliminated formwork for concrete, reduced steel to the minimum and was light and easy to assemble on site. The combination of precast elements and in situ work lowered costs. Shells were cast in a separate yard and transported to the site in trucks. Casting was done while the foundations were being laid and walls were being built. The delivery of material and site construction was coordinated with precision. The project was a good example of application of research done in an academic institution, but could only have been implemented because the Army has an organised workforce.

While research on low-cost building materials during this time was mostly on technology that used inexpensive materials like stabilised soil, bamboo, fly ash and husk, there was also work done on precast concrete technology. The new technology interested engineers who were keen to know more about design, manufacture and material handling systems for assembly. Many architects mistakenly thought that precast construction was the way to overcome the housing shortage; they believed that quality would improve with reduced in-situ construction and components manufactured off-site, and that the new technology for assembling preformed elements would help complete projects more quickly. However, precast construction also had its share of problems: joints between components require sealing, and the cement grout used for this proved ineffective. It was not until the 1990s that efficient sealants were developed in India, by which time the enthusiasm for prefab housing had waned.

There were other problems in precast technology. The process of manufacturing components in a factory has its own challenges – the components have to be designed and detailed like industrial products for

Dharavi, termed 'Asia's largest slum', is in fact a thriving informal town with streets and houses that have grown over time. It has an organic quality.

efficient production, shipping to a site and assembly by people trained in the technology. It also involves specialised after-sales service. Moreover, a building with assembled factory-made components is more expensive because manufacturing costs include excise duties and local taxes and a higher transport cost. Precast technology for mass housing is viable only if the project is large and on a single site since the cost of infrastructure and material-handling systems require extensive repetition for it to work economically.

In schools of architecture and among architects, there was always a debate going on about the use of advanced technology (or mechanisation) versus human labour in construction. Most of my fellow students as well as socially conscious architects were opposed to mechanisation and the loss of employment that this entailed. Technology which reduces labour, however efficient, fast and modern, comes at a great human cost, besides making buildings expensive. What everyone overlooked was the glaring anomaly in the structure of state levies. A component made in a factory attracted excise duty while the same component made on site did not. And that was one of the main reasons for increased cost.

However, those who argued for maintaining human labour dismissed any alternative that brought in improved productivity and increased wages. They did not give enough thought to the deficiencies of the system of tendering and construction and worn-out procedures. A large workforce at the site, less than a third of which is skilled, makes the process of construction time-consuming and laborious. Most of the unskilled labour is employed in material-handling, which, because of inefficient tools and methods, does not add much value to the project. Those who were in favour of mechanised construction used this point in their arguments: they said that unskilled labour, in addition to handling materials, could develop skills in

Dharavi, like other slums, has been dismissed as illegal when in fact all of these have thriving economies and provide employment to many. Redevelopment of these informal settlements should include places for work in addition to living spaces.

using equipment and assembling components. They claimed that a smaller but trained workforce would ensure a better built and finished building. Buildings would also come up faster.

The one common factor that both sides agreed on was the use of concrete for all buildings since everyone, whatever his ideological persuasion, wants a floor and roof that is durable. Concrete roofs had become standard construction procedure by then, and both poor and rich had one thing in common: they wanted RCC roofs over their heads. In the city, this has become a kind of social leveller unlike in the village where a person's position in the social order is determined by the kind of roof over his or her head.

Slums And Redevelopment Schemes

People who build houses for themselves respond directly to their own needs, unlike architects who design for preconceived needs. You see this in slums, which are an indigenous collection of huts built cheaply with recycled or disused materials that come up with amazing speed on public or vacant lands. However, since slum dwellers always have the fear of eviction looming large, they are reluctant to improve their surroundings though they use great ingenuity in making the best use of interior space.

Slums are an explosive political issue since slum-dwellers are a big vote bank. In Bombay, slumlords, who are invariably connected to the political class, grab land and either build huts that are rented out or let people build their own huts, for which they extract payment. The larger slums, like Dharavi, often have workplaces within them. The western media refers to Dharavi as 'Asia's largest slum' but it would be more

In slum rehabilitation schemes, builders allot less land for rehabilitation and take the larger portion for commercial sale. Slum dwellers are housed in high-rise buildings built so close to one another that they seriously compromise safety, light and ventilation. The slum has only become vertical.

A rare scheme in Wadala allotted more land to rehouse the slum dwellers. They were in low-rise buildings with open space around them. Two tower blocks with high-end apartments were the sale component.

appropriate to call it 'Asia's largest informal town' since it has a thriving economy with small-scale industries and commercial enterprises. Houses were added on here over the years.

Slums which are said to make up 50 per cent of Bombay's housing needs have attracted widespread attention for years. Slum rehabilitation schemes have been attempted by the government over the decades, the most recent model being one in which the Slum Redevelopment Authority (SRA) gives incentives to private developers to build 225-square-feet tenements that are given free of cost to slum dwellers. In return, the developer gets to build for free sale an area equal to the rehabilitated areas. He does not pay for the land, yet his profit margin includes a return on the market value of land since that is included in the price of the sale flat. The redevelopment policy was first introduced in 1991 to benefit slum dwellers but it has turned out to actually benefit developers enormously – a developer does not pay upfront for land, gets additional FSI and relaxed norms in respect of setbacks, heights and distances between buildings.

Despite the huge benefits, developers have not done justice to slum redevelopment projects, cutting costs to further add to their own profits. SRA buildings are often built so close together that the slum dwellers' basic right to light and air and safety, which the bye-laws protect, is seriously compromised. This is a clear abdication of social and moral responsibility by the government – many of the rehabilitation buildings are more like vertical slums. Yet, for the slum dweller, redevelopment is a reprieve from the threat of eviction. The move from a hut to a free tenement with a pucca roof may be more important to him than the loss of light and air or even fire safety.

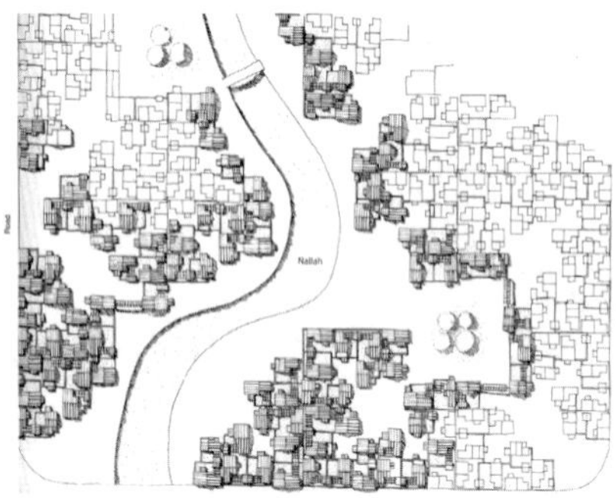

In housing, built areas and open spaces are closely interlinked. In this housing scheme by Charles Correa in New Bombay, groups of houses on individual plots are arranged around a courtyard, which, in turn, leads to a larger open space. Plots are approximately of the same area so that there is equity in land-holding. Space outside the house is shared.

The 'vertical slum' is a product of inequitable sharing of land. The developer allots the bare minimum land required to house slum dwellers, leaving the rest for sale flats or for future use or value additions like a club house, a swimming pool or gardens for the sale flats. A more equitable distribution of land need not compromise the sale portion of a project, however. An example of this is Rangari Chawl at Wadala where the architect, Suresh Mhatre, allotted 60 per cent of the land for rehabilitation and 40 per cent for free sale, resulting in two seven-storeyed buildings and two more upscale high-rises with apartments for sale. The space around the buildings is sufficient for light, air and fire safety for both the rehab and sale parts of the project. The rational, holistic and humane approach that the architect and developer took in this case showed that schemes under SRA rules can succeed without being inequitable.

Ideas For Low-Cost Design

A Gandhian idea that was prevalent during the early years of our practice was that housing should be 'by the masses and not for the masses'. This meant people could build their own houses instead of waiting for public agencies to develop and allot housing estates. This idea appealed to me and some of my peers. We worked out several solutions for self-made housing for a variety of plot sizes ranging from 80 square metres to 200 square metres. We liked the idea of letting people take charge of their living environment.

My friends and I frequently discussed this idea during tea sessions at Annapurna, an open-air cafeteria at Cross Maidan. One of the ideas we discussed was that small plots with individual houses could be developed to get dense but decent housing. The Bangalore City Improvement Trust had demonstrated

Self-help housing by groups is an alternative strategy to tackle the housing shortage. In this design for a part of Dharavi Koliwada, land owners rationalised the boundaries of their sites and agreed to build their houses according to the community's needs.

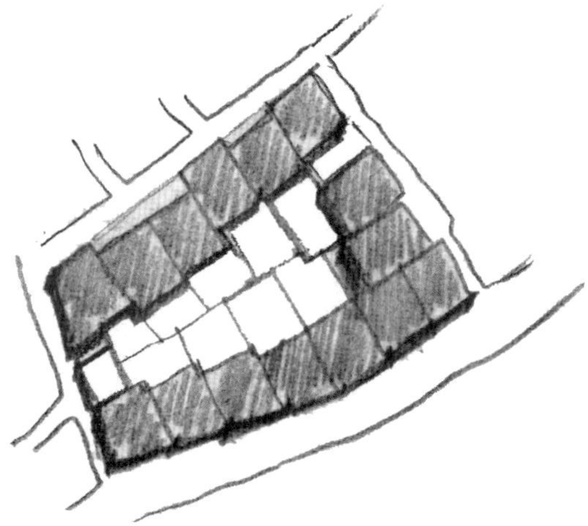

The rules were simple. A house occupied only half the site and the rear setback was larger than the front. The rear setbacks of all the houses were grouped together to make a courtyard for community use, especially for women and children.

this in the 1950s in an area it laid out with plots of 82 square metres, on which houses were then built by individuals.

Charles Correa, who also took part in these discussions, later wrote an essay about equity plots in his book 'The New Landscape'. He demonstrated the idea in his scheme for incremental housing in New Bombay, called 'Artists' Village' where he arranged houses around a courtyard, several of which were in turn grouped to form a larger courtyard and to the larger community space. Plots varied only slightly in area and there was, therefore, more equity in individual ownership of land. Over the years, though people made changes to their houses – for instance, a house that initially occupied only half the area of the plot was extended to cover it fully, and in some cases a floor was added – the overall layout and open spaces remained unaffected since the changes were within the plots allotted to individual owners. The design of the Artists' Village was more about the arrangement of plots and spaces between and around them than individual buildings. Therefore, despite alterations, the village has retained its character, and people like staying there.

Group housing schemes, in contrast, do not accommodate changes easily since land is not parcelled to individual owners, and buildings are two or more storeys high with several occupants. Additions and alterations take place in unpredictable ways that may end up in disorder or encroach on common open spaces. Post-occupation audits are never done to review if the design norms adopted were adequate. In the few that have been done for low-cost State housing projects, people complained that limited space resulted in cramped living conditions. However, even the better-off residents of these projects could not

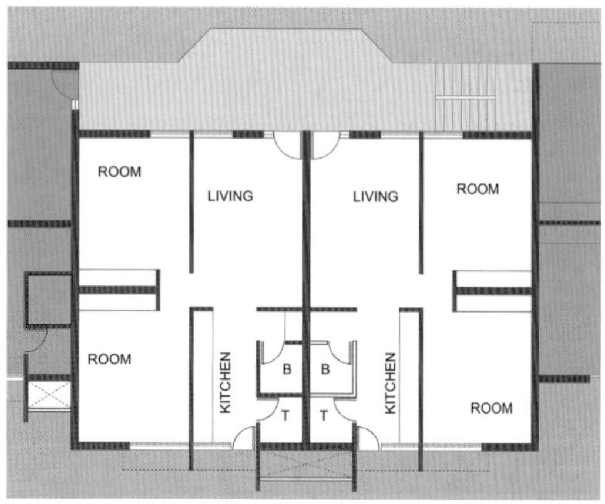

Many Dharavi residents are self-employed and earn enough to afford a pucca house but cannot find a place to work in. A covered space open on all sides over the top floor of the house can be used as a workplace and a sleeping space at night.

move into bigger apartments because of the high prices. The gap between market prices and improved affordability can be bridged only if public housing is continuous and supply of land is ensured at moderate prices. This is well within the competence of the government.

In March 2008, Sytse de Maat, Vytautas Baltus, Ashwin Karjatkar and I formed a study group in a workshop conducted by Urban Typhoons, a body of individuals interested in urban issues. We worked with the residents of Dharavi Koliwada to help them choose between making incremental changes in their village and accepting the Dharavi Redevelopment Plan proposed by the government. They were opposed to the Plan because it deprived them of their traditional rights over the land and gave them, instead, apartments of 30 square metres in high-rise buildings. Their rejection of the government's plan prompted them to look for alternatives.

To gain their confidence, we showed, through computer images, how the environment around their houses could improve merely by having good roads and pavements. We then worked on a plan to group plots that adjoined one another and rationalised their boundaries and areas into buildable equivalents. Houses were designed to have common walls, occupy a maximum of 60 per cent of the plot, have a small setback on the roadside and a larger one at the rear. Taking a cue from Ballard Estate, the rear setbacks were amalgamated to form a courtyard where children could play and women could meet their neighbours socially. Many in Dharavi are self-employed and they need workplaces, so a covered space open on all sides was provided over the top floor of the house for use as a workplace during the day and for sleeping at night. Claude Batley had suggested a similar idea in his alternative plan for Back Bay and his report for setting up housing standards in the Greater Bombay Plan.

We found that in a people's approach, rules have to be minimal. They need to be limited to ground coverage, minimum setback on the front and height of the building. Setbacks on the side and rear and any feature affecting the cluster of houses would have to be accepted by adjoining neighbours. This could bring in some of the same 'looseness' that towns that have grown organically over time possess. A house built in this way involves several people: the owner and his architect and his neighbours and their architects, all of whom have a face. This is unlike a centrally planned scheme where all decisions are made at the Planning Office. Of course, even a project of this nature needs someone to work out the size and shape of plots, lay them out and decide where and how much to build. That has to be done by an architect. A 'bottom-up' approach also needs the government's help to obtain land and arrange institutional finance. It means a paradigm shift in public housing policy which is within the government's power, provided there is political and bureaucratic will.

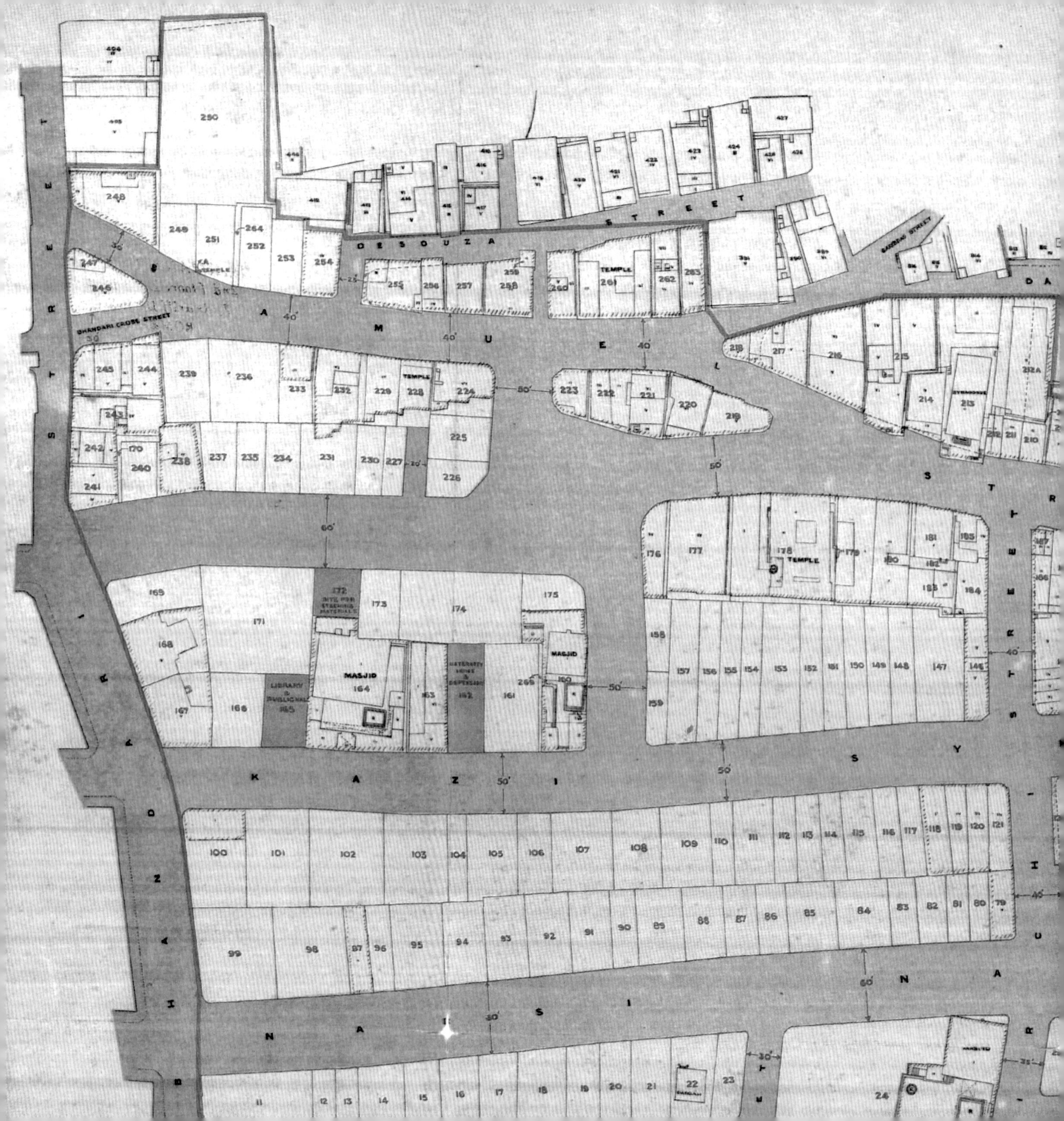
DESOUZA STREET
SAMUEL STREET
KAZI SYED STREET
NARSI NATHA STREET
BHANDARI STREET
BHANDARI CROSS STREET
TEMPLE
MASJID
SYNAGOGUE
LIBRARY & PUBLIC HALL
MATERNITY HOME & DISPENSARY
SITE FOR STACKING MATERIALS

Policies Affect The Urban Fabric

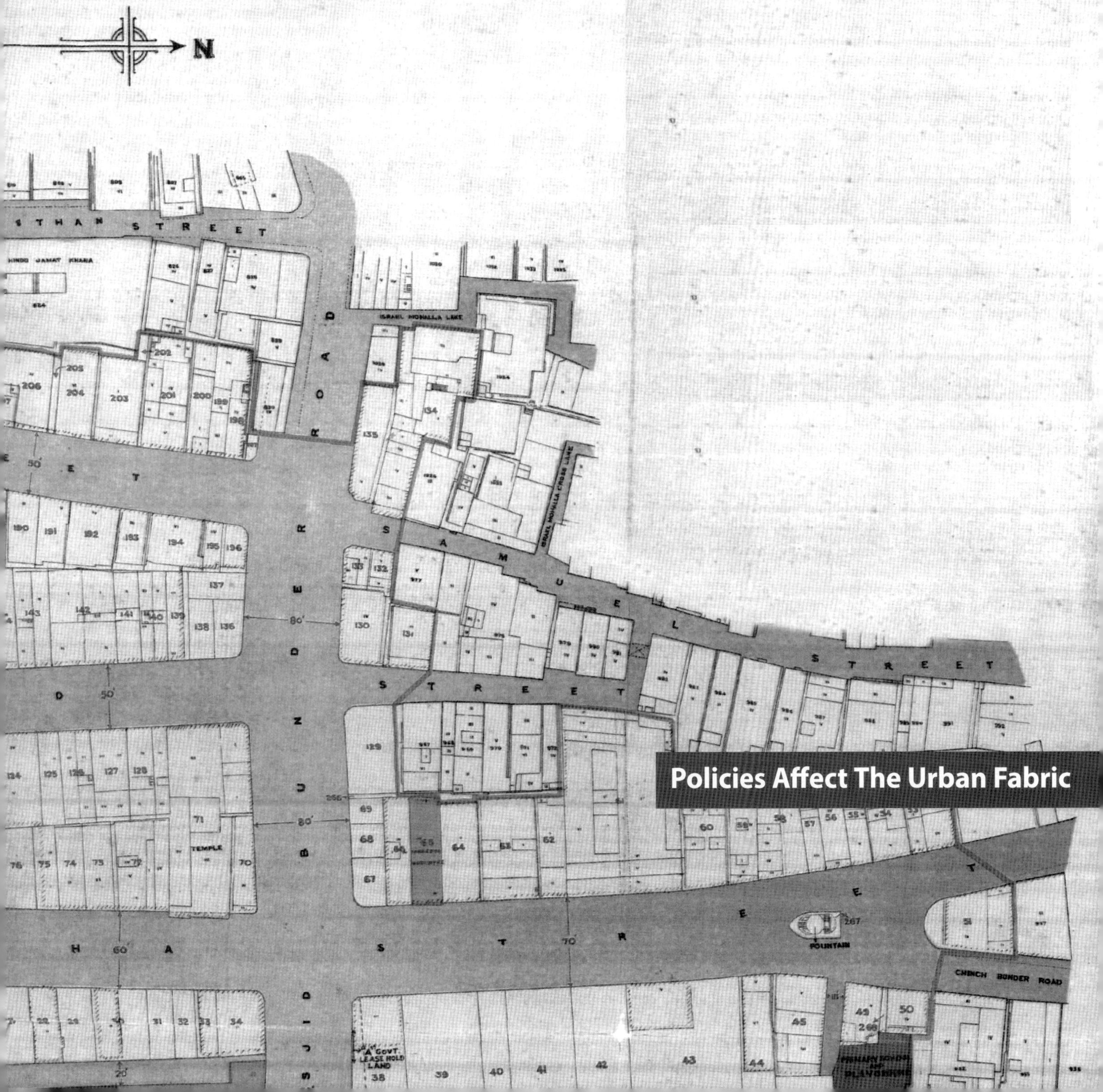

Policies Affect The Urban Fabric

As a young man, I often walked around town on Sundays with my friend Gopal, an airman posted at the Air Force base at Cotton Green. On one of our walks, we discovered a bridge located at the end of Wodehouse Road in Colaba, under which lay the rails of the old Churchgate-Colaba train service. The train service ran from 1867 to 1930, after which it was discontinued under pressure from land owners in Cuffe Parade who wanted an exclusivity that would enhance the value of their property.

Gopal and I often sat on a bench on this bridge. After a few years, in the early 1950s, I noticed the bridge was gone. Two decades later, I met the then chief engineer of Central Railway, Radhakrishnan, and found out why it had been dismantled and how the bureaucracy works to its own advantage. The state government had planned a wide road to connect Wodehouse Road to Cuffe Parade, for which Wodehouse Bridge and the land under it had to be acquired from the Railways. The Railways accepted the proposal, dismantled the bridge and handed over the land under and adjacent to the bridge to the government. Subsequently, the road plan was realigned, leaving the Wodehouse Road site vacant. Senior bureaucrats promptly got a block of apartments built for themselves on this plot, making sure, of course, that procedures were followed and all the paperwork was in order!

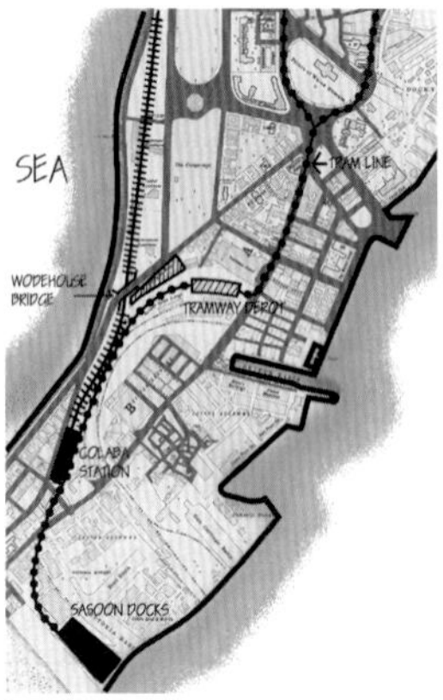

Wodehouse Bridge, under which trains between Churchgate and Colaba ran till the 1930s, was dismantled in 1950 to widen the road connecting Wodehouse Road and Cuffe Parade. The bridge had benches on which you could sit and watch the trains go by.

A city is built by the State and the community. In 'State', I include planners, politicians and the bureaucracy who together formulate policies. These policies are also subject to pulls and pressures from different interest groups – as we saw in the demolition of the Wodehouse Road bridge, this string-pulling even from bureaucrats is not new. Official policies and their interpretations affect the way people live.

Two laws were especially important in shaping Bombay housing – both in their observance and their misuse. The Bombay Rents, Hotel and Lodging Houses Rates Control Act, 1947, caused stagnation in rental housing that would later lead to a policy of reconstruction which would, in turn, forever alter housing in the city, taking it from low-rise to high-rise. The Urban Land Ceiling and Regulation Act of 1976 (ULCRA) also had a far-reaching effect on the city's growth and form, raising the cost of land and making flats unaffordable. Both were examples of how laws brought in by a government to fulfill social obligations do not always work.

Rental Housing

In the case of the Rent Act, which froze rents at levels prevailing in 1940, the law was more breached than observed. The act was intended primarily to protect the tenancy rights of low-income residents and to prevent landlords from exploiting the housing shortage brought about by the influx of refugees after the partition of the country. Rent control did protect the low-income group but middle- and upper-class people who occupied large flats and who could afford to pay more for them also benefited from rents that were kept artificially low. Many landlords who depended on a rental income were ruined since the meagre rents could not support the increasing cost of living. The act also gave rise to corruption inasmuch as very many illegal transfers of tenancy rights took place, from which both vacating tenants and landlords benefited.

However, there is another side to the rental housing story. Most landlords, after the Rent Control Act came into being, let their buildings deteriorate, claiming that the rents were too low for them to maintain the property. But while this may have been true in the case of chawls and small, low-rent buildings, landlords, as a rule, were not known to be particularly concerned about their tenants even before the Rent Control Act. Most landlords of buildings in the inner city and around the docks, mills and factories used to cram as many rooms and tenants as possible into their buildings, making for living conditions that were abominably unhealthy. Many did not even visit their buildings and dispatched a collector to get the rent and deal with complaints – complainants, on their part, were either ignored or threatened with eviction. There was neither a system of house or estate management nor was there any provision for a sinking fund for replacement after 60 years though the rent was supposed to include contributions to that fund. Landlords' successors inherited buildings without the money to maintain them. The result was indifference and disregard for the safety of tenants. In effect, therefore, the deterioration of housing stock had begun before rents were frozen. N V Modak, in a note appended to his 1946 report on 'Greater Bombay', wrote about deterioration of housing stock due to neglect and lack of funds for replacement. He titled his note 'Slum creation due to non-provision of sinking fund'.

The socialistic piece of legislation gave rise to a host of illegal practices. Secured tenants of larger flats sublet rooms to 'paying guests' or portions of their flat for 11 months at a time for a fee (the charge for letting out was termed 'fee' since 'rent' was protected by law). This was higher than the rent paid to the landlord. Offices, also within the ambit of the Rent Act, were similarly sublet. Invariably, the license fee was raised every time the agreement was renewed. However, landlords also benefited whenever a tenant vacated his flat and illegally transferred his tenancy right to someone else for a monetary consideration called 'pugree'. The pugree was shared between the vacating tenant and the landlord in a 60:40 ratio. The transfer was always paid in cash since it was illegal to put a price on a right protected by law. Most landlords thus recovered the original cost of their building through illegal transfers of tenancies, since the 'pugree' was based on prevailing market prices that were always higher than the original cost.

Yet another instance of the misuse of the Rent Act involved the many flats that the British government in India had requisitioned during the second world war to house serving officials and those on war duty. Although this was intended to be only for the duration of the war, the officers, both Indian and British, continued to occupy the flats for years afterwards. The post-independence Indian government, in many cases, obliged its retiring officers by coercing or mildly forcing landlords to transfer tenancies without a monetary consideration.

The Rent Act led to decades of stagnant rents that eventually resulted in the deterioration of rental housing stock. The timber posts and joists in buildings built before the 1930s rotted from dampness. Every monsoon, there were house collapses. To prevent the loss of property and lives, the municipality set up the Bombay Buildings Repair and Reconstruction Board in 1969 and began to charge tenants a repair cess. The Board's mandate was to make dilapidated buildings structurally sound, but it ran into problems soon enough – contractors were reluctant to take on this job since it was difficult to move tenants out and working conditions were difficult and risky. Many contractors were more interested in retrieving good timber from the buildings. Projects were either abandoned midway or, if completed, were shoddy pieces of work. Even today, house collapses take place every monsoon.

The failure of the Repair Board led to the municipality coming up with a policy to incentivise landlords to redevelop old properties. In 1991, it amended the bye-laws, thereby permitting a tenanted, cessed building (where the rent included a repair cess) to be demolished and rebuilt with incentives strong enough to attract developers. In the reconstructed building, tenants were to be given flats with an area ranging from 23 square metres to 73 square metres (248 square feet to 785 square feet) at no cost to them.

The incentive for the builder or landlord was a free sale component – an area at least twice the existing area of the building, if not more, to be sold in the market for profit. On the face of it, everybody seemed to gain by this policy. However, it had its pitfalls. Building setbacks were reduced, affecting the quality of light and air coming into the houses and increasing the risk of fire. Streets designed for a certain volume of traffic became inadequate while amenities like recreation grounds, schools and health clinics designed for a smaller population now had to be shared by many more. There would be houses for people to live in but life outside could be worse – unless reconstruction policies considered the neighbourhood as a whole.

Way before government policies led to the crisis in rental housing, there was another movement which gave citizens access to an ownership home – the cooperative movement of the early twentieth century. The Cooperative Societies Act, a piece of legislation by which an activity or industry or property could be jointly owned and developed and its profits shared, was enacted in 1906. The Saraswat community was among the first to explore the concept of cooperation in banking, property ownership and credit systems. The Saraswat Cooperative Housing Society, formed in 1915, was the first society registered in the country, and its housing colony, built at Gamdevi in 1915, was the first of its kind in the city. This was followed by another one at Santa Cruz in 1919. The success of these projects lead to more – Shripad Talmaki, a prominent Saraswat, promoted projects like Anandashram at Proctor Road and Talmakiwadi at Tardeo.

Other than those promoted by specific communities, cooperative societies were invariably started by individuals who identified a piece of land, paid an advance for purchase and set about forming a society, after which the project commenced. Most promoters were individuals with very little financial backing,

The Saraswat community was a pioneer in the cooperative movement which included banking, property ownership and credit systems. The Saraswat Cooperative Housing Society, the first of its kind in the country, was built at Gamdevi in 1915. It was the first instance of cooperative ownership of property.

and projects often took long to complete. Despite efforts, the cooperative sector could not make good the shortfall in housing and it was the developer who had to bridge the gap by bringing in capital and business capability.

Unlike the cooperative model, the developer model of housing construction which emerged in the 1960s was strictly for profit. Builders brought in very little capital. To begin with, they paid only a small part of the land cost as a token of 'intention to buy'. An 'agreement to sell' was then entered into with the land-owner, in which the price and time for completing the sale was specified. With this agreement, the builder made plans and got them approved by the municipality. The scheme was then advertised. Prospective buyers paid advances, which were used partly to pay instalments for the land and partly to begin work. The building was erected with payments from prospective buyers at different stages of its construction.

It was a win-win situation for builders; not so much for buyers, who, lured with low prices to book early, were the ones to take the risk. In many cases, they had to face the brunt of buildings left incomplete either because of defective title deeds or problems in getting planning approvals. Often, payments from buyers investing in one property were diverted towards the purchase of land for development of other properties. Many builders were unethical in their dealings with buyers, selling them substandard buildings. It was thanks to this situation that a developer's credibility in the twin matters of timely completion and payments commensurate with progress became more important than the design and quality of construction of a building. The Rahejas, one of the leading builders in the city, acquired a reputation for reliability and their projects thus got ready buyers.

Most projects promoted by builders had a cash component in the price – buyers were forced to pay part of the cost of a flat in unaccounted-for cash. Now and then a project would be advertised giving details of the project with special emphasis on the words, 'Only cheque payments will be accepted'.

A major factor in real estate transactions, which affected the price of housing, was the exchange of cash. Not only did genuine buyers have to shell out a part-payment in cash for the flats they booked but real estate also became an investment ground for those with excess cash, the latter being a byproduct of high taxation, controls and restrictions in economic activity. People began diverting the cash component of profits from their businesses into real estate projects promoted by builders, which were safe places to park illicit money. Flats that were booked when a builder announced a scheme would change hands quite a few times even before the building was finished. The 'sale' was done by the exchange of papers, generally allotment letters, and almost always paid for in cash.

Despite the proliferation of developers in the 1970s, the housing shortage persisted and flat prices continued to climb. Developers chose to put the blame for this on ULCRA, the 1976 legislation which ordained that a person could hold only 500 square metres (5,380 square feet) of vacant land in a metropolitan city; anything in excess of this would be acquired by the government for low-income housing. In reality, however, very little land was acquired, and owners of land had to apply to the government for permission to hold whatever land they had. Arriving at the area of vacant land was a convoluted exercise, and scrutinising plans and calculations involved delay and corruption.

While developers continued to perpetuate the spurious notion that flats were expensive because of a shortage of land, the rise in apartment prices continued even when more land came into the market after the closure of textile mills and industries through the 1990s and 2000s. The shortage, notional as it might be, suited developers because they could keep the price of apartments high and pressurise the government to increase FSI, ostensibly to make housing affordable.

Among other things in an advertisement was a standard line: 'All rooms have a panoramic view.' What was not mentioned was that the view was of the adjoining building.

From the 1970s to the present day, with a brief period from the late 1990s to around 2004 when flat prices crashed from their artificial highs, it was a sellers' market and the developer called the shots. He priced a flat on a unit cost per square foot that varied depending on when the flat was booked. The rate was low if the booking was done before construction began which, in a way, meant the buyer was financing the builder. Computation of area started with 'carpet' or actual usable space; later, builders began including the thickness of walls, both inside the flat and those enclosing it, in their area calculation, calling this 'built-up area'. A few years later, to increase their profit even more, they added a portion of common amenity spaces to the area of the flat, calling this 'superbuilt-up'. 'Superbuilt-up' was up to 40 per cent more than carpet area, with the result that a buyer was shelling out 40 per cent more money for the same living area. Builders claimed they were keeping the unit price constant without mentioning that the living area of the flat was getting smaller and smaller. Moreover, the customer was paying upfront for a portion of a plan and not for a finished product. He did not get guaranteed quality for what he bought nor did he get protection under the Consumer Act, which is competent only to determine deficiency in service and not the quality of a product.

For the private developer, housing is a business of making a product and selling it. Yet, he does not see it that way because to do so would mean investing in design and technology and in good-quality construction and marketing. That would be a major shift from the present situation where the buyer funds the project to a great extent without getting any assurance of timely delivery and quality.

The Development Plan And FSI

In the first half of the twentieth century, the city grew incrementally through planning initiatives at different places and times and not from a master plan. New precincts came up unobtrusively without changing the character of earlier settlements, adding to the multi-layered character of the city. In a way, the city's growth was organic. That kind of growth became obsolete when in 1967 the first Development Plan and Development Control Rules for Bombay were approved. Unlike planned precincts and interventions by the Bombay Improvement Trust and Bombay Development Department, which were area-specific, the Development Plan and Rules were applied uniformly all over Greater Bombay. It was a 'one size fits all' approach.

When the government decided to extend the city limits, new systems were necessary to develop and administer the extended area called Greater Bombay. This meant making a master plan. The first plan, drawn up by N V Modak and Albert Mayer in 1948, sought to improve the old city and plan the new additions to the city – the suburbs beyond the island. This was a tough job, as the plan had to provide for a less developed area along with an overgrown city. The main concerns dealt with in this first plan were overcrowding, slums, housing, densities, zoning and transportation. Of all the problems that Bombay faced, the most serious one was overcrowding. The bye-laws of the Bombay Municipality enforced from 1919, prescribed a minimum area of 25 square feet (2.30 square metres) and 250 cubic feet (7 cubic metres) per person – that was lower than the minimum prescribed in the Bombay Jail manual which was 40 square feet (3.70 square metres) and 560 cubic feet (15.80 cubic metres) per prisoner. A prisoner enjoyed more living space than a householder! In 1939, the municipality revised the living space rate to 36 square feet per person and the area of a tenement to 180 square feet. Every now and then, changes were arbitrarily made without any rationale. Of these revisions, Modak, perhaps in desperation, said, "No other town in India has attempted to prescribe a standard for overcrowding."

The report accompanying Modak's plan incorporated several recommendations of the Housing Panel, of which Batley was a member. Modak set out some ideals that he hoped would be translated into a workable plan. He increased living space to 45 square feet per person and recommended that as part of the planning process, slums should be rehabilitated and not merely cleared. He also related zoning to use, density and height. In a way, this implied area-specific rules since the coverage, size and height of buildings determine the volume of traffic and hence road widths. The report warned against arbitrary or piecemeal or partial zoning. Modak and Mayer's report presented a growth plan based on observation and assumptions. It was not detailed and did not specify the methods to be used for achieving the ideas and ideals it laid out.

None of this was reflected in the Development Plan and Rules that followed. The DP specified zoning, land use within a ward and, significantly, the concept of FSI, which is the ratio of the total built-up area of the building to the area of the site. The ratios were specified for different zones.

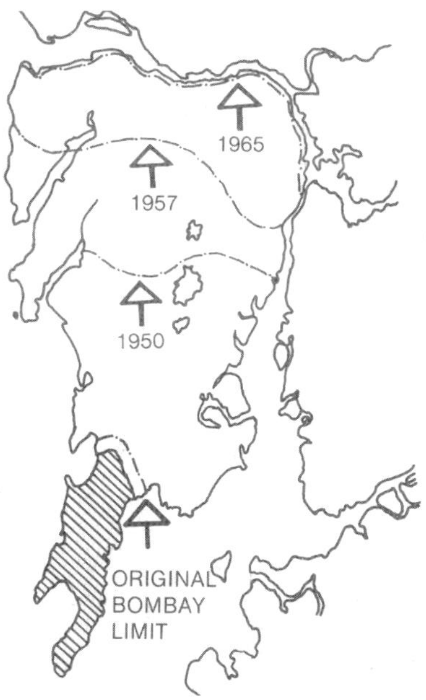

The 1967 Development Plan for Greater Bombay extended the limits of the city. A master plan and rules to suit it were introduced. It was a 'one size fits all' type of development unlike the earlier incremental growth through site-specific solutions.

Prior to the drafting of the Development Plan, architects in the 1950s were clamouring for change in the bye-laws so that they would be free from the building volumes prescribed earlier. These derived from specific setbacks, footprints and heights. The argument was that the earlier rules brought in order only by dint of dull repetition – if, instead, the building volume was derived from ratios like FSI and setbacks, and if open spaces became relative to height, there would be variety with order of a different kind. Planners also agreed that changes were necessary and the earlier restrictions pertaining to volumes and setbacks had to be amended to enable optimum growth. The argument was accepted and the Development Plan and Rules were drafted and submitted for government approval. In the meantime, there was an interim supplement to the existing bye-laws which specified open spaces around a building, depending on the user. Floor space indices were limited to 1.00 in all cases except in gaothans where the FSI was 1.20. An interesting rider was that the commissioner could condone an error of 1 per cent in computation of areas. Needless to say, the permitted margin of error was always availed of.

By itself, FSI was a good tool for planning – but applying the same ratio for all areas in the city, regardless of ground realities, created anomalies, especially in localities where existing built areas exceeded what was permitted. Renovation or reconstruction in those localities was ruled out. FSI based on the area of a ward instead of individual sites might have been more rational. Where an area is to be conserved for its neighbourhood character, like the gaothan, traditional design standards for heights, coverage and setbacks appears a more effective approach. The concept of FSI also had some contradictions within itself. In most countries, FSI or FAR (Floor Area Ratio) includes all the area within the footprint of the building without any exclusions. In Bombay, several elements are excluded in computation that helps increase saleable areas. Elements shown in the plans as "architectural and elevation features", which are exempted from area calculations, are converted and added to built areas fraudulently. Numbers, instead of being a means to an end, have become an end with a price tag attached.

After the Development Plan and Rules came into being, FSI and its price became the prime motivator of development. A property was only worth the area that coult be built on it. Location could help in enhancing the unit price of the FSI but ultimately only the saleable area decided a property's value. Over the years, the relationship of built area to density eroded, especially since FSI norms are uniform across neighbourhoods, regardless of population size. A concept which started as a measure to manage density has become a numbers game, and the demand for more built-up area continues unabated, supported by the builders' specious argument that higher floor space indices make the land component more affordable. This is a myth created by vested interests for whom additional saleable area helps keep the price of properties high. Indeed, with higher FSI, more area becomes available for sale to investors – not for those who need a place to live.

FSI has become a saleable and tradable commodity in the real estate market. As in many businesses, there are corrupt and criminal practices here that try to circumvent the rules. Take the case of Pratibha, a building in Cumballa Hill that was promoted in the 1980s as an apartment building for high-income buyers. The developer and his architect, in collusion with officials in the District Land Records office, altered the area of the site and forged land documents to get additional area. Through this, several floors were added to the building, bringing with it a lot of extra saleable area. When the fraud was discovered, the state government considered regularising it, provided the additional area was handed over to accommodate government employees. The argument was that if the developer did not benefit and if he bore the cost, the offence could be condoned. There was a public outcry against such a move. The suggestion was flawed because it condoned a crime and turned a blind eye to the violation of municipal bye-laws which were for the city's good. FSI and the manipulation in its interpretation and computation has played havoc with the growth and form of the city – and continues to do so.

Opportunities For Growth

Opportunities For Growth

In the sixties, with the advent of the new Development Plan and Rules, including FSI, architects felt the need for the city to grow beyond what was possible by conventional planning. There was a need for fresh ideas, and one of these came in the form of 'a city across the harbour.'

A New Town

The genesis of New Bombay (Navi Mumbai) goes back to Modak's plan for Greater Bombay, which mainly looked at the development of the area north of Mahim Creek. Modak's report also referred to an idea mooted by H Foster King in his speech at the Indian Institute of Architects in July 1945 that the only logical way for Bombay to grow was to spread to the mainland so that new areas would be more easily accessible to the office district in the Fort area. King, who also opposed tall structures on the western edge of the island city as they would block the sea breeze from entering the inner city, thought of the new areas as a dormitory town. He argued that the cost of opening up areas in the mainland was cheaper than reclaiming land from the sea, and suggested connecting these new areas with the city through an undersea tunnel,

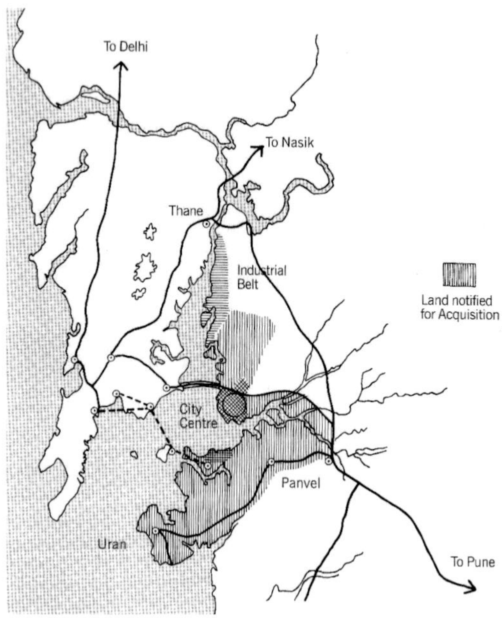

The Modak-Mayer plan for Greater Bombay was limited to the area north of the island city. But the authors of the plan realised its limitations. The city had to grow across the harbour, and the idea was initiated in 1945. However, it remained a mere talking point until Correa and his colleagues made a plan. They conceived the new city as a self-sufficient one with jobs, opportunities and a transport system - not a dormitory town depending on Bombay for its sustenance.

which would be safe in times of war. He ruled out transport by sea, as boats were slow and unusable during the rainy season. Arguments against the tunnel focused on its high costs and its usefulness being restricted to vehicle owners. J G Bodhe, a civil engineer, revived the idea of a new town in the early 1960s with his suggestion to connect Apollo Bunder to Uran across the harbour. His interest, however, was only in the design and construction of the bridge, not so much in the new city. Everyone opposed his bridge because the location could affect shipping lines and also create traffic congestion in South Bombay.

The idea of a new city was also mooted by others but it remained notional until Charles Correa took the wind out of everybody's sails by presenting a comprehensive plan that was radically different from previous ideas. The plan, co-authored by Pravina Mehta and Shirish Patel, proposed a city that was not just a dormitory town but a self-sufficient township with places for work, living and shopping. The plan for the new city was structured around an efficient mass transport system that would enable nodes to develop independently. The city centre, developed around a lake created out of a natural feature, would also be the locus for three trains going outwards, giving dynamic energy to the centre, like a pinwheel. The city centre was to be located close to the sea, creating an image as powerful as Marine Drive. The plan visualised developed waterfronts similar to Apollo Bunder, and ferries plying between the two cities with the Elephanta Island as a mid-point. Correa, perhaps basing his design on the time-honoured tradition of venerating water as a source of life, called his plan 'A City On The Water'. After much debate, the Maharashtra government accepted the New Bombay plan and assigned the task of developing the new city to the City and Industrial Development Corporation of Maharashtra Ltd (CIDCO), a public limited company owned by it.

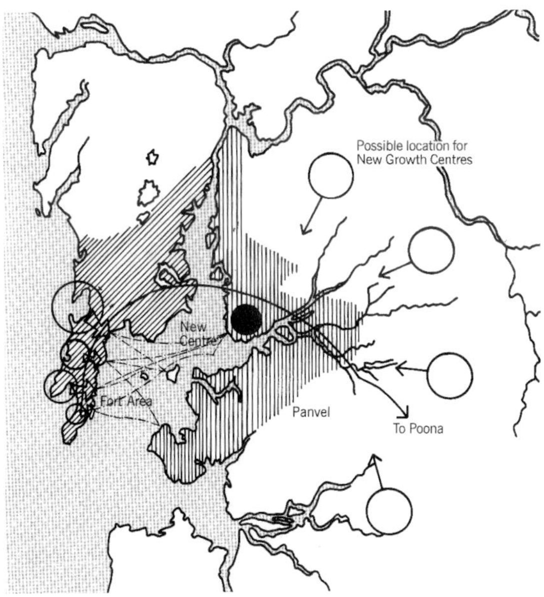

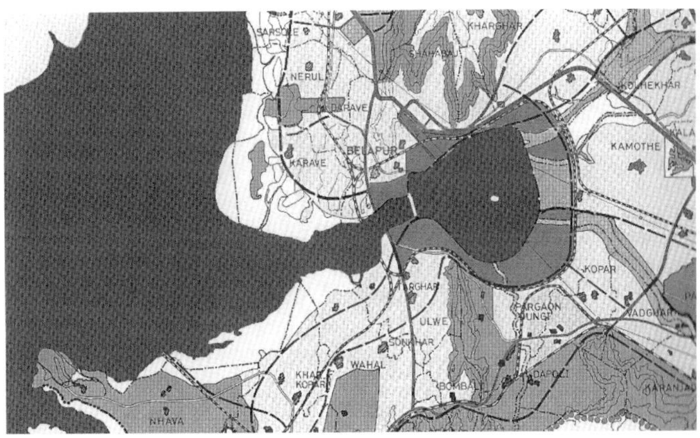

The plan for New Bombay visualised development of its seafronts and using water transport between Bombay and the new city. It was mainly structured as nodes strung along a transport corridor. The city centre was around a natural water body, which prompted the authors of the plan to call it 'A city on the water'.

The idea of a new city across the harbour showed one way for Bombay to grow. The government's acceptance of the ambitious and comprehensive plan for a new town was seen as a positive move and suggested that similar forward-thinking steps would be taken for planned growth and improved housing within Bombay too. The opportunity to do so rose in the 1980s and '90s when land began to be freed up with the shutting down of old textile mills in central areas of the island city.

The Mill Lands

Bombay's growth from the eighteenth century onwards was driven by commerce, shipping and manufacturing. Of these, the textile industry, which employed a large workforce that lived around the mills, contributed the most to the prosperity of the city. By 1900, Bombay had the largest number of textile mills in a single city anywhere in the world.

In 1919, the congestion and pollution caused by the mills in the centre of the city prompted the government, possibly on the advice of the Improvement Trust, to consider shifting them out of Bombay to Badlapur. The city had already started growing northward but no mill owner was willing to shift since there was no infrastructure available in Badlapur. The government did not pursue it either, and for the next four decades the mills flourished.

In the 1950s, the textile industry could neither expand within Bombay because of restrictions set by the Congress government nor close down because of the latter's political compulsions, one of them being

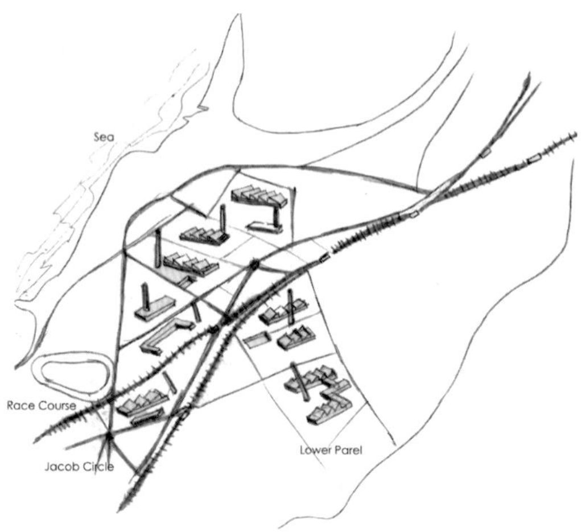

The textile industry was allowed to die out for a number of reasons, the principal one being potential profits on real estate.

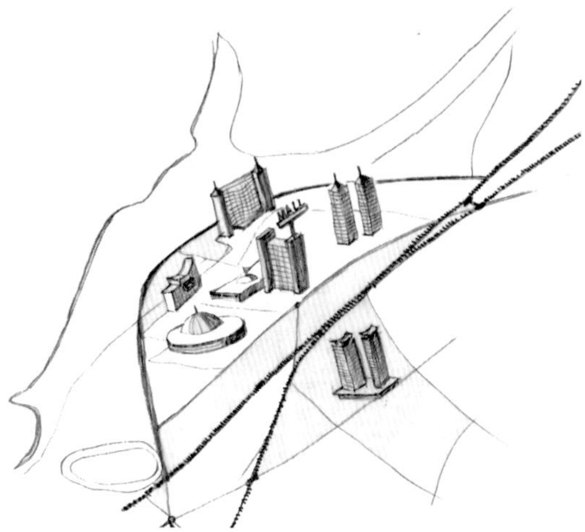

Land available in the city after the closure of the textile mills was large enough to make a big difference to the city.

that the main union was controlled by the party. Moreover, mills in the city were classified as large-scale industry and were thus unable to compete with the small-scale power looms in nearby Bhiwandi which were subject to far less taxes and duties. By the 1970s, textile manufacturing in the mills had become unviable, and they survived only because of a badly paid labour force. Many mills turned sick and were nationalised so that workers could keep their jobs. The decline of the industry and the rise of land prices in Bombay convinced mill owners that developing real estate was more profitable than running their factories.

In 1982 the textile workers' union led by Datta Samant, a strident labour leader, went on a strike for higher wages. The strike lasted for 18 months, the mills closed down and thousands of workers were left jobless.

In 1991 the Development Control Rules were amended to permit piecemeal development of vacant mill land in order to raise money for reviving or modernising the mills. However, this concession was misused and development was haphazard. The government, therefore, set up a study group in 1996 to advise it on proper land use, additional urban facilities and a suitable urban form.

Bombay's mills occupied about 600 acres of land in the heart of the city, which was more than the areas of the entire Fort, Ballard Estate and Nariman Point put together. This land resource could be recycled to revitalise the city, provided it was planned as an important part of the whole city and not a stand-alone development. The study group entrusted with the job was headed by Charles Correa. It drew up a plan in which lands belonging to the National Textile Corporation were amalgamated and developed according

THE SALE OF LAND WILL BE PERMITTED ON THE BASIS OF A SIMPLE FORMULA WHICH MAY PERHAPS BE AS FOLLOWS:

(i) ONE-THIRD OF THE LAND (WITH A MINIMUM OF SAY ONE ACRE) IS SURRENDERED TO BOMBAY MUNICIPAL CORPORATION FOR PROVISION OF PARKS, SCHOOLS OR OTHER SOCIAL AMENITIES.

(ii) ANOTHER ONE-THIRD OF THE LAND IS USED FOR LOW INCOME HOUSING AS PER THE STIPULATED GUIDELINES (OR IS SURRENDERED TO MAHARASHTRA HOUSING AND AREA DEVELOPMENT AUTHORITY FOR THIS PURPOSE).

(iii) THE REMAINING ONE-THIRD LAND, TOGETHER WITH THE FLOOR SPACE INDEX ON THE LAND SURRENDERED TO BOMBAY MUNICIPAL CORPORATION, CAN THEN BE SOLD AT MARKET PRICES AND USED FOR HOUSING (WITHOUT SPECIFYING THE INCOME LEVEL).

THUS THE SELLER SHOULD BE ABLE TO GET TWO-THIRDS OF THE CURRENT MARKET VALUE OF THE LAND (SINCE HE WOULD BE TRANSFERRING TWO-THIRDS OF THE F.S.I. TO THE BUYER). SUCH A POLICY WOULD

(i) INCREASE LAND FOR AMENITIES IN THE CITY WHERE IT IS MOST NEEDED.

(ii) PROVIDE LOW-INCOME HOUSES CLOSE TO WHERE THE JOBS ARE.

(iii) CONTRIBUTE TO THE RESOURCES AVAILABLE FOR THE DEVELOPMENT OF THE BOMBAY METROPOLITAN REGION

The report by a study group appointed by the government in 1996 proposed an equitable sharing of land.

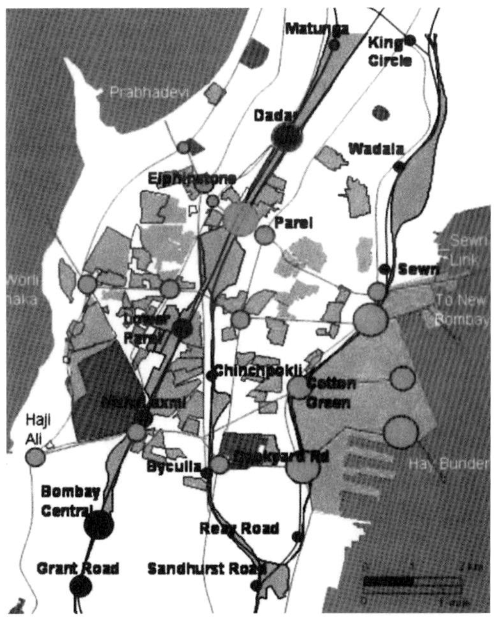

The plan accompanying the report contained East-West road connections to ease the traffic, connect railway stations and link them to the eastern waterfront

to the formula devised in 1985 by the Bombay Metropolitan Region Development Authority. The formula was simple. It divided the land three ways, in which a third was made over to the municipality for parks and civic amenities, a third for public housing and the residue for commercial exploitation together with the FSI of the plot surrendered for civic amenities. This would have kept price of the land at reasonable levels and provided citizens with desperately needed open space. The more important part of the plan made by the study group was the east-west road connections that would ease traffic flow, connect railway stations and provide access to the eastern waterfront and on to the rest of the metropolitan region like New Bombay. It was a fantastic opportunity to majorly restructure the core of the city and was possible only because the mill lands became available. However, this vision of a comprehensive redevelopment of the area was not implemented by the government, which only accepted the main recommendation of how the land would be recycled if a mill were to shut down.

What unfolded later was an incredible story of opportunity lost due to political and bureaucratic malfeasance, sheer greed and a court's judgment that missed the wood for the trees. In 2001 the rule pertaining to mill redevelopment was surreptitiously amended with disastrous results for the city. The three-way division of land, which initially included the entire area of a site, now excluded the land under a structure even after its demolition. This considerably reduced the amount of land for public use, leaving the bulk of it with the mill owners for commercial exploitation.

Civil society challenged the legality of the amendment and made a plea to the Bombay High Court that the government had failed in its duty to protect citizens' right to open space, clean air and protection

For over a hundred years the textile industry was one of the major engines of growth in the city. It was a principal employer and the city's social structure thus had a sizeable working-class segment. When the mills shut down, land that should have been available to all was used for luxury apartments, shops and malls, pushing those needing housing further away and also depriving the city of desperately needed open spaces.

Chawls where mill workers lived now stand cheek-by-jowl with swanky towers, making for an incongruous and somewhat tragic image.

and improvement of the environment. But although the High Court ruled in favour of the petition, the Supreme Court failed to see the larger picture and protect the interests of the majority. Instead, it looked at the legal issues concerning the competence of the government to amend a regulation, the definition of open lands and other technical matters. It paid little attention to the issue of open spaces needed for the city nor did it consider the environment an important issue unless there were effluents or other health hazards that affected the citizens. The last straw was the contention that mill lands were only a small fraction of the area of a ward and an even smaller one of the city. Change in their land use was of little or no consequence to the entire city.

The judgment sealed the fate of the textile industry in Bombay and ensured that an opportunity for planned redevelopment in the core of the city was lost.

For over 150 years the cotton mills were the mainstay of Bombay's economy. Built with some capital and a lot of human labour, the mills are etched deeply in the city's memory. When they closed, capital multiplied many times over but a century of toil came to naught. The court's judgment ensured that the mills' sirens went silent, the chimneys stopped spewing smoke and the memory of the cotton mills and people who worked in them was erased.

A resource that could have eased the housing shortage for the less privileged, created open spaces which the city is starved of and provided a new and efficient network of roads and transport corridors, was lost. What has resulted is skewed and ad hoc development, with the area now dominated by commercial

Spaces where once machines and men worked are now abuzz with another kind of activity. Toil has been replaced by leisure.

In the redesigned spaces a mill chimney reminds us of an era gone by.

complexes, high-end offices and gated residential enclaves – all for the few who can afford them. Paradoxically, politicians elected by the majority amended the rules for the few who may not even have voted for them.

Planning And Built Form

The built form we see in the city today is not the sole creation of the architect though it is his work that is the most visible. The architect comes in only after sites are laid out, municipal facilities are put in place and rules for development are set out.. He is like the actor who plays his part only in the last scene but as in the grand finale in a play, his work can make all the difference. For him to perform well, however, the play needs a good script, lighting, props and direction. The contribution of all the others, though invisible, is equally, if not more, important. In a city, built form rides on the back of planning decisions.

Unlike a design brief for a building worked out by a client and his architect, the process of drawing up a brief for the city is far more complex. The State must balance physical conditions and the pulls and pressures of different stakeholders and vested interests with political compulsions and State interests. The more powerful groups wield greater influence and the political class that controls land – a city's biggest resource – is always under pressure from the real estate lobby. The introduction of FSI and the changes to it and the Development Rules have led to a big change in the form of the city.

The planned interventions by the Improvement Trust and the Development Department had a recognisable urban form because their rules and design controls were based on an envisioned built form. Violations and deviations from approved plans became conspicuous and were easy to detect and prevent. The development was largely people-oriented in its planning objectives, though, paradoxically, a lot of people were displaced when schemes were taken up for execution. The present Development Plan does not envision a form because it is based on a set of abstract ideas like FSI that cannot predict a form. It is a free-for-all situation in which there are many voices screaming for attention. It is not community- or people-oriented. Planning which relates only to abstract ideas without regard for people is actually responding to commercial exploitation. When that happens, the city becomes unlivable.

The Changing Role Of The Architect

The role of an architect in a project has also changed from a 'beautifier' of buildings to sole designer to a leader of a team. When he was a beautifier, an engineer was in charge and the architect was a one-man office. When a client put him in charge, he needed assistants; a quantity surveyor and an engineer to design the structure. Smaller buildings were designed and supervised by small practices. The larger offices were either partnerships between an architect and engineer in which both partners handled their areas of specialisation or group practices in which partners worked independently but shared office premises and administrative and support staff. In such offices, the principal would decide on all major issues in a project, leaving a senior architect to oversee all details, including drawings prepared by the structural consultant. Design, estimates and tenders for services like electrical, plumbing and air-conditioning were drawn up by specialist vendors. The architect became a leader of a team when projects became complex and demanding.

The nature of practice changed in post-independence India. In the 1950s, when we started working, three major streams of practice or sources of work had emerged. The first was clients who used architects to design and oversee the interiors of houses, offices, restaurants, shops and showrooms, a job which till then was done by furniture-makers. The larger furniture companies like Kamdar or John Roberts retained designers, mostly Europeans, to design the interiors, present them to clients, and give advice on the procurement of artifacts and selection of upholstery, drapes and carpets. They also designed and detailed furniture and oversaw the work on site. Architects were now given these assignments, and work was carried out like building projects with drawings, tenders, site supervision and certification of bills. Clients became aware that an architect could be useful in interior projects.

The next set of clients who offered projects to architects were industrialists. In the '50s, the government planned to widen the industrial base of the country by restricting imports and insisting that these goods be manufactured in the country. This helped the economy to grow, and architects had more projects than they could handle. Manufacturing units came up in zones set up for industries. State-owned companies acquired land and developed them into sites for industries.

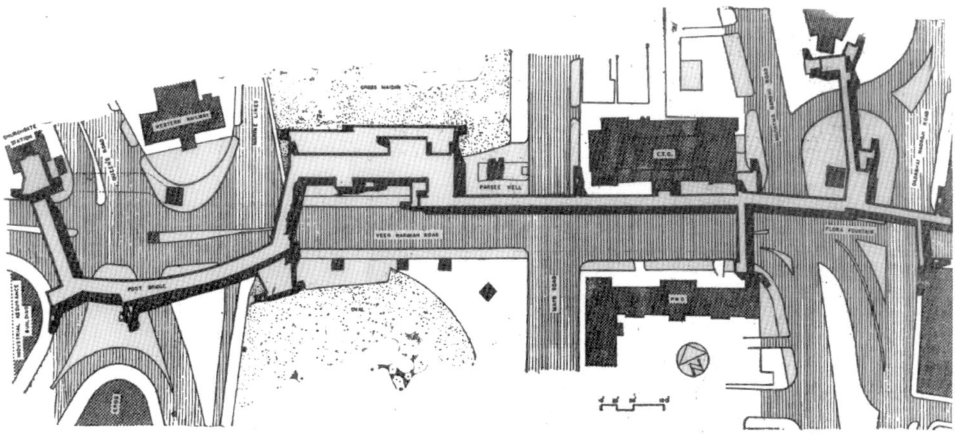

The idea of skywalks goes back to the 1960s. Here is a proposal for one from Churchgate station to Flora Fountain. Skywalks built many decades later have been unsuccessful because people are reluctant to climb stairs.

Industrialists preferred purchasing land from the state industrial development companies although this was more expensive than buying from private land-owners. This was because many of the latter did not have clear titles to their land, and purchase procedures were therefore cumbersome and time-consuming – they entailed verifying the ownership of the land, surveying boundaries, giving notices for purchase, negotiating prices and going through lengthy land-use conversion procedures in case the land was agricultural. The delay caused by all these procedures far outweighed the benefit of the relatively lower cost of the land. Moreover, land obtained from private owners was undeveloped while industrial estates had the necessary infrastructure. Only individual or family-owned companies generally bought land from the open market because the sellers were mostly farmers and their land boundaries and records could easily be fudged for a little extra cash.

The initial phase of industrialisation saw both multinational and Indian companies set up units. Multinational companies had adequate capital and their projects were well funded since they had to conform to standards prevailing in their home countries. Indian companies were generally undercapitalised and projects had low budgets within which buildings had to be made. Industrial projects needed multi-disciplinary teams; user departments, consultants for the structure, services, machinery and public utility servers. Industrial projects demanded completion within a strict time and cost schedule as well as efficient coordination between users, consultants, contractors and vendors. For the architect, it required adjustment to a different work culture. His role now was that of a team leader, not the sole decision-maker, and his office thus had to be restructured. The nature of practice changed. Buildings had to be efficiently designed to suit a programme structured around requirements that were strictly functional and oriented to a manufacturing process. Projects were complex and large. They had to be dealt with impersonally and professionally, which most offices were not equipped for. Only the large firms with a corporate structure could compete and get the major projects. But there were plenty of small and medium-sized jobs available. The architect was now neither a beautifier of buildings nor one with sole authority in a project. He was part of a corporate team and had to adhere to its culture.

The third set of clients for architects were real estate developers. The early developers were not sure of the role of architects and their usefulness in their projects apart from the statutory requirement of getting plans approved by the municipality. They provided young architects with work and got them to make plans for approvals, paying them low fees and promising them more work. Developers then gave architects freedom to make elevations that would attract buyers while keeping a tight control on the plan arrangement and saleable areas. The architect once again became a beautifier of building facades, coming back to where he had started.

The Architect And The City

Several Bombay architects have, over the decades, made proposals to improve the city. Most of these proposals were ignored but some have been implemented, albeit years later. For instance, in the 1960s, *The Times of India* reported on an idea for grade separation of the main road between Charni Road Station and Opera House. The suggestion was to segregate vehicular and pedestrian traffic by raising the road just high enough to let pedestrians use the lower level of the street. The road would have to be raised only 2.5 metres and the cost of doing this would be lower than a vehicular flyover. The idea was ignored then but was implemented on the Western Express Highway at Santa Cruz (East) 50 years later.

Similarly, in 1964 Charles Correa proposed a skywalk from Churchgate Station to Flora Fountain to provide safe passage for train commuters exiting the terminus on to a busy street. The idea of separating pedestrian and vehicular traffic with skywalks was popular in Europe at that time. (The elevated street already existed in Bombay from the 1930s – for instance, Tilak Bridge connecting East and West Dadar, and the skywalk connecting East and West Matunga.) Critics of Correa's proposal noted that most pedestrians were reluctant to climb stairs, and might not want to give up walking along the relatively shaded, pleasant path from Churchgate to Fountain with its statues, Parsi well, and pavement book sellers.

Years later, Correa also came to believe that segregating pedestrians was a poor solution to the congestion caused by permitting cars to come into the city centre. Many cities across the world have restricted car traffic in their business districts. In 2008, when the Mumbai Metropolitan Region Development Authority (MMRDA) proposed a skywalk from Churchgate to CST, Correa agreed with heritage activists who opposed it because they thought it would ruin the skyline. Although the Churchgate skywalk was never built, the city now has many skywalks for commuters coming out of train stations, many of which are not used. By providing skywalks, planning authorities are only compounding the mistake of allowing indiscriminate use of private car traffic.

Some architects and activists have also played a role in reviving derelict sea fronts. But these are local developments that do not affect policy, which is where the core issues affecting the city lie and which is currently shaped mostly by the State and vested interests.

Most architects in the city today are preoccupied with designing iconic towers – unlike when I started practice in the 1950s when there was a greater concern with the overall built form and with public housing. Changes in building typology and form are certainly a sign of urban growth. But those transformations need to go beyond the design of stand-alone buildings. Architects could help make a change in the way Bombay is growing if they look beyond the drawing board and reflect on the change in the urban fabric brought about by the Development Plan and Rules.

Epilogue

A city changes constantly – and it must do so to stay relevant to the times. But how has Mumbai changed? In the decades prior to the introduction of the Development Plan, the urban fabric provided a lot of opportunity and space for face-to-face social interaction, which suited a community-based society. That has given way to islands of habitation connected by streets that are suitable only for fast traffic. Bombay was more egalitarian than other cities and had more mixed localities than most. Now, the city is more stratified. Planning tools like FSI have helped bring about this state of affairs by promoting the dominance of only one housing typology – the tall tower block, its residents gated and isolated from their surroundings. Unfortunately Bombay citizens today – including architects – take this housing form to be a sign of progress, the marker of a global modern city.

Bombay needs to reinvent itself but without imitating models elsewhere. To quote from the Modak-Mayer report: "Of equal importance is the expression of physical and functional considerations in architectural form and organisation which makes a direct and lasting impression on the people who see, live and work in them. People want to live in a great city, a city of dignity, grace and inspiration; not only an efficient city."

For this to happen, planners, architects and all those concerned about the city need to put on their own thinking caps – not the caps imported from Dubai, a city with a collection of buildings from everywhere that belong nowhere. We need to initiate and debate a new set of ideas about urban form to help move the city to its next stage of growth. After all, a city can become only as great as its residents make it.

Glossary

Baug
Literally meaning 'garden', a baug in Bombay refers to a gated housing colony generally occupied by the Parsi community

Bhisti
A community of water-sellers who carry water from place to place in a goatskin bag

BIT
Bombay Improvement Trust, a body set up by the Government of Bombay in 1898 to develop the city

BDD
Bombay Development Department, a development authority that succeeded the Improvement Trust

Cantilevered verandah
A balcony that projects from the building without supports

Chhajja
A projecting or overhanging weather shade for a roof or window

Chhatri
A rooftop architectural feature used in Mogul and Rajput buildings to emphasise their corners

Chawl
A building containing small two-roomed tenements with a common corridors and toilets

Chowk
Literally meaning 'square', this refers to an open space, either a courtyard in a building or a public space in a town

DC Rules
Development Control Rules of the Municipal Corporation of Greater Mumbai which lay down the dos and don'ts of how structures can be built

DP
Development Plan of the Municipal Corporation of Greater Mumbai

Darwaza
Literally meaning a gateway or door, the word generally refers to entrances to forts or towns

Doubly curved shell
A concrete roofing component that is curved in both directions

Elevation
A view of a building seen from one side, a flat representation of one façade

Eaves board
A vertical edge to a sloped roof

Fanlight
A small rectangular window placed directly above a main door or window which provides ventilation even when the main door or window are shut

Footprint
The area of ground occupied by a building

FSI
Floor Space Index, which refers to the ratio between the area of a site and the area built on it

Gaothan
A particular type of village-like housing existing within Mumbai city

Glossary

Greenfield project
A project built on an unencumbered site

Infill Estate
A planned intervention in an existing built-up area

Joists
Small, parallel beams of timber, steel, reinforced concrete etc, for supporting floors, ceilings or the like

Kaccha
Literally meaning 'unripe', can be taken as 'makeshift' in the context of roads or housing

Katta
A Marathi word for 'platform' which, in the public space, refers to a low wall where people sit during leisure hours and interact

Lintel
A load-bearing building component or a decorative architectural element often found over portals, doors and windows

Load -Bearing Wall
A wall that takes the entire load of the floor or roof uniformly

Louvre
A window-shading device with slats that can be angled to admit or keep out air and light

Mandala
A diagram of the cosmos often used in planning a Hindu temple

Nahani
A washing space (also called 'mori') usually referring to a kitchen sink

Naka
An intimate public space, usually a street corner in a neighbourhood, where people meet

Otla
A platform or plinth usually in the front portion of a traditional house where visitors are received

Pitched roof
A sloping roof

Pucca
A Hindi word that means 'permanent'

Roof cornice
A horizontal ornamental moulding that crowns a building

Setback
The distance between a building and the boundaries of the site on which it stands

Shikhara
A tower over the sanctum housing the main deity in a temple

Single-loaded corridor
A corridor that has rooms only on one side

Wadi
An enclosure containing a group of houses or a plantation

Credits

The author gratefully acknowledges the contribution of the following people:

Photos:

Abhijeet Doshi
Anil Nagrath
Anuradha Murthy
Ashok Kulkarni
B Shirazi
Chandroo Iyer
Hemangi Kadu
Ipsita Mahajan
Kaiwan Mehta
Prateek Banerjee
Sandeep Talpade
Smita Dalvi
Suresh Mhatre
Sytse de Maat
Vivek Sheth, NID report

Drawings:

Ashwin Karjatkar
Vytautas Baltus
Charles Correa
NID report
4 from the fifties, 20CASI
Measured Drawing by students of Sir J J College of Architecture, Prerna Khilari, Surbhi Dolas and others

Sketches:

Author
Anant Raje

Published Sources:

Bombay: A Photorama, MCGM
Dinodia.com
The Modern House by F R S Yorke
The Natural House
4 from the fifties, 20CASI
TISS Archives
Higginbotham
Cement Marketing Company of India
Bombay Art Deco Architecture by Navin Ramani
Industrialised Buildings by R M E Diamamt
Mill for Sale - The Way Ahead ede Darryl D'monte